The Effective SENCO

The Effective SENCO
Meeting the Challenge

Janice Wearmouth

Open University Press
McGraw-Hill Education
McGraw-Hill House
Shoppenhangers Road
Maidenhead
Berkshire
England
SL6 2QL

email: enquiries@openup.co.uk
world wide web: www.openup.co.uk

and Two Penn Plaza, New York, NY 10121-2289, USA

First published 2016

A catalogue record of this book is available from the British Library

ISBN-13: 978-0-33-526204-5
ISBN-10: 0-33-526204-x
eISBN: 978-0-33-526205-2

Library of Congress Cataloging-in-Publication Data
CIP data applied for

Typeset by Aptara, Inc.

Praise for this book

"The 'Effective SENCO' is an essential resource for every SENCO, especially those studying on the National Award for SEN Co-ordination. It skilfully links up-to-date SEND legislation and policy with reflective practical approaches that will help SENCOs lead their schools in developing effective whole school practice. The wealth of audit tools, templates and examples offer a rich source of ideas for creating support for children within all education settings."

Professor Gill Richards, Professor of Special Education, Equity and Inclusion, Nottingham Trent University, UK

"This book combines theory and practice in a thoughtful way to underpin the work of SEN coordination in schools. In a climate where teachers more than ever need to reflect on their practice, it combines reflective and discussion activities with checklists, audit tools and case studies. This is exactly what trainee and experienced SEN coordinators need to support them in their roles."

Brahm Norwich Graduate, Professor of Educational Psychology and Special Educational Needs, School of Education, University of Exeter, UK

"This book provides exactly the type of information, suggestions and analysis which SENCOs need to help them meet the challenges in an inclusive school. This book will be essential for both the experienced SENCO and those new to the role. Janice Wearmouth explains complex concepts and guides the reader to reflect on the key issues in the field making this a book that every teacher must read!"

Dr. Gavin Reid, Author and Independent Educational Psychologist

Contents

Foreword

Special Educational Needs Co-Ordinators (SENCOs) play a vital role in the shaping of the future of so many of our country's children and young people. From both my professional and personal experiences, effective SENCOs successfully manage to combine the qualities of compassion, organisation, strong leadership, and unshakeable resolve to do the right thing by those in their care.

In an ever changing field, SENCOs must constantly meet the challenge of delivering first-rate educational provision for children with special needs and disabilities. The magnitude of the responsibility on the shoulders of SENCOs can often be extremely daunting and I am delighted that Janice Wearmouth has produced this accessible compendium to assist this band of often unsung heroes and heroines in their work.

John Bercow
Chancellor, University of Bedfordshire

Acknowledgements

I would like to thank all those who have assisted with the production of this book, especially the special educational needs co-ordinators who have taken the National Award for Special Educational Needs Co-ordination at the University of Bedfordshire over the past six years and so generously shared their knowledge and experience. In particular I would like to acknowledge the contributions to the text of Louise Bell, Karen Brindley and the senior management team at The Peckover School, Nickie Chamberlain, Anna Fenelon, Vanessa Leaves, Claire Mythen, Ragny Sharma and Jenny Taylor. I would also like to acknowledge Martha Smith's contribution in the area of autism. Thank you!

I would like to dedicate this book to my mother, Dora Ruth, and to all those women in my family who have gone before.

How to use this book

Very simply, the aim of this book is to help you carry out your role as special educational needs co-ordinator (SENCO) effectively. If you want to know how to carry out your duties successfully, then this is the book for you. Its aim is to provide you with a straightforward and practical guide that will give you confidence in the development and improvement of special needs and disabilities (SEND) provision in your school, whether you are new and in training or more experienced. The chapters, which cover a broad array of topics encountered by SENCOs, are deliberately short and accessible and are informed by current legislation, practice, theory and critical understanding of the issues in the field. It is a book that can support you both during your studies for the National Award for SEN Co-ordination and in your day-to-day role, using its rich array of tools and resources.

These valuable tools and resources have been included to support you in your SENCO role whether you are in training, in your early career or more experienced, or responsible for professional development in SEND in schools and colleges. If you are in training and studying for the National Award for SEN Co-ordination, the content of the book comprehensively covers the learning outcomes (LOs) for the Award. For easy reference, Appendix A1 contains a mapping of the learning outcomes against the content of the chapters. You can use this as a checklist that these LOs have been achieved, where appropriate.

You may also like to think of this book as your tool chest where you will find helpful tools to develop and implement SEND provision for the unique needs of your school. Throughout the book you will find a number of features, as well as tools and resources, for you to have on hand either for your own use or for use as professional development with other members of staff, including:

- *reflective activities* that invite reflection on policy and practice in SEND provision, and on personal positions, values and beliefs regarding the rights and legal entitlements to education of all young people, in particular those with SEND;
- *activities for discussion* with other staff members in your school or college;
- *checklists* of effective inclusion practices as tools for 'learning walks' or staff professional development;

- *audit tools* to help you contribute to your school's self-evaluation of the quality of SEND provision and the extent to which your school conforms to the requirements of the 2014 legislation (to be used, for example, prior to OFSTED inspections);
- examples of completed *policy documents*, e.g. SEND policy, dyslexia policy;
- examples of classroom and individual student *observation tools*;
- *templates* for understanding and assessing difficult behaviour and planning for improvement.

Finally, to exemplify practice in the various areas of SEND provision, we have threaded through the chapters a number of *case studies* of effective small-scale research projects to develop SEND provision, and examples of *individual learning and behaviour plans* that are focused on assessed needs. A number of these are taken from excellent practice identified among the cohorts of SENCOs who have successfully taken the NASC course at the University of Bedfordshire.

Getting to grips with the role of the SENCO is both a great challenge and a great privilege. We hope that this book will help you meet that challenge so that you may thrive and flourish in your role.

Introduction

The co-ordination of special educational provision in schools is multi-faceted and challenging. New legislation in England, the Children and Families Act, introduced in September 2014, strengthens and extends the legal requirement to ensure the availability and effective co-ordination of high quality provision for special needs and disabilities (SEND) in schools and, for the first time, in further education colleges. *The Special Educational Needs and Disability Code of Practice 0–25 years* (DfE, 2014a) is an overt component of central government policy in the area of special educational needs with its status of statutory guidance. Teachers in schools and colleges continue to be expected to provide effective learning opportunities for all their students, including those who have special educational needs and disabilities. Schools, colleges and other settings have clear duties under the statutory guidance of the new Code and must 'have regard' to its contents. They should do what it says or be able to explain why they have not done so and explain the alternative provision that has been made. It is no longer sufficient, however, simply to ensure that young people with SEND have access to an appropriate education. Instead, Section 19(d) of Part 3 of the 2014 Children and Families Act specifies access that enables young people to 'achieve the best possible' educational and other outcomes. This reflects a new and higher level of outcome required by law.

Effective co-ordination of SEND provision therefore continues to be high priority for senior management teams, governors, parents and politicians. School governors also have particular responsibilities towards young people with SEND in schools. Section 66 of the 2014 Act contains a key duty on the governing body of a school – and this includes the proprietors or management committee where relevant – to use their 'best endeavours' to secure special educational provision for all children or young people for whom they are responsible. It is essential that all involved understand what 'having' a special educational need or disability means for the young person and his or her family, and what addressing such needs and disabilities entails in schools.

At the same time the requirement for all new special educational needs and disability co-ordinators (SENCOs) to take the National Award for SEN Co-ordination (NASC) has remained in place. Included in the new learning outcomes of the NASC which have been revised in light of the recent amendments to the law is a revision of what is required in terms of professional knowledge and understanding for the SENCO role.

This book has therefore been designed as an accessible, well-theorised and practical resource to help new and experienced SENCOs and those in training to carry out their duties in supporting the development and improvement of SEND provision from a thoughtful and confident position that is very well informed in current legislation, practice, theory and critical understanding of the issues in the field. It therefore provides a well-balanced and accessible overview of the following:

- the new (2014) legislation related to SEND provision and the new SEND Code of Practice and the implications for schools and colleges, and the role of the SENCO in particular;
- key challenges of the SENCO role, as identified by experienced, effective, practising SENCOs, and how these might be addressed;
- what SENCOs really need to know and what they can and should do in order to co-ordinate provision for SEND properly and effectively.

It also comprehensively covers the (2014) learning outcomes of the National Award for Special Educational Needs Co-ordination.

Current legislation promotes the inclusion of (almost) all young people in mainstream schools and colleges. However, this has to be implemented within a national context of school and college 'improvement' and competition and market-oriented practices where young people with SEND may not be able to contribute positively to a school's position on league tables of achievement. Such challenges are not necessarily insurmountable, however, and the book discusses the debates and dilemmas and offers practical suggestions to address these.

Chapter 1, 'Setting the scene', includes a discussion of the concepts of 'special educational needs', learning difficulties, disabilities, 'challenging' behaviour and how these are used and understood. Included also is an outline history of special provision to contextualise discussion of, and enable reflection on, the law, policy and practice in the following chapters.

Chapter 2, 'Models of learning and behaviour in the SEND field', comprises an overview of common frames of reference that are used to interpret learning and behaviour in the area of SEND and that are crucial to understanding the difficulties that are experienced as well as ways to address these.

Chapter 3, 'Current statutory and regulatory frameworks for SEND', includes discussion of essential features of Part 3 of the Children and Families Act (2014), and of the 2010 Equality Act as part of the legal framework for disabilities, and associated regulations and statutory guidance documents and their implications for schools and colleges that is contextualised within an understanding of underpinning intentions. It goes on to consider the role of the SENCO, school management teams and governing boards in implementing SEND legislation, the challenges experienced in these roles and ways that some of these challenges can be addressed. Included also is the role of OfSTED in ensuring the law is implemented.

Chapter 4, 'Understanding communication and interaction needs', Chapter 5, 'Understanding cognition and learning needs', Chapter 6, 'Understanding social, emotional and mental health needs', and Chapter 7, 'Understanding sensory and physical difficulties and needs' comprise a focus on each of the four areas of need outlined in the 2014 Code. This includes discussion of current research and practice related to identifying and making effective provision for needs within each area, including difficulties in receptive and expressive language, autism, profound and multiple difficulties in learning, dyslexia, AD/HD, Tourette's, visual, auditory and multi-sensory impairments, and physical difficulties, in particular, muscular dystrophy.

Chapter 8, 'Assessment of learning, behaviour, physical and sensory needs', discusses types and purposes of assessment and the functions it serves, for example, the learning environment as the context for differentiated teaching, assessment of the strengths and difficulties experienced by individual students, including concepts of formative, criterion-referenced, summative and standardised forms of assessment and entitlements, issues and challenges. Also discussed are ways to approach eliciting pupil 'voice', and approaches to the assessment of challenging behaviour.

Chapter 9, 'Planning provision for individual needs, makes links between the identification of need and the planning of provision: the 'assess–plan–do–review' cycle advocated in the 2014 Code of Practice. It also highlights good practice in developing learning and behaviour plans at different ages and stages for improved access to the curriculum with examples of the individual planning process and resultant plans in a number of areas. The requirements and process for developing formal Education, Health and Care Plans are also outlined.

Chapter 10, 'Achieving coherence and cost-effectiveness in provision', comprises discussion and examples of ways to achieve coherence and cost-effectiveness in provision across the school and college: the purpose and function of provision-mapping, examples of good, clear, coherent provision maps and the process by which they were developed in practice and checklists of effective interventions to audit cost effectiveness. It also considers ways to achieve good communication across the school and college and provides examples of effective practice.

Chapter 11, 'Policy-making in SEND provision in schools and colleges', focuses on the principles of effective leadership in schools and colleges together with a discussion of the process and practice of policy-making in the context of statutory requirements in the area of SEND provision. It also includes an outline of the requirements of SEND policies and provides examples of clearly written SEND policy documents.

Chapter 12, 'Working with families', begins by outlining the background to current policies on families' rights in decision-making about SEND provision for young people. It goes on to discuss the legal requirements in relation to partnership work with families and carers and some of the challenges in meeting these, with examples of effective practical initiatives designed to enable more positive working relationships between schools and home.

Chapter 13, 'Collaborating with other professionals', sketches the range of people with whom SENCOs might be expected to work and their likely role: teaching assistants (TAs), outside agencies (Health and Social Care in particular), and so on. It will go on to discuss research associated with the usefulness and cost-effectiveness of TAs in addressing the needs of young people with SEND in classrooms, the challenges raised by some recent research studies and ways that some experienced SENCOs have addressed these challenges. It also includes the role of specialist external agencies in supporting provision for SEND in schools and colleges, including consideration of the issue of the 'Local Offer'.

Chapter 14, 'Developing effective SEND provision', focuses explicitly on clear, high quality examples of initiatives taken by SENCOs to develop SEND provision across their schools. It indicates ways in which practising SENCOs have identified areas of provision requiring improvement, identifies the specific weaknesses in these areas, presents the designed interventions to address these weaknesses, sets out the aims and objectives against which the SENCOs might later evaluate their interventions, implement and assess their work and set out the implications for future developments in their school and college SEND provision and ways in which these might be included in the subsequent School and College Development Plan.

There are 11 Appendices to help you:

Appendix A1 National Award for Special Education Needs Co-ordination learning outcomes mapped against chapters
Appendix B1 Access to Learning Plan strategies
Appendix B2 Example of an individual provision map for an autistic young man
Appendix B3 Annotated class provision map
Appendix B4 Year 8 pilot provision map
Appendix B5 Evaluated school provision map for cognition and learning needs
Appendix B6 Factors influencing the effectiveness of interventions, and next steps
Appendix B7 Example of completed template for a school or college SEND policy and Information Report
Appendix B8 Lesson observation pro-forma
Appendix B9 Whole-school needs analyses
Appendix B10 Behaviour Support Plan

1

Setting the scene

Introduction

In a book that is designed to address issues of challenge in the co-ordination of in-school and college provision for students' 'special educational needs' and 'disability' (SEND), it is really important to have a very clear view of what it is, in educational terms, that we are trying to achieve for all young people and, within this, for those identified as 'having special educational needs' and disabilities. In this introductory chapter we address the following questions:

- What do we mean by the terms 'special educational needs', learning difficulties, disabilities?
- How are these terms used and understood in schools and colleges?
- How did special educational provision evolve over time?
- Are there examples from different times and places to contextualise our understanding of current policy, provision and the legislative framework?

Reflection 1.1: What is 'inclusion' in schools and colleges?

Just take a few minutes and think about what, for you, are the important features of 'inclusion' in schools and colleges. What are the features of an 'inclusive' school, in your view?

Comment

A number of SENCOs were asked the same questions and came up with the following comments. How far do you agree with them?

- All children having equal opportunities to participate in all areas of broad balanced curriculum and feel valued, which implies:
    - removing barriers to learning so everyone can access the curriculum and make progress regardless of any circumstance – health, finance, behaviour, etc.;
    - treating young people differently according to various needs and adopting a holistic approach to support a tailored, individual approach to the curriculum;

  - differentiation in classrooms and awareness of how the learning context supports inclusion or excludes some children;
  - acceptance of diversity without negative comments or notice, with care taken regarding the language used about others;
  - a sense of belonging, taking account of the individual's feelings;
  - all young people know they have a voice;
  - young people with needs have access to appropriate provision (internal and external) to meet those needs, irrespective of location;
  - deliberate consideration of strategies, procedures, resources and people to make it happen.
- Schools getting to know families really well, understand their backgrounds and engage positively with parents or guardians to ensure they are actively involved with all decision-making and communication, so they are confident that:
  - they know they are listened to by the school;
  - they can support their children and feel a part of the community;
  - they understand their responsibility and that of the school.
  - Supporting pupils and staff to create a safe environment for learning for everyone where everybody has a positive attitude towards everyone else and there is mutual respect.
- Schools having high expectations, enabling a high level of achievement for all, which implies:
  - progress data are taken often and analysed by department or leadership teams and used to inform staff, the parents and the students and put appropriate, thoughtful interventions in place where progress is not at the level expected of individual pupils;
  - progress towards self-directed learning to become functioning members of society.

What is 'special' about 'special educational needs'?

We often use the term 'special educational needs' as if we all know what it means, while at the same time we all know that we can define 'need' in different ways. At this point, therefore, we consider what is meant by 'need(s)', 'special educational needs' and 'disability'. Only when we have a clear definition can we begin to answer questions about how those 'needs' can be addressed and 'special' educational provision co-ordinated.

Reflection 1.2: Learning from personal 'special needs'

Why some pupils fail can be explained in a range of ways. The problem might be interpreted as rooted in social factors, for example, family poverty and unemployment or in cultural differences in understanding and expectations between family and school. Alternatively, the child's difficulties might be seen as arising out of the immediate learning environment, for example, inappropriate teaching methods or texts, or inadequate school resources. Another view might be to see the problem as located at the level of the learner himself or herself and an individualised approach taken to identifying and assessing his or her 'special' learning needs.

- Take a few moments to reflect on what was the hardest thing you have ever tried to do.
- What it was that made it so hard?
- Did you succeed?
- If so, what helped you to do this?
- If not, how did it make you feel? What might have helped you?

Comment

Several colleagues as well as myself have tried answering these questions on a number of occasions. Responses to what it was that made the task so hard seemed to fall into a number of categories:

- too big a gap between current level of understanding and skill and what was required to complete the task;
- poor level of teaching or support on offer;
- lack of confidence or belief that we would be successful;
- excessive anxiety that filled our heads and prevented us from thinking clearly;
- prior belief, gained from previous experience of failure, that we would fail again.

For me, the hardest text I ever tried to read was Shakespeare's *Macbeth* in school at the age of 13 – with no introduction or explanation. I remember feeling bemused, and then frustrated and stupid by turns, by the unfamiliar language and vocabulary of the play. I certainly did not want to admit out loud to any of my classmates that I could not cope with the text. I became completely hostile to the suggestion of anything Shakespearean for years afterwards – until a very good live production and excellent acting made the plot clear and undid the damage.

We can only make sense of new ideas and information in terms of what we already know. It is hard to learn unless what we are reading about, listening to or looking at makes sense to us. Without a way of a way of relating to the words and the ideas in a passage, we are not likely to be interested in it. Learning happens in the same way for all students of any age. What would have helped me to make more sense of *Macbeth*, and what I needed, was a clear introduction at the beginning, perhaps watching a film of the play (had it been available at the time) and teacher explanation of the vocabulary.

How far do you think any of this might relate in any way to the learning of pupils you teach who experience difficulties of some sort?

Special educational needs

In England, Northern Ireland and, until very recently, in Wales also, legislation, government publications, Regulations, official circulars, consultation, advice and guidance documents, academic texts and articles, on the topic of 'special educational needs' and 'disability' reinforce an impression that there is common understanding of what the term implies and that the term is neutral. The expressions 'children with special educational needs', 'SEN(D) children', or, even, 'SENs' are often used in educational contexts. However, this apparent consensus may serve to conceal the complexity of meaning underlying this term.

As we discuss more fully in Chapter 2, schools are required to operate within the law which pertains to SEND. In England, the legal definition of SEN has remained largely the same since the concept was introduced in the 1981 Education Act, following recommendations in the Warnock Report (DES, 1978). Under the terms of current legislation, the Children and Families Act, 2014, Part 3, §20 (1), a child or young person has special educational needs if he or she has a learning difficulty or disability which calls for special educational provision to be made for him or her. That is, a young person only has 'special educational needs' when special provision is required to meet them; learning difficulties do not in themselves constitute the need.

What is meant by 'learning difficulty' is not as straightforward as it sounds. In law, a child or young person may be seen as having such a difficulty if

(a) he or she has 'significantly greater difficulty in learning than the majority of' same-age peers, or
(b) he or she has a disability which prevents him or her from making use of (educational) facilities 'of a kind generally provided for' same-age peers in mainstream educational institutions.

(Children and Families Act 2014, Part 3, §20 (2))

In law, a learning difficulty creates a need but that need is only 'special' if the provision required to satisfy it is 'special'. A student might have a 'learning difficulty', for example, if he or she has a specific literacy difficulty which makes it hard to engage in the same learning activities as other students. This much is fairly obvious – but a child might also have a 'learning difficulty' if he or she has a physical disability that creates a barrier to moving around the school or classroom to participate in those activities with peers.

This way of defining a learning difficulty raises a number of questions. Included in them are how to measure 'significantly greater difficulty in learning' and how to compare one student to the majority. Comparing individuals against what we feel most people at that age should be learning and the way they should be learning it is bound to lead to mistakes, leaving some children without support and others with support that is unnecessary. Then there is a question of how to gauge the contexts in which a difficulty becomes significant, for example, whether remembering names is difficult only in examinations, or in everyday learning situations also. Finally, there is the question of what is meant by a general level of provision. Some schools have facilities for particular activities, others do not.

It is not simply the complexity of the term within the legal definition that is challenging, but also its associations. The notion of fulfilment of 'need' may convey a sense of benevolence. In practice, however, particularly in the past, what was termed 'need' was often not negotiated with learners and their parents or carers. An assumption of agreement between all the interested parties about what is 'needed' may ignore crucial issues of the degree of power allowed to pupils and parents in the decision-making process (Wearmouth, 2009).

As Corbett comments, students can become marginalised by schools through discourse that prejudices our view of them:

> What does 'special' mean? If we detach this word from its anchor in 'educational' we can see that 'special' does not mean especially good and valued unless we use a phrase like, 'you are a special person'. It is linked to 'needs' which implies dependency, inadequacy and unworthiness.
>
> (1996: 3)

Reflection 1.3: Marginalising discourse: the example of Down's syndrome

Some of the ways in which children with Down's syndrome were portrayed in the past, the treatment that some received and the terminology that was used illustrate a number of the issues related to marginalisation and values discussed above. For example, owing to his perception that children with Down's syndrome shared physical facial similarities such as folds in the upper eyelids (epicanthal folds) with those of the Mongolian race as identified by the German physiologist and anthropologist, Johann Friedrich Blumenbach, John Langdon Down used the term *mongoloid*. He wrote in 1866:

> A very large number of congenital idiots are typical Mongols. So marked is this, that when placed side by side, it is difficult to believe that the specimens compared are not children of the same parents. The number of idiots who arrange themselves around the Mongolian type is so great, and they present such a close resemblance to one another in mental power, that I shall describe an idiot member of this racial division, selected from the large number that have fallen under my observation.
>
> (Down, 1866: 259)

With the rise of the eugenics movement in the first half of the twentieth century, a number of countries, including certain states in the USA, began programmes of forced sterilisation of individuals with Down's syndrome. 'Action T4' was a programme of the systematic murder of individuals with Down's syndrome and other comparable disabilities in Nazi Germany, for example (Lifton, 2000). Since the Second World War, however, laws relating to such sterilisation programmes have been repealed.

In 1961, a number of geneticists wrote to the editor of *The Lancet*, suggesting that Mongolian idiocy had 'misleading connotations', had become 'an embarrassing term', and should be changed (Gordon, 1961). *The Lancet* advocated using the term Down's Syndrome. The World Health Organization (WHO) officially dropped references to mongolism in 1965 after a request by the Mongolian delegate (Howard-Jones, 1979).

Down's syndrome cannot be cured, but the learning and other difficulties associated with it can be addressed if people with the syndrome are offered appropriate help and if other people accept and include them. Above all it is important to stress that children with Down's syndrome are individuals with their own abilities and achievements (Wearmouth, 2009).

Constructions of difference between people

Over the years, different social or psychological perspectives on the root of the difficulty have given rise to different approaches. Particular approaches to provision for pupils seen as 'having difficulties' may often be interpreted as reflecting the norms and values of society as much as what might be in the long-term interest of future life chances.

Reflection 1.4: Discourses on difference

Fulcher (1989) has identified four discourses reflecting a range of ways in which differences between individuals with disabilities have been conceptualised. The distinctions she makes can also be applied to the varying ways that 'special educational needs' have been viewed. As you read the outlines below, you might like to consider whether there are parallels in the ways in which 'special educational provision' and students with SEND are regarded in educational institutions in your experience:

- *the medical discourse* which sees difficulties as diseases or deficits to be treated. The language of this discourse depends on the notion of deficiency and negativity, which, in turn, has connotations of being in some way inferior or distant from the norm (like dis-, un-, -challenged, difficulty, impairment). This why the 'medical model' of students' difficulties is identified with a 'deficit model';
- *the charity discourse* which assumes those in difficulty need the help of others. This may be seen to embody paternalistic values of nurturing and care (Corbett, 1996);
- *the lay discourse* which is associated with the fearful, prejudiced or resentful response of the ordinary person towards the disabled, giving rise to the view that children who are different must be separated off from the majority;
- *the rights discourse* where, as Garner and Sandow (1995) point out, lobby groups representing the interests of 'minority' groups have presented issues related to provision and participation in terms of human rights. However, policy-makers and service providers have tended to be preoccupied with provision, and in viewing people as consumers, have seen those same issues as problems only for the organisation concerned.

From my own experience of teaching in eight different schools, it appears to me that pupils who experience difficulties or who may seem threatening to the system are often seen from one of these four perspectives that sometimes clouds our professional judgment.

All of this is of crucial importance because the way in which we see the root of a difficulty has a very strong impact on what we see as an appropriate way to respond to it. The relationship between educational expectations related to how we describe students and student achievement, self-esteem and development, for example, has been well documented since the seminal work of Rosenthal and Jacobson (1968).

The lens through which we view any situation carries with it its own constraints and limitations. It is pertinent, therefore, to examine what might lie at the root of difficulties in learning faced by individuals and groups of pupils from a broader perspective. One might ask, for example, what part economic deprivation and poverty play in creating these difficulties, and think about the extent to which 'learning difficulties' might be seen as 'obstacles to learning' arising from the society in which they live. Figures from the National Statistics Office (DfE, 2010), for example, show very clearly that students in the least deprived areas continue to outperform those in the most deprived areas, and those eligible for free school meals perform less well than those who are ineligible.

Lessons from history about the 'special' education sector

To understand current provision, it is important to be aware of its historical origins. The way in which educational provision is currently organised is a product both of its own history and of the values, beliefs and political ideology of our society (Wearmouth, 2009). Special provision has been characterised by a number of recurring themes that have echoed down the years, including:

- whether to separate young people who experience difficulties in learning and behaviour into segregated provision, or integrate them into mainstream;
- whether the curriculum should be the same for all students, or different for some groups, reflecting discussion around the academic-vocational/manual divide;
- whether, and how, to classify children into the various groupings of difficulties. As a corollary of this, what characterises the differences both between the groupings and between the students so classified and others;
- differential valuing of young people in the various groups;
- whether all young people are educable in any form recognisable as 'education'.

Other on-going debates include the question why the special education sector was developed in the first place:

- Were special education systems created by caring professionals wishing to address the needs of children in difficulty more effectively?
- Is special education provision essentially benevolent?
- Did special educational provision develop primarily to serve the economic and commercial interests of society? Did these interests dictate that as many people as possible with difficulties should be productive and contribute to an industrial society? Certainly businessmen 'played a part in the founding of pioneer establishments for the deaf and for the blind, and... throughout the 19th century trade training took up much of the lives of the handicapped attending them' (Cole, 1990: 101).
- Did it develop to provide a means to exclude troublesome pupils, or pupils who required a lot of the teacher's time, from mainstream classes? For example, when a new national system of secondary schools was designed in the 1944 Education

Act, did the smooth running of those schools demand the exclusion of some pupils, for example, those categorised as 'educationally subnormal'?

- Is it in the vested interest of, for example, the medical profession and psychologists who support the existence of special provision?

The early years of special education provision

As the Warnock Report (DES, 1978: Chapter 2) notes, early institutions for children who experienced difficulties of various sorts were founded by individuals or by charities and catered only for a few. Later, central government intervened, initially to support and supplement what was provided through voluntary agencies. Later still the government created a national framework for special education provision, but it was not until the 1970s that this framework included the entitlement of all children to an appropriate education.

The early institutions were designed to focus on moral improvement, training in work skills, and the Christian religion (Oliphant, 2006) rather than education. In Britain, they began in the second half of the eighteenth century, first, with schools for blind and deaf children, for example the School of Instruction for the Indigent Blind, established in 1791 in Liverpool. Oliphant (2006: 55) notes that this school was, according to its founding plan, intended, along with religion, 'to furnish the blind with employment that may prevent them from being burdens to their family and community'. 'Habits of industry' should be formed with men making baskets, tablecloths and whips while the women spun yarn, made sail-cloths and picked oakum. As recipients of public charity, the inmates had little freedom of choice. It was not until other schools were founded thirty years later that educational aspects were introduced into the curriculum, for example, in the London Society for Teaching the Blind to Read in 1838. Even so, most blind children's prospects were 'pretty grim' (Bell, 1967: 11). Worcester College remained the only route for blind children to achieve higher qualifications and entry into the professions until after the Second World War. The first schools for the deaf were also very limited in the education they offered.

Attempts were made to teach a trade to girls with physical disabilities from poor homes in the Cripples' Home and Industrial School for Girls established in Marylebone in 1851, and to boys in the Training Home for Crippled Boys, founded in Kensington in 1865.

For those children who experienced serious difficulties in learning, until the end of the nineteenth century there was little provision apart from workhouses and infirmaries for those who needed secure care. The first specific provision made for them was the Asylum for Idiots established at Highgate in 1847 which took in people of all ages. By 1870, there were five asylums. Only three professed to offer any kind of education. Parents had to agree to them being certified as 'idiots' for children to be admitted to these institutions. This descriptor was hated by many (Cole, 1989: 22).

Implications of universal education

In 1870, the Forster Education Act in England and Wales established school boards charged with ensuring provision of elementary education in places where voluntary enterprise had not provided enough. Only a few school boards admitted blind and deaf children to ordinary elementary schools. In 1880, a further Education Act finally made school attendance compulsory between the ages of 5 and 10, or the age of 13 for those who had not achieved the standard of education required by local byelaws. Further legislation in 1893 extended the age of compulsory attendance to 11, and in 1899 to 12.

As a result of the introduction of compulsory schooling, large numbers of children came to school for the first time. Many appeared to have poor intellectual ability and made little or no progress. In the large classes that existed in public elementary schools, their presence was often felt to be holding others back. National level funding for individual schools and, therefore, teachers' salaries, depended in part on the outcomes of examinations of pupils conducted by school inspectors as, for example, in England between 1863 and 1890 when the policy was abandoned. The question therefore became what to do with these children.

In 1889, a Royal Commission, cited in the Warnock Report (DES, 1978: 4), distinguished between three groups of children with varying degrees of learning difficulties: 'feeble-minded', 'imbeciles' and 'idiots'. Feeble-minded should be educated in 'auxiliary' schools away from other children, imbeciles should be sent to institutions where education should concentrate on sensory and physical development and improved speech. 'Idiots' were not thought to be educable. This same Commission recommended compulsory education for the blind from age 5 to 16, and for the deaf from age 7 to 16. Deaf children, generally considered slower to learn on account of difficulties in communication, were to be taught separately by teachers who should be specially qualified to do so. (It is interesting to note that teachers in special schools for children with visual and auditory impairments still require specialist qualifications but those in some other kinds of special educational institutions do not.) Legislation followed in England and Wales in 1893 with the Elementary Education (Blind and Deaf Children) Act. It was not until 1938 when the (1937) Education (Deaf Children) Act came into effect that deaf children were compelled to attend school from the age of 5.

In 1896, a Committee on Defective and Epileptic Children recommended that school authorities should make provision for all 'defective' children in their area and be able to make attendance compulsory. This included children with physical disabilities. Many parents felt that there was a stigma attached to their child's placement in a special class, and resisted it, however. One witness to the Sharpe Committee said that parents 'will admit anything except that their children are defective in intellect' (Cole, 1989: 40).

The Mental Deficiency Act of 1913 required local education authorities in England and Wales to ascertain and certify which children aged 7 to 16 in their area were defective. Those judged by the authority to be incapable of being taught in special schools were to pass into the care of local mental deficiency committees. Interestingly, Cyril Burt, later Sir Cyril, was appointed to a part-time position of school psychologist for the London County Council in 1913, with the responsibility of picking out the 'feeble-minded' children, in accordance with the 1913 Act.

In 1921, an Education Act consolidated previous legislation, requiring children in the four categories of blind, deaf, mentally and physically defective (but not 'idiots' or 'imbeciles') and epileptic to be educated. 'Defective' and epileptic children should be certified by local education authorities and then educated in special provision, of which there was a whole range made by both voluntary bodies and local education authorities. As the Warnock Report (DES, 1978) comments, the statutory foundation of special provision continued broadly until the 1944 Act. The parents of children in any of the four categories were required to see that their child attended a suitable special school from the age of 5 in the case of blind or deaf children, or 7 for other children, until the age of 16.

Reflection 1.5: Contextualising provision for 'delicate' children

For several decades in the twentieth century a particular form of special provision, open air schools, existed to provide for 'delicate' children. Their form and organisation are tied to the social, political and ideological context within which they originated (Wearmouth, 2009). In Britain, these schools were founded at the beginning of the twentieth century in the context of national concern over the poor physical well-being of large numbers of children, particularly in the cities where living conditions were often wretched. Recruitment of soldiers to fight in the Boer War had highlighted concerns about young adults who were medically unfit to fight (Cole, 1989). Consequently the government passed the Education (Provision of School Meals) Act in 1906 to enable local education authorities (LEAs) to provide school lunches and, in 1907, the Education (Administrative Provisions) Act to require LEAs to carry out medical checks on all their pupils.

Open-air schools were modelled on a German example, where the first such school was established in 1904 in pine woods in Charlottenburg (Gamlin, 1935) with a regime of careful supervision, good food and exercise. The first British open-air school was Bostall Woods, founded in Woolwich, in 1907, soon followed by others. These children were subjected to a 'somewhat Spartan regime' with lessons 'out of doors or in three-sided rooms, with meals provided and a compulsory rest period in the middle of the day' (Cole, 1989: 51). Classrooms in Aspen House open-air school in Streatham, London, had floors and roofs but no walls, so, if it snowed in winter, the children might have to clear it off the tables and chairs before they could start lessons. However cold it became, lessons continued and pupils just had their clothes and blankets to keep warm. The numbers of children who fitted the criteria and the cheapness of buildings, effectively three-sided sheds with corrugated iron roofs, led to an expansion of numbers, and by the 1930s there were 4000 children a year from London who were sent to such schools. They were funded by LEAS, charities or private philanthropists, for example, the Cadbury family.

Doubts about the efficacy of these schools began in 1930 when a report from the Industrial Research Board questioned being out of doors in all weathers. Doubts increased when medical officers surveying open-air schools for the Ministry of Education in 1949–50 commented: 'When the canvas curtains were drawn, rain drove in and above the curtains so that the floor and furniture were often wet. We saw children scraping frozen snow off the desks and chairs before they could be used' (Cole, 1989: 113). Even so, in 1955, 12,000 'delicate' children were still being educated in open-air schools in England and Wales. Subsequently, however, open-air schools gradually became redundant. Medical opinion had moved away from encouraging such schools, and children's health and physical well-being had improved as a result of better standards of living, slum clearances, the advent of the National Health Service, the arrival of antibiotics that reduced the incidence of tuberculosis, and the provision of milk and meals in schools.

Different curricula for different learners

Towards the end of the Second World War, a coalition government reorganised the education system through the 1944 Education Act in England and Wales and sought to develop a common national framework for the education of a diverse student population. The statutory system of education was to be organised 'in three progressive stages to be known as primary education, secondary education, and further education' (1944 Education Act, Part 11, §7).

The government advised LEAs to 'think in terms of three types' of state secondary schools in circular No. 73 (12 December 1945). A booklet, *The Nation's Schools*, explained that the new 'modern' schools would be for working-class children 'whose future employment will not demand any measure of technical skill or knowledge' (MoE, 1945, quoted in Benn and Chitty 1996: 5). This booklet was withdrawn but the same policy was restated in *The New Secondary Education* two years later (Wilkinson, 1947). A report by Sir William Spens in 1938 had recommended a tripartite system of secondary education, with grammar schools for the most able, secondary modern schools for the majority, and secondary technical schools for those with a technical or scientific aptitude. The 1944 Act itself never mentioned the words 'tripartite', 'grammar schools' or 'secondary modern schools', but this system was quickly adopted by many LEAs. Selection of pupils was through an examination at the age of 11 (the 11+) based on a belief that psychometric testing was reliable and valid and could differentiate between different 'types' of learners whose aptitudes suited them to different kinds of schools. Within individual mainstream schools, students were selected and placed in ability 'streams' and academic or work-related programmes, according to their measured 'ability'.

In the area of special education, the 1944 Education Act, Sections 33 and 34, and associated Regulations, also assumed that reliably categorising young people was both possible and appropriate. The duty of LEAs to ascertain which children required special educational treatment was extended to children with all types of disability, generally described in the Act as 'pupils who suffer from any disability of mind or body'. The Handicapped Students and School Health Service Regulations (1945) in England and Wales developed a new framework of eleven categories of students: blind, partially sighted, deaf, partially deaf, delicate, diabetic, educationally subnormal, epileptic, maladjusted, physically handicapped and those with speech defects. Maladjustment and speech defects were included for the first time. The regulations required blind, deaf, epileptic, physically handicapped and aphasic children to be educated in special schools. Children with other disabilities could attend mainstream if there was adequate provision (DES, 1978: 2.46).

Official guidance in 1946 estimated that the number of children who might be expected to require special educational treatment, not necessarily in special schools, would range from between 14 and 17 per cent of the school population.

During the years which followed, the two groups which continually expanded in numbers were those students considered 'educationally sub-normal' (ESN) and those identified as 'maladjusted' (DES, 1978):

> The category of educationally sub-normal children was seen as consisting of children of limited ability and children retarded by 'other conditions' such as irregular attendance, ill-health, lack of continuity in their education or unsatisfactory school conditions. These children would be those who for any reason were retarded by

> more than 20 per cent for their age and who were not so low-graded as to be ineducable or to be detrimental to the education of other children. They would amount to approximately 10 per cent of the school population.
>
> (DES, 1978: 2.48)

The number of children in ESN special schools nearly doubled between 1947 and 1955 from 12,060 to 22,639. As the Warnock Report (DES, 1978) comments, post-war planners assumed that ordinary schools would have the major share in making provision for those young people with difficulties in learning and behaviour. However, during the war, a lot of accommodation in schools had been destroyed, many schools that survived were in a bad state, raising the school-leaving age meant that additional buildings were needed, secondary modern schools in particular often had large classes, and suitably trained teachers were in short supply (DES, 1978: 33–40). The outcome for special educational provision was that the planners' intentions were not wholly fulfilled, and provision in ordinary schools failed to develop as expected.

The Education (Handicapped Children) Act 1970 removed the power of health authorities to provide training for children who experienced the most serious difficulties in learning (deemed 'mentally handicapped') and required the staff and buildings of junior training centres to be transferred to the education service. Around 32,000 children in institutions of various sorts, together with an unknown number at home, now became entitled to special education. In future, they were to be regarded as 'severely educationally sub-normal' (ESN(S)), as opposed to the moderately educationally sub-normal (ESN(M)) group who had previously made up the ESN category.

Reflection 1.6: The construction of a category: the case of 'maladjustment'

'Maladjustment' is an interesting category, the use and demise of which in special education illustrate how far labels become pervasive and fixed to suit the existing national context. The 'maladjusted' label is one with 'which has a powerful history of stigma, being associated with undesirable personal and social characteristics' (Galloway et al.. 1994).

After 1945, all LEAs had a responsibility to establish special educational treatment in special or ordinary schools for pupils defined as maladjusted. However, such was the uncertainty around what constituted 'maladjustment', that the Underwood Committee was set up in 1950 to enquire into 'maladjusted' students' medical, educational and social problems. The Underwood Report (1955: Chapter IV, para. 96) lists six symptoms of 'maladjustment':

- nervous disorders, e.g. fears, depression, apathy, excitability;
- habit disorders, e.g. speech defects, sleep-walking, twitching and incontinence;
- behaviour disorders, e.g. defiance, aggression, jealousy and stealing;
- organic disorders, e.g. cerebral tumours;
- psychotic behaviour, e.g. delusions, bizarre behaviour;
- educational and vocational difficulties, e.g. inability to concentrate or keep jobs.

In our view, a child may be regarded as maladjusted who is developing in ways that have a bad effect on himself or his fellows and cannot, without help, be remedied by his parents, teachers and other adults in ordinary contact with him.

(1955: 22)

There has never been a consensus on what defines 'problem behaviour', of the sort categorised by the term 'maladjusted'. It was 'a ragbag term describing any kind of behaviour that teachers and parents find disturbing' (Galloway and Goodwin, 1987: 32) and could be used to justify special provision. Between 1945 and 1960, the numbers of pupils classified as maladjusted rose from 0 to 1742. Estimates at the time of Rutter et al.'s (1970) epidemiological study varied from 5–25 per cent of the child population. By 1975, there were 13,000 pupils labelled as maladjusted (Furlong, 1985) – but now there are none. The term 'maladjusted' has been replaced by ill-defined terms such as 'emotional and behavioural difficulties' which was first formally used by Warnock (DES, 1978) and which enabled pupils to be removed from the mainstream.

Concerns around issues of equity

Although the system established after 1944 seemed stable, as Clark et al. (1997) note, many educators began to see that selection within the tripartite system was not as fair as it might appear. Differing proportions of students were selected for each type of school in different areas of the country, and considerable doubt was increasingly cast on the reliability and validity of the psychometric test procedures used to discriminate between children (Wearmouth, 1986). A growing concern for equality of opportunity in society at large led some researchers to comment that the system was divisive and functioned to sustain the position of some already advantaged societal groups. For example, Douglas (1964) and Hargreaves (1967) found a disproportionate number of middle-class children in grammar schools.

The result of all this was, beginning in the 1960s and increasingly in the 1970s, the establishment of comprehensive schools, the introduction of special classes and 'remedial' provision in mainstream, and the integration of some children from special to mainstream schools.

Introduction of the concept of special educational needs: the significance of the Warnock Report

In November 1973, Margaret Thatcher, then Education Secretary in the Conservative government, announced that she proposed, in conjunction with the Secretaries of State for Scotland and Wales, to appoint a committee of enquiry chaired by Mary Warnock:

> To review educational provision in England, Scotland and Wales for children and young people handicapped by disabilities of body or mind, taking account of the medical aspects of their needs, together with arrangements to prepare them for entry into employment; to consider the most effective use of resources for these purposes; and to make recommendations.
>
> (DES, 1978:1)

The report, published in 1978, introduced the concept of 'special educational needs', recommending that it should replace the categorisation of handicap and suggesting that up to 20 per cent of pupils might have a 'special educational need' at some time in their school career. A study by Rutter, Tizard and Whitmore (1970), mentioned above, had enquired into the incidence of difficulties in learning in the school population. The report from this study showed teachers' perceptions that, on average, 20 per cent of their students were experiencing difficulty of some kind. Since that time, the same figure has been used to estimate the number of children nationally who might experience difficulties. Of the total number of students, approximately 2 per cent are seen by policy-makers as likely to have difficulties which require additional or extra resources to be provided. This figure of 2 per cent is clearly useful to resource-providers, for example, LEAs, to estimate what proportion of their resources they are likely to have to set aside for individual students' educational needs. However, it is an arbitrary one, drawn from a count of students in special schools in 1944 (DES, 1978). The law, focusing as it does on individual need, gives no such figures for the incidence of children likely to need statutory assessment.

Warnock's radical recommendations formed the basis of the 1981 Education Act. Under the terms of this Act, the 11 categories of handicap were replaced with the view that pupils' difficulties occur on a continuum, and that a 'special educational need' exists if a child has 'significantly greater difficulty in learning' than peers, or a disability that hinders him or her from using educational facilities normally available in the local school. Local education authorities were given responsibilities to identify needs which called for provision in addition to that normally available in the school. This Act affirmed the principle of integration. All children should be educated in mainstream schools but with certain provisos: that their needs could be met there, and that it was compatible with the education of other children and with the 'efficient use of resources'. It also introduced the system of 'statementing' to give children a legal entitlement to special educational support.

Differences in views: inclusive or special schools?

The tension between including children with difficulties and segregating them into special provision has repeatedly surfaced. 'In every age, many concerned professionals have been reluctant to segregate the handicapped' (Cole, 1990: 106). The Sharpe Report of 1898, for example, contains a report from Dr James Kerr of the Bradford Schools Board that teachers wished 'to get rid of these [so-called 'feeble-minded] children' so that they would have fewer problems in schools and classrooms (Education Department, 1898: 19). However, another contributor to the report stated that opinion was divided on the subject. 'There appears to be amongst the teachers... a general agreement that the children, where they are tractable, are as well, if not better, in the ordinary schools under ordinary arrangements' (Education Department, 1898: 216). Indeed, many teachers were reported as wanting 'to exclude only the openly disruptive children and the severely handicapped' (Cole, 1990: 102).

Decisions about whether inclusive mainstream, or special schools, are more likely to meet children's learning needs are not always clear-cut. Two groups of students about whom teachers these days often express very serious concerns are those whose experience profound and complex difficulties in learning, who may also have acute physical disabilities, and those whose behaviour is perceived as very threatening and disruptive (Wearmouth, 2009). It may be that some students are so vulnerable that the overriding consideration for them is a protective environment where their individual care needs can be considered together with their education. Whether the actual location is a mainstream or special site may be of less relevance than other considerations. The quality of the specialist facilities to support children's physical requirements, the level of understanding between students and staff and the effectiveness of the system of communication between home and school are very important, irrespective of location. In relation to the second condition, the proviso that students 'with special educational needs' should be educated in mainstream schools provided that this is compatible with the education of peers is often seen as the justification for placement in an alternative location.

The Ofsted (2010) review found that no one model – such as special schools, full inclusion in mainstream settings, or specialist units co-located with mainstream settings – worked better than any other. It became apparent during the review that the pattern of local services had often developed in an ad-hoc way, based on what had been done in the past rather than from a strategic overview of what was needed locally. The effective practice seen during the review encompassed a wide range of models of provision, often with significant flexibility in the way in which services were provided within any one local area.

Summary

Over the years, the ways in which differences between people have been conceptualised, notions of entitlements and human rights have developed, and the focus of, and on, education itself has altered, have all contributed to the complexity and changing nature of the field of special educational needs.

The term used in legislation since 1983, 'special educational needs', is part of the discourse which, to some, may sound derogatory. At the same time we must recognise, along with the Disability Movement, that failing to acknowledge difference can be counterproductive to the learning needs of a student and be interpreted as disrespectful to that person's life experiences. Whatever an individual's view, parents, teachers and other professionals in education have to conform to aspects of official definitions when engaged in formal processes under the law.

Sometimes, ensuring that a pupil is identified as 'having a special educational need', perhaps even that his or her needs are specified on a Statement, now reconceptualised as an Education, Health and Care plan and thus risking labelling, could be the best way to protect a mainstream placement for a child experiencing difficulties. Paradoxically, 'including' a child in a mainstream school might need to be accompanied by more labelling and categorising of individual pupils, using basically the same medical and psychological perspectives that would be the case if the same learner attended a special school.

2

Models of learning and behaviour in the SEND field

Introduction

Crucial to understanding difficulties in learning and behaviour and ways to address these is familiarity with the model, or perspective, within which that learning and behaviour is viewed. In this chapter we address the questions:

- What are the most common frames of reference currently used to interpret learning and behaviour in the SEND field?
- What are the implications of these frames of reference?

There is an important, though in some ways simplistic, distinction that we can make between the view that the mind is a passive recipient of knowledge and merely reacts to outside influence, and the view that it is pro-active in interpreting and constructing the world. In terms of frames of reference from educational psychology, a passive view of the human mind is most commonly reflected in the behaviourist model. Here all behaviour is assumed to be learned. What underlies behaviour principles is a basic concern with observed events, that is what people actually do, not with assumptions about intentions or feelings. In the world of special needs provision, individual education plans have often been drawn up with interventions designed to shape learning and behaviour that are 'done to' the child. The opposite view of the human mind, that it is active in reaching out and constructing meaning, is reflected in models most commonly associated with constructivist and sociocultural views of learning.

A behaviourist view of learning

It is particularly important to be familiar with the principles linked to behaviourist psychology (Skinner, 1938, 1953; Baer et al., 1968) that have often dominated thinking about assessment and intervention in terms of learning and behaviour in educational institutions (Dwivedi and Gupta, 2000). The behavioural model works on the principle that all behaviour is learned through a process of conditioning, and that responses (or behaviours) are strengthened or weakened by their consequences.

Early work, for example, Skinner (1938) relied on experiments with laboratory animals. In a famous sequence of trial-and-error learning tasks, rats learned to press levers in order to find food (Skinner, 1938). Learning involved the formation of a stimulus-response association in the rats' memory: pressing the lever would result in finding food. Reinforcement through a reinforcer, in this case, food, strengthened the stimulus–response association. If the association was broken by removing the reward, the rats' behaviour would gradually cease through 'extinction'. The opposite of positive reinforcement is negative reinforcement. Undesirable behaviour is discouraged and desired behaviour encouraged through putting a stop to something unpleasant. Where something unpleasant occurred as a result of an action, it is viewed as 'punishment'.

When behavioural principles are applied in school settings, behaviour experienced as disturbing is seen as having been learned through positive reinforcement in some way. To address this situation, the reinforcing conditions or consequences of behaviour as well as the physical and social context in which the behaviour occurs can be systematically modified in order to bring about improvement in students' behaviour. Most work using this model has been based 'on behavioural management approaches (which employ strategies such as positive reinforcement, response cost, extinction and so on) where the reinforcing conditions or consequences of a behaviour are adjusted in order to moderate its frequency' (Dwivedi and Gupta, 2000: 76). The key to all this is consistency on the part of teachers.

Operant conditioning – reinforcing what teachers want their students to do again, ignoring or punishing what they want students to stop doing – has been widely applied in teaching in UK classrooms since the 1970s (Merrett, 1985). One way to address undesirable behaviour is therefore to ensure that whatever is rewarding and reinforcing is removed so that the behaviour is extinguished. In addition, whenever individuals behave in ways that are seen as more appropriate, they should be rewarded in a way that clearly recognises the greater acceptability of the new behaviour within contexts where that behaviour is clearly acceptable. Another way is to identify and alter the stimulus context or setting (the 'setting conditions') in which that behaviour occurs. Behavioural principles can be applied to changing behaviour at individual or group level. Rogers (1994a; 1994b) encourages adopting a behavioural approach towards teaching primary school pupils whom he describes as 'behaviourally-disordered' (BD) to take responsibility for their own behaviour. He notes: 'While most students respond to the normal socialisation into rights-respecting behaviour, some will need to be *specifically taught*.' He goes on to comment: '[L]earning targets can be developed as specific *behaviour* plans that involve teacher modelling, student-rehearsal and feedback and encouragement in the natural setting of the classroom' (Rogers, 1994c: 166–7).

Task analysis and precision teaching

Behavioural approaches have often been used in the SEND area for precision teaching consequent on task analysis. Here the skills underpinning particular tasks or component elements of a new concept are broken down into small precisely defined stages in a hierarchy of learning. Pupils learn and practise each stage to mastery level. This often requires repetitive practice, such as learning multiplication tables, spelling, phonic work and word recognition. Correct responses are rewarded and reinforced.

Critiques of behavioural techniques for controlling and shaping behaviour

A number of criticisms of behaviourist techniques for controlling and changing behaviour have been commonly expressed. For example, behavioural approaches might serve teachers' wishes to manage students rather than responding to individual needs (Hanko, 1994) and engaging students' interests. These approaches might also lead children into becoming overly dependent on praise. In any case, inappropriate use of praise can be damaging to some students for two reasons. If it is not sincere, students may well see through it. Also, students who have learned from previous experiences that they are likely to find learning activities in school difficult will be very discouraged by teachers' obvious lack of understanding of their situation. Consequently, 'a praise-refusing student's determination not to be lured into the risks of failing yet again may be further reinforced' (Hanko, 1994: 166). In every school I taught, I met praise-refusing students who have, seemingly, shut themselves off from teachers. Many have been socially isolated and, to judge by body language, feel appalled at their own loneliness yet cannot do anything about it. I well remember the case of Paul, undernourished, dirty, smelly, and always alone, but hovering as close to the entrance of the school building as he could manage. No amount of attempts by me to 'shape' his behaviour through praise would have enabled him to socialise more with his peers.

Behavioural approaches might also encourage students into unthinking conformity to authority (Milgram, 1974). There is an assumption that the school curriculum to which students are expected to comply is appropriate and relevant and that school and teacher processes and practices are equitable and reasonable for all students but we all know that this is not necessarily the case. Furthermore, these approaches tend to ignore the importance of cultural and community contexts, together with the traditional values, in which behaviour is defined and understood (Glynn and Bishop, 1995; Macfarlane, 1997; 2000a; 2000b). There is an assumption that teachers know which types of rewards and sanctions are 'meaningful' to individual students as positive or negative reinforcers. Where teachers do not understand the cultural norms of their students, they may 'mis-cue' in their application of behaviour management strategies. Gee (2000) illustrates this point vividly with an example of a small girl who told a story at the class 'sharing time'. The story was full of rhythm, pattern and repetition and would have been highly valued in the child's family and local community, where oral performance was prized according to its entertainment value. The teacher, however, was anticipating a different (unarticulated) style of oral performance, that of being informative, linear and succinct, and did not appreciate the child's form of story-telling. Subsequently this child was referred to the school psychologist for telling tall stories.

Sometimes, too, behavioural approaches fail to take adequate account of the emotions. As Hanko comments:

> Emotional factors affect learning, especially if we see only their provocative or withdrawn facade which usually hides children in constant misery, loneliness, self-loathing and fear... teachers are frequently baffled by children who 'don't respond even to praise', 'spoil their work the moment I praise it', 'just shrug it off' and 'don't seem to care'.
>
> (1994: 166)

Cognitive-behavioural approaches

Recent years have seen a move away from strict behaviourist approaches towards alternative ways of understanding learning that take greater account of how individuals construct reality for themselves. Cognitive-behavioural approaches have emerged from behavioural psychology and have a number of additional key characteristics, one of which relates to a focus on the way the mind processes information. Cognitive-behavioural approaches can incorporate a wide range of cognitive processes, including the use of perception, language, problem-solving, memory, decision-making and imagery. For example, in the school situation when students begin to pay attention to 'the stream of automatic thoughts which accompany and guide their behaviour, they can learn to make choices about the appropriateness of these self-statements, and if necessary introduce new thoughts and ideas' (McLeod, 1998: 72). This can result in behaviour more appropriate to the school context and lead to a higher level of academic achievement.

Reflection 2.1: Focusing on solutions

In the area of student behaviour in schools, a number of researchers have employed the concept of meta-cognitive awareness (that is, awareness of one's own thinking, feelings and emotions) in the area of emotional regulation, or self-management in order to cope with feelings such as violence, bullying, disaffection or isolation (Meichenbaum and Turk, 1976; Shapiro and Cole, 1994). De Shazer's (1985) 'solution-focused brief therapy' (SFBT) continues to be employed in some places. SFBT is focused on solutions rather than problems, hence the main task is to help a student imagine how he or she would like things to be different, and what it would take for them to be so. The best-known technique is that of the 'miracle question' (de Shazer, 1988). A paraphrase of this might be, 'If one night, while you were sleeping, a miracle happened and the problem that brought you here was solved but you didn't know that the miracle had happened because you were asleep, what would be different when you woke up in the morning that would tell you that the miracle had taken place?' As de Shazer et al. (2007: 40) comment: 'Ultimately the miracle question is not so much about figuring out what would be a "dream come true"...as it is about discovering...and replicating the effects of it.'

Also important are the 'scaling questions':

- On a scale of 1 to 10, where 1 is the worst it's ever been and 10 is after the miracle has happened, where are you now?
- Where do you need to be?
- What will help you move up one point?
- How can you keep yourself at that point?

In the context of schools, students are invited to work out ways of reaching a positive outcome and to use their responses to learn ways of behaving more appropriately in school and achieve more highly in academic terms.

Constructivist approaches

In recent years there has been an increasing interest in constructivist views of learning with a focus on ways in which individuals actively construct their understanding of the reality in which they live. There is a recognition here that 'the emotional and behavioural difficulties which people experience in their lives are not caused directly by events but by the way they interpret and make sense of these events' (McLeod, 1998: 71–2). How young people think of themselves in school has an enormous impact on their learning and behaviour. Pollard comments that some might be 'highly anxious and continually under-value themselves'. Some can seem 'over-confident and extremely resilient'. Some may know their own strengths and weaknesses while others 'may seem to have relatively naïve views of themselves. Children may be gregarious, or loners, or they may be lonely' (Pollard, 2002: 97–8). Learning is highly dependent on both the context, what the learner makes of the situation in which he or she finds himself and the interaction between them (Greeno, 1998; Lave and Wenger, 1998).

In this view, difficulties in learning and behaviour 'problems' in schools are also situated in the interaction between the context and the perceptions of students (Mehan, 1996; Lave and Wenger, 1998; McDermott, 1999). It is important therefore for adults to understand how children make sense of their own circumstances and what impression is conveyed to students of others' views of them. Adults in schools have to be concerned all the time with the sense that children are making of their worlds, their experiences, tasks in classrooms, and so on. Being open to this demands careful and sensitive listening, observation and reflection. It appears obvious that taking the young person's view seriously is essential to any consideration of how we might reduce obstacles to students' learning (Hart, 1995). Learning programmes are likely to be more effective when students have some sense of ownership over them.

Children, like the rest of us, come to decisions about what learning is worth investing in. They judge whether the benefits of any given learning situation outweigh the time, effort and (in some classrooms) the risk of being wrong and exposing themselves to public humiliation in being thought stupid. Questions of value-to-oneself are at the heart of the learning process. Young people may not make the effort if they do not perceive it as worthwhile in relation to the effort that is required. All learners are active, all learners think about their learning, all have views about it and all have feelings about it, no matter what the context. All learners have some power and control. They may enthusiastically comply with the demands set for them or may outwardly comply but inwardly be resentful. They may be unco-operative or disruptive and resist the demands made on them. For young people in schools, feeling that they have some control over their learning, understanding why they are learning something, choosing how to do it and when to do it, may be important. Allowing learners some degree of choice in, or power over, what they learn and how they learn invites them to take control over their learning. This is not always easy in busy classrooms. However, offering some choices that can be accommodated within the school day gives learners responsibility and acknowledges that they have preferences, dislikes and ideas.

Reflection 2.2: When difficulties are not just literacy-related

Arnold was another student about whom I had many concerns. Over the two years I worked with him in a comprehensive upper (13–18) school, his written work showed just how little progress he seemed to have made in literacy skills. He just did not seem to care. He came to school in a shirt that was always dirty. He smelled of body odour and nicotine. I never knew what Arnold was thinking. I never knew what he felt about his own lack of literacy. If we had known, it might have made a difference either to our approach or to the outcome educationally. Arnold left school functionally illiterate.

(Adapted from Wearmouth, 2009)

Constructing understanding

While Skinner's work was seminal to advances in understanding learning from a behaviourist perspective, a number of researchers have contributed to the way we often think about children's learning from a constructivist view. Two of the foremost theorists are Jean Piaget (1896–1980) and Lev Vygotsky (1896–1934). Other leading educationalists, for example, Jerome Bruner, have picked up and developed Vygotsky's ideas.

Jean Piaget

Jean Piaget, a Swiss psychologist, was one of the theorists who contributed a lot to the thinking that children learn by doing. From his work with his own children, Piaget (1954; 1964; 1969) concluded that there were four universal stages of learning:

- *Sensorimotor (0–2 years)*. The child is born with a set of reflex movements and perceptual systems, learning is, in general, through trial and error learning and there is quick development of direct knowledge of the world as the child relates physical actions to perceived results of those actions.
- *Preoperational (2–7 years)*. The child develops the ability mentally to represent events and objects (the semiotic function) and to engage in symbolic play but is not yet able to see others' point of view which is characteristic of 'egocentrism'.
- *Concrete operational (7–11 years)*. The child develops the ability to use logical thought or operations (rules) but can only apply logic to physical objects, hence the term, concrete operational. The child also becomes less ego-centric and begins to be able to see things from the viewpoint of others. He or she starts to develop an understanding of conservation of number, area, volume, orientation and reversibility, but is not yet able to think abstractly or hypothetically.
- *Formal operational (11+ years)*. The child acquires the ability to use abstract reasoning and manipulate ideas in his or her head, without being dependent on concrete objects, for example, to combine and classify items, do mathematical calculations, think creatively, and imagine the outcome of particular actions.

Piaget's work has been criticised in a number of respects. For example, his work implies that child development occurs in discrete stages, but actually, of course, it is uninterrupted, continuing throughout adulthood. In basing his research on his own children, he was using a skewed sample of the child population from which to draw his conclusions. He also appears to have underestimated children's abilities at different ages (Wood et al., 2001). In addition, there is insufficient consideration of different social or cultural contexts in which children in general live and grow. Further, some of the methods for the research on which these conclusions were based have been questioned (Donaldson, 1984). However, despite these criticisms, Piaget's conclusions that learners construct knowledge by interacting with their environment and that they re-construct their thoughts in the light of new experiences, have made a strong contribution to practice in primary schools, in particular. Linking learning to direct experience with the environment has been influential on primary practices in organising rich classroom learning environments replete with concrete materials and resources.

Lev Vygotsky

Akin to Piaget's model of constructivism but developed in a very different context, that of Soviet Russia, is the social constructivist model of Lev Vygotsky. As Vygotsky (1962), suggested, language is also important to the sense-making process, in addition to a carefully organised rich learning environment. Vygotsky concluded that it is through interacting with a more informed/knowledgeable other that learning is developed. This means that relationships among learners themselves and between learners and adults that are bound up with the learning environment are also important.

The next steps in learning of which a child is capable, and the range of knowledge and skills that learners are not yet ready to learn on their own but can learn with support from, and in interaction with, more informed and experienced others, for example, adults, is called the 'zone of proximal development' or ZPD in this model. Within the zone, the more experienced other is central. Learning involves practice within the zone, for example, to encourage the development of skills to automatic level. One important reason why Vygotsky's views have become popular in education circles in recent years is that they give a clear role for the teacher in the person of this more informed other.

The view of learning just described emphasises the social and cultural context of learning and the role that adults play in supporting that learning, and is often called 'socio-constructivism' (the construction of knowledge in a social context), or is referred to as taking a sociocultural perspective on learning. The ideas from this view of learning underpin much of the current work on formative assessment – 'assessment for learning' – that is discussed in Chapter 8 of this book.

Jerome Bruner

Bruner (1966) outlines three modes of representation of reality used by humans as they develop their conceptual understanding of the world which, like Piaget's model above, move from the concrete 'learn by doing' to the abstract:

- *The 'enactive' mode of representation* works through action. We 'do' and then we understand and know. In their very early years, young children rely on enactive modes to learn. As they learn to move, they learn to do so through their own actions without the need for verbal and written and physical symbols. Children unable to experience their world by sight, hearing, taste, touch or smell, or unable to move easily will be less able to understand and know through 'doing' unless special efforts are made to enable them to access their world otherwise.
- *The 'iconic' mode* is a visual representation of the real object. Images therefore stand for the physical object. Using this mode of representation, children learn to understand what pictures and diagrams are and how to do mathematical calculations using numbers and without counting objects.
- *The 'symbolic' mode* is an abstract representation of something else. Abstract symbols are 'arbitrary', meaning that they do not necessarily bear any resemblance to whatever it is that they represent. For example, commonly in spoken language the sound of a word bears no resemblance to reality, unless it is onomatopoeic.

Children's learning involves becoming proficient in each of these increasingly more complex modes, but they may experience difficulty at any point in their development. A common feature in children who experience cognitive difficulties is weakness in understanding and remembering that a symbol can 'stand for' something else, for example, something concrete or an action. Teachers might need to build in strategies to classroom teaching which facilitate access to the curriculum in ways that address these difficulties, for example, much more time to acquire concepts through experience of using and manipulating concrete objects.

Summary

Over the years, the ways in which differences between people have been conceptualised, notions of entitlements and human rights have developed, and the variety of models of learning and behaviour that are used, have all contributed to the complexity and changing nature of the field of special educational needs.

3

Current statutory and regulatory frameworks for SEND

Introduction

As we saw in Chapter 1, in England and Wales, the 1981 Act is seen by many as the key piece of legislation concerned with children and young people who experience difficulties or have disabilities in education. Education Acts related to SEND and subsequent to the 1981 Act should be seen in the light of other education law that, following the Education Reform Act of 1988, encouraged a neo-liberal market-driven approach to education which led to competition, consumer choice and pressure on resources. Features of the 1988 Act that are relevant to SEND provision include the introduction of the National Curriculum, local management of schools, Grant Maintained Status and open enrolment in schools. Examples of curriculum requirements that had far-reaching consequences for students who experience difficulties are the introduction of the compulsory, subject-based curricular framework and a national system of assessment based on norms and focused on results which could be used to evaluate the 'effectiveness' of schools. The increasing focus on 'norms' inevitably led to a greater emphasis on making additional provision for those pupils who experience difficulties in the attempt to attain these norms.

In this chapter we will do the following:

- contextualise the development of current legislation by outlining law in the SEN field that preceded it;
- focus on features of Part 3 of the Children and Families Act (2014) and associated regulations and statutory guidance documents and their implications for policy and practice in schools and colleges;
- outline the requirements of the 2010 Equality Act as part of the legal framework for disabilities;
- consider the role of the SENCO, school management teams and governing boards in implementing SEND legislation;
- outline aspects of the role of OfSTED in ensuring the law is implemented.

The law relating to special educational needs

The 1993 Education Act replaced the 1981 Education Act and covered much of the same ground. It introduced the *Code of Practice for the Identification and Assessment of Special Educational Needs* (DfE, 1994), designed on the model of industrial codes of practice, to provide a shared text for use at tribunals, should there be any dispute between parents or carers and the school and the local education authority (LEA) (now the LA) with regard to decisions about their children in assessment and statementing. The previous local educational authority appeals panels which heard complaints from parents were replaced by 'independent' tribunals chaired by lawyers. Local authorities should provide education for excluded pupils in Pupil Referral Units which must offer a broad balanced curriculum, but not necessarily the full National Curriculum.

The 1993 Act was repealed and replaced by the 1996 Act in November 1996, with Part 4 of the new Act incorporating all the provisions of Part 3 of the 1993 Act. The 1996 Act remains the basis for education-related law in Wales, but the law in England changed substantially in 2014 with the Children and Families Act. The two Codes published since 1994 reflect changes in legislation, first, in relation to the 1996 Education Act and, most recently, to the Children and Families Act, 2014 (DfE, 2014a).

The Children and Families Act (2014)

The Children and Families Act (2014) has brought about some changes in the law in England. The new system of supporting children and young people with SEN now applies to young people from birth to 25 years, as long as they stay in education or training. This issue of age is important. In law, a child becomes a young person when he or she is no longer of compulsory school age (that is, when he or she became 16 before the last day of the summer term (Section 83(2)). Once a child becomes a young person, he or she can take decisions in relation to the Act on his or her own behalf, rather than their parents, subject to a young person 'having capacity' to take a decision under the Mental Capacity Act (2005). If young people do not have the mental capacity to make a decision on their own, their parents will automatically be assumed to be making the decision on their behalf unless the Court of Protection has appointed a deputy. A deputy is usually a young person's parent. The decision about whether young people have mental capacity to make a particular decision is something that they and their parents should make in the first instance. Mental capacity needs to be considered for every decision that a young person needs to make regarding their education. It can never be assumed by a school or college that a young person does or does not have the mental capacity to make a decision.

This new system will not cover children or young people if they are disabled and have health and social care needs but no SEN.

Section 19 of Part 3 of the Act requires that the views, wishes and feelings of children, young people and their parents, and their participation, must be central to every decision the LA makes in regard to assessing a child or young person's SEN and how to support them. Not to do so is illegal and can be open to challenge.

It is the LA's duty to ensure they identify all children and young people who have or may have SEN and disabilities in their geographical area. A child or young person with SEN is entitled to support that enables them to achieve the 'best possible educational and other outcomes'. The school or college that a child or young person attends should put support in place to make sure this is happening. If it does not, the LA has the responsibility to ensure it does.

Statutory assessment of special educational needs that previously might have resulted in a Statement of SEN, now may result in an Education Health and Care plan (EHC). If the young person has a statement of SEN, he or she must be transferred to an EHC unless his or her needs have changed and he or she no longer needs a statement. A young person in further education is now legally entitled to the special educational provision specified in their EHC plan, but EHC plans do not apply to higher education. Only the LA can carry out an EHC needs assessment to identify needs and provision to meet those needs. If an EHC plan is then issued, the LA has the legal duty to ensure that the educational provision is made. If a school or college's actual resources – finances or teaching expertise – cannot make the provision outlined in the plan, the LA must provide it. This duty can never be delegated to a school or college, no matter what funding arrangements are in place. Where there is health provision in an EHC plan, the local health commissioning body – usually the Clinical Commissioning Group – has the duty to provide it. It is also the local authority's duty to provide the social care provision in an EHC plan if it results from an assessment under social care legislation.

The school or college staff must tell the parent if the child or young person has been identified as having SEN, whether or not they have an EHC plan. They must identify their needs to the best of their ability and they must put the right support in place to make sure the child progresses and achieves the specified outcomes. All this information should be documented in a clear record that should be available to the parent(s) on request. Previously this would have been the individual education plan for a child without a statement, but the 2014 legislation no longer requires any particular format for this. The school must meet with the parent(s) at least three times a year to discuss this record.

Every LA must develop and publish a 'Local Offer' (§30) that sets outs the services and provision it expects to be available both inside and outside the LA's area for children and young people with SEN and a disability. The Local Offer should make clear what special educational provision it expects the schools and colleges in its area to make from their existing budgets. Local authorities have a duty to publish comments about the Local Offer from children, young people and their parents, and the action they intend to take in response (§30(6)).

The LA is obliged to consider identifying a personal budget (§48) for educational provision for a child or young person if the parent requests it when they are carrying out an EHC needs assessment or when they are reviewing an EHC plan. The personal budget is the notional amount of money that would be needed to cover the cost of making the special educational provision specified in the EHC plan. However, a head teacher or principal has a veto if they do not agree to a direct payment being made for special educational provision which would need to be delivered in their school or college.

When LAs take decisions about assessment or an EHC plan, they are required to inform parents and young people of their right to mediation ((§52(2)). This is arranged by the LA, except for health-related issues. The mediator must be independent. Parents and young people can only bring an appeal to a tribunal about the SEN element of a plan if they can demonstrate that they have considered mediation. We discuss the implications of the increased focus on parental entitlements in Chapter 12.

Responding to individual needs

When a teacher is seriously concerned about the progress made by a child in a classroom, it is very important to be aware of the process that should be followed to maintain the child's access to education. Schools, further education colleges and other settings have clear duties under statutory guidance in the *Special Educational Needs and Disability Code of Practice: 0 to 25 Years* (DfE, 2014a) and must 'have regard' to its contents. The link between the Code and its purpose in providing a shared framework should parents or families wish to make an appeal is made clear in the reference to the First-tier Tribunal: 'The First-tier Tribunal must have regard to any provision of the code that appears to it to be relevant to a question arising on an appeal under this Part' (§77 (6)).

In the next section, the content and implications of the 2014 Code are reviewed.

The Code of Practice 2014

The *Special Educational Needs and Disability Code of Practice: 0 to 25 Years* describes the principles that should be observed by all professionals working with children and young people who have SEN or disabilities. These include:

- taking into account the views of children, young people and their families;
- enabling children, young people and their parents to participate in decision-making;
- collaborating with partners in education, health and social care to provide support;
- identifying the needs of children and young people;
- making high quality provision to meet the needs of children and young people;
- focusing on inclusive practices and removing barriers to learning;
- helping children and young people to prepare for adulthood.

Changes from the previous Code which was published in England in 2001 reflect the new (2014) law and include:

- guidance on provision for disabled children and young people from 0–25 years, as well as those with SEN, to improve outcomes;
- a stronger focus on the participation of students and their families in decision-making (see Chapter 12 in this book);
- guidance on joint commissioning of services to ensure co-operation between education, health services and social care, and a new co-ordinated assessment process with Education, Health and Care plans to replace statements (see Chapter 13 in this book);

- guidance on what must be included in the Local Offer (see Chapter 11);
- advice for schools and colleges to adopt a graduated approach to identifying and providing for students with SEN with four stages of action: assess, plan, do, review, to replace the previous 'School Action' and School Action Plus' categories (see Chapters 8 and 9 in this book). The first step to supporting individual children's needs is high quality teaching by classroom teachers, differentiated for individual students.
- guidance on access to impartial advice that LAs must provide for families and students with SEN;
- advice on how to provide for four areas of special educational needs: communication and interaction, cognition and learning, social, emotional and mental health difficulties, and sensory and physical difficulties;
- guidance on record-keeping, with evidence of pupil progress, a focus on outcomes, and a rigorous approach to monitoring and evaluation of support that has been provided (see Chapter 10 in this book);
- guidance on funding. The notional SEN budget is not ring-fenced. The school should provide high quality support from the whole budget. The school should provide additional support up to a nationally prescribed threshold with the LA providing top-up funding where the cost of the SEN provision exceeds the threshold.

Individual plans for children and young people

The Code (§6.17) advises class and subject teachers, supported by the senior leadership team, to identify pupils who make less than expected progress by making regular assessments of the progress of all pupils.

> In deciding whether to make special educational provision, the teacher and SENCO should consider all of the information gathered from within the school about the pupil's progress, alongside national data and expectations of progress. This should include high quality and accurate formative assessment, using effective tools and early assessment materials.
>
> (Dfe, 2014a: §6.38)

Gathering of information about pupils should include discussion early on with both the pupil and their parents so that everyone can be clear about the pupil's areas of strength and difficulty, any concerns the parent(s) might have, the outcomes agreed for the child, and what the next steps will be. If a pupil is identified as having SEN, schools are exhorted to remove barriers to learning and put effective special provision, to be known as 'SEN provision', in place through a graduated approach in the form of a four-part cycle of assessment, planning, intervention and review (assess→plan→do→review) where previous decisions and actions are revisited, refined and revised as staff and parents understand more about what supports the pupil in making good progress. This approach should utilise more frequent review and more specialist expertise in successive cycles as required to match interventions to the educational needs of children and young people.

Where, despite appropriate interventions, a pupil continues to make less than expected progress, the school should consider involving specialists, including from outside agencies. Together, the SENCO, the class teacher, the specialists, and the parents/family, should consider a range of approaches to support the child's progress and agree the outcomes and a date by which progress will be reviewed.

If the child or young person still does not make the progress that is expected, the school or parents should consider requesting an Education, Health and Care needs assessment and provide evidence of the action taken by the school as part of its SEN support. Guidance given in the 2014 Code about EHC plans is discussed in the section on statutory assessment below.

Statutory assessment of special educational needs and disability

According to Ofsted (2010), about 1.7 million school-age children in England, that is, just over one in five pupils, were identified as experiencing special educational needs of various kinds. The Code of Practice makes the assumption that teachers will offer differentiated learning opportunities to all students, including those with special educational needs and disabilities. For example, the 2014 Code (§6.12) reads:

> All pupils should have access to a broad and balanced curriculum. The National Curriculum Inclusion Statement states that teachers should set high expectations for every pupil, whatever their prior attainment. Teachers should use appropriate assessment to set targets which are deliberately ambitious. Potential areas of difficulty should be identified and addressed at the outset. Lessons should be planned to address potential areas of difficulty and to remove barriers to pupil achievement. In many cases, such planning will mean that pupils with SEN and disabilities will be able to study the full national curriculum.

If, however, a child fails to make adequate progress, then additional or different action should be taken. The Code defines inadequate progress as progress which:

- is significantly slower than that of their peers starting from the same baseline;
- fails to match or better the child's previous rate of progress;
- fails to close the attainment gap between the child and their peers;
- widens the attainment gap.

(DfE, 2014a: §6.17)

Of the children that schools identify as having SEN, those who have longer-term or more severe disabilities or difficulties may be the subject of statutory assessment.

Education, health and care plans

Schools and colleges should identify and support young people with SEN and a disability, either from their own resources under what is now to be called 'SEN Support' or, where the degree of need is such that it requires a higher level of resourcing than is available from these resources, through an Education, Health and Care (EHC) plan. Local authorities, not schools, colleges or parents, have the legal duty to carry out an EHC needs assessment, issue an EHC plan and ensure the special educational provision that has been specified in an EHC plan. An LA has a clear duty to assess a child's or young person's education, health and care needs where he or she may have SEN and may need special educational provision to be made at a level or of a kind which requires an EHC plan. An EHC needs assessment can only be requested if the young person has or may have educational needs, NOT where there are only health and care needs, no matter how severe.

The test which local authorities must apply in coming to a decision about an EHC plan is set out in the Children and Families Act 2014 (§37 (1)). Based on the evidence gathered:

1 Where, in the light of an EHC needs assessment, it is necessary for special educational provision to be made for a child or young person in accordance with an EHC plan –
   (a) the local authority *must* secure that an EHC plan is prepared for the child or young person, and
   (b) once an EHC plan has been prepared, it must maintain the plan.

Further details about the required content of EHC plans are given in Chapter 8 in this book.

The special educational needs co-ordinator (SENCO)

The role of the special educational needs co-ordinator (SENCO) originally was set up in response to the Education Act of 1981. In many places, the role of the SENCO has developed considerably since that time. The new (2014) SEN and Disability Code of Practice highlights the strategic nature of the role at the level of the senior management team in a school or college:

> The SENCO has an important role to play with the headteacher and governing body, in determining the strategic development of SEN policy and provision in the school. They will be most effective in that role if they are part of the school leadership team.
>
> (DfE, 2014a: §6.87)

The day-to-day responsibility of the SENCO is outlined as: 'the operation of SEN policy and co-ordination of specific provision made to support individual pupils with SEN, including those who have an EHC plan' (DfE, 2014a: §6.88).

Key responsibilities can include:

- overseeing the day-to-day operation of the school's SEN policy;
- co-ordinating provision for children with SEN;
- liaising with the relevant Designated Teacher where a looked-after pupil has SEN;
- advising on the graduated approach to providing SEN support;
- advising on the deployment of the school's delegated budget and other resources to meet pupils' needs effectively;

- liaising with parents of pupils with SEN;
- liaising with early years providers, other schools, educational psychologists, health and social care professionals, and independent or voluntary bodies;
- being a key point of contact with external agencies, especially the local authority and its support services;
- liaising with potential next providers of education to ensure a pupil and their parents are informed about options and a smooth transition is planned;
- working with the headteacher and school governors to ensure that the school meets its responsibilities under the Equality Act (2010) with regard to reasonable adjustments and access arrangements;
- ensuring that the school keeps the records of all pupils with SEN up to date.

(DfE, 2014a: §6.90)

We discuss the management role of the SENCO and its implications for policy and practice related to SEND provision in schools and colleges in more detail in Chapter 10.

The role of the Area SENCO

Local authorities often make use of Area SENCOs to provide advice and guidance to, for example, early years providers on the development of inclusive early learning environments. In the Code §5.56, the role is outlined as, typically,

- providing advice and practical support to early years providers about approaches to identification, assessment and intervention within the SEN Code of Practice;
- providing day-to-day support for setting-based SENCOs in ensuring arrangements are in place to support children with SEN;
- strengthening the links between the settings, parents, schools, social care and health service;
- developing and disseminating good practice;
- supporting the development and delivery of training both for individual settings and on a wider basis;
- developing links with existing SENCO networks to support smooth transitions to school nursery and reception classes;
- informing parents of, and working with, local impartial Information, Advice and Support Services, to promote effective work with parents of children in the early years.

Current definitions: areas of 'need'

The 'need' which assessment and subsequent provision should address is conceptualised somewhat differently across the UK. The current *SEN and Disability Code of Practice 0 to 25 Years* (DfE, 2014a: §5.32) recommends that assessment and provision should focus on four broad 'areas of need' described as 'communication and interaction', 'cognition and learning', 'social, emotional and mental health', and sensory and physical. Clearly there is a lot of overlap between these areas, as we note in Chapter 4 in this book.

The Equality Act (2010)

Other legislation may well affect the teaching role in schools. Since 2000, a number of pieces of legislation relating to disability equality have been passed across the UK, in 2001, 2005 and, most recently, in the Equality Act, 2010, the aim of which was to consolidate previous disability legislation. The Equality Act passed into law on 6 April 2010. It stresses planned approaches to eliminating discrimination and improving access, and is nationwide (including private education), imposing duties on schools and local authorities. In other words, organisations such as schools and colleges are expected to be proactive in anticipating and responding to the needs of their disabled students.

A child or young person is disabled under the Equality Act 2010 (section 6) if he or she has a physical or mental impairment which has a substantial and long-term adverse effect on his or her ability to carry out normal day-to-day activities. 'Substantial' means more than minor or trivial and 'long-term' means lasting more than one year or likely to last more than one year. Not all children or young people with special educational needs will be disabled and not all disabled children or young people will have special educational needs. The vast majority, however, will fall under both legal definitions.

Early years settings, schools, colleges and local authorities have clear legal duties to act to prevent unlawful discrimination, whether directly or indirectly. For example, Paragraph 85 of the Equality Act 2010 states that there must be no discrimination by a school, for example

2 (a) in the way it provides education for the pupil;
(b) in the way it affords the pupil access to a benefit, facility or service;
(c) by not providing education for the pupil;
(d) by not affording the pupil access to a benefit, facility or service.

Educational institutions must therefore ensure that they do not treat children and young people with disabilities less favourably than others. Over time, the law has now been changed to increase children's rights to be educated in the mainstream. Stronger rights to a place in a mainstream school have made it unlawful for schools and LAs to discriminate against disabled students, particularly in relation to admission arrangements and the educational provision in school. Paragraph 85 of the 2010 Equality Act, for example, also states that there must be no discrimination by a school against a young person:

3 (a) in the arrangements it makes for deciding who is offered admission as a pupil;
(b) as to the terms on which it offers to admit the person as a pupil;
(c) by not admitting the person as a pupil.

A child who has SEN and an Education, Health and Care Plan must now be educated in mainstream school subject to two conditions: the wishes of the child's parents and the provision of efficient education of other children.

Schools and colleges also have a duty to make reasonable adjustments – to change what they do or were proposing to do–to ensure a child or young person is not disadvantaged. This includes the provision of aids and services to support a child or young person. Schedule 13, of the Equality Act 2010 reads:

4 In relation to each requirement, the relevant matters are —
   (a) deciding who is offered admission as a pupil;
   (b) provision of education or access to a benefit, facility or service.

The Act gives parents the right of appeal to a Tribunal, if they feel their child has suffered discrimination.

Summary

The law currently relating to special educational needs and disabilities is the Children and Families Act (2014), Part 3. Statutory guidance in the new Code highlights clear duties laid on schools, colleges and other settings to ensure that young people with SEND have access to an education that takes account of their needs. 'Appropriate' education is no longer sufficient, however. Section 19(d) of Part 3 of the Children and Families Act (2014) specifies access that enables young people to 'achieve the best possible' educational and other outcomes. This reflects a new and higher level of outcome than previously anticipated.

The Equality Act (2010) consolidates previous disability-equality and discrimination legislation and is nationwide, operating across all four countries of the UK.

4

Understanding communication and interaction needs

Introduction

The 'need' which assessment and subsequent provision should address can be conceptualised in a variety of ways. In England, the new Code of Practice (DfE, 2014a: §5.32), outlines the following four broad areas of need and support:

- communication and interaction
- cognition and learning
- social, emotional and mental health
- sensory and physical needs

Clearly. there can be a lot of overlap between these areas. Statutory advice in the current Code (DfE, 2014a: §5.33) clearly acknowledges that individual needs may not be confined to one discrete area but can span these areas.

This chapter will discuss research and practice related to identifying and making effective provision for needs in the first of the four areas, communication and interaction. It will include particular discussion of difficulties in receptive and expressive language and autism.

The importance of communication

Communication is a vital part of building relationships, sharing experiences and learning. A number of conditions are associated with difficulties in this area, for example, pragmatic language impairment, autism and profound and multiple learning difficulties. There is a close link between communication and language, but they are not synonymous. 'Communication is really more the means by which we convey language, both to get our meaning across and to understand the meaning of others' (National Deaf Children's Society, 2010: 8). It involves not only language, but also 'other things like eye contact, gesture, tone of voice, facial expressions and body language'. Language is 'the words (vocabulary), phrases, grammar and expressions we use and how we organise them to communicate' (National Deaf Children's Society, 2010).

English as an additional language and special educational needs

The various Codes of Practice across the UK note that the identification and assessment of the special educational needs of young people whose first language is not English require particular care. The 2014 Code in England (2014: § 5:30), for example, advises that

> [P]ractitioners should look carefully at all aspects of a child's learning and development to establish whether any delay is related to learning English as an additional language or if it arises from SEN or disability. Difficulties related solely to learning English as an additional language are not SEN.

We cannot assume that their language status or unfamiliar or conflicting expectations are the only reason for students who learn English as an additional language making slow progress. They may also experience general cognitive difficulties. This may be a very sensitive area that requires specialist help. If by providing contextual support, cognitively demanding tasks can be accomplished, the needs are linguistic; if not, they may be educational. It is important always to try to obtain a first language assessment. Standardised tests are often culturally or linguistically biased so it is also important to check whether norm-referencing was on a bilingual population.

Language impairment

Difficulties in language acquisition may involve receptive (comprehending what is said and written) or expressive (putting thoughts coherently into words, verbal or written) language impairments. The former is less obvious than the latter and can create barriers to learning if overlooked. Young people experiencing pragmatic language impairment (PLI), previously called 'semantic-pragmatic' disorder, have special challenges with using language appropriately in social situations and with semantic aspects of language, that is, the meaning of what is said. Such an impairment can create challenges in the classroom, given that so much of the teaching in schools and colleges depends on spoken and written forms of language (Smedley, 1990; Adams and Lloyd, 2007). Children who have PLI have difficulties developing conversational skills, such as turn-taking and adhering to the topic of the conversation (Bishop, 2000). Some are insensitive to their listeners and talk endlessly about their own preoccupations and interests. Some experience problems understanding discourse and telling stories in a logical order (Norbury and Bishop, 2003); and have problems with over-literal use of language (Leinonen and Letts, 1997). Some are competent in using the formal structure of language, spoken and written, but experience difficulties in semantic understanding (Rapin and Allen, 1983).

Pragmatic language impairment is one of the difficulties often experienced by autistic children (see below).

Addressing language impairment

Structured programming

Adams and Lloyd (2007: 229–30) describe a highly structured classroom intervention to address PLI, using 'modelling and individual practice; role-play; practising specific pragmatic skills in conversations;...promoting self-monitoring and coping strategies...to make both immediate and hidden meanings of language and communication explicit', as well as the pragmatics of grammatical structure:

- First, good practice 'in interacting at an appropriate social and language level with the child' was established. The language demands in the classroom were modified, typically by 'having an assistant translate language into short meaningful utterances' accompanied by a visual demonstration.
- Next, the children were taught 'the vocabulary of social situations and insight' into others' emotions. Changes to routines were added in small steps, and discussed before they were implemented. Children were supported to understand 'social and verbal inferences, metaphors and hidden meaning in language'.
- Finally, work on the pragmatics of language focused on 'explicit exercises and classroom support in exchange structure, turn-taking, topic management, conversational skills, building sequences, cohesion and coherence in narrative and discourse'.

Alternative and augmentative communication (AAC)

Alternative and augmentative communication (AAC), any kind of communication that replaces standard means of communication such as speech, is often used where young people experience particular difficulties in verbal communication. Alternative and augmentative communication systems are designed to complement and enhance standard means of communication (see http://www.autism.org.uk/living-with-autism/strategies-and-approaches/alternative-and-augmentative-communication/picture-exchange-communication-system.aspx). One form of AAC is the Picture Exchange Communication System (PECS) in which a child is taught to communicate with an adult by being given a card with a picture on it. In PECS, the adult teaches the child to exchange a picture of something for an item he or she wants, for example, to exchange a picture of a drink for a real drink. Pictures can be used progressively to make whole sentences or express preferences, but it may take a long time to reach this stage of development in communication.

Developing expressive language

Students who experience difficulty in expressing themselves need frequent opportunities for exploratory talk in every area of the curriculum in order to put new information and ideas into their own words and to link subject matter to what they already know. Strategies that facilitate oral language development might include exploratory talk in small groups, problem-solving aloud, explanations of how something is made, or how and why things happen, dramatisation and role-play, interviews (live or taped), and group discussion.

Objects of reference and symbol systems

Objects of reference and electronic banks of pictograms are forms of AAC that are also often used to assist children with varying degrees of difficulties in communicating. 'Objects of reference' refer to physical objects used to represent those things about which humans communicate: activities, events, people, ideas, and so on. These objects can be used as a 'bridge' to more abstract forms of communication such as sign, symbol or word. Objects of reference are often chosen because of their multisensory properties to give the individual a clue about what is about to happen, for example, a piece of soap to signify that washing is about to take place, or a seat buckle to signify a car journey. It is essential that the same item is always used to signify the same event. The contexts in which various objects gain significance and meaning are obviously different for different people.

Symbol-based language programs have been developed over many years. For example, Widgit Software has produced an array of software that uses pictorial symbols to support the development of communication skills. Widgit symbols have a consistent visual structure with a wide vocabulary that can be used in a combined sequence to convey a broader meaning and build more precise information. Widgit describes its Symbol Set as 'comprehensive collections of images' designed to 'support text, making the meaning clearer and easier to understand' by providing a 'visual representation of a concept'. The Symbol Set often 'follows a schematic structure, or set of design "rules"', that enables the reader to develop his or her own receptive and expressive language skills (see http://www.widgit.com/symbols/about_symbols/accessed 1 June 2015).

The experience of 'autism'

In 1943, Leo Kanner identified a difficulty in a small group of young children which was marked by their inability to relate to people and social situations. profound 'aloneness', failure to use language fluently to communicate and anxious and obsessive desire to maintain sameness, fascination for objects which are handled with skill in fine motor movements, a good rote memory, over-sensitivity to stimuli and, often, difficulties in learning, some at a severe level. He called it 'early infantile autism' from the Greek αυτος (autos) meaning 'self' to denote excessive focus on the self (Kanner, 1943).

Around the same time, Hans Asperger in 1944 used the term 'autistic' to denote a range of traits in some ways similar to those commented on by Kanner (Wing, 1996). Additional features identified by Asperger were unusual responses to some sensory experiences: auditory, visual, olfactory (smell), taste and touch. He also noticed an uneven developmental profile, a good rote memory, circumscribed special interests, and motor co-ordination difficulties. People with Asperger Syndrome tend not to experience similar levels of learning difficulties that are associated with autism, and often have measured levels of intelligence that are average or above (National Autistic Society (2015a), http://www.autism.org.uk/about-autism.aspx, accessed 1 June 2015).

Building on previous work, Wing and Gould (1979) identified a 'triad of impairments' in a broad group of 'autistic' children:

- *difficulty in social interaction, difficulty with social relationships*, for example, appearing aloof and indifferent to other people, that clearly affects interactions with other children and adults, difficulty in understanding unwritten social rules, recognising other's feelings, or seeking comfort from others. Grandin (1996) recalls pulling away when others tried to give her a hug because being touched over-stimulated her senses and overwhelmed her. She remembers always wanting to participate in activities with other children but not knowing how and never fitting in. She tried to work out how to behave from observing other people and learning through trial and error.
- *social communication problems, both verbal and non-verbal*. People on the autistic spectrum often find it hard to understand the meaning of gestures, facial expressions or tone of voice.
- *lack of social imagination*, which means inability to think and behave flexibly. This may result in restricted, obsessional or repetitive activities and difficulties in developing the skills of playing with others. Children often find it hard to understand and interpret other people's thoughts, feelings and actions, predict what will or could happen next and understand the concept of danger. They may also find it hard to engage in imaginative play, prepare for change and plan for the future, and cope in new or unfamiliar situations.

In addition to this triad, repetitive behaviour patterns are a notable feature, as well as a resistance to change in routine.

Approaches to addressing autism

What is needed in educational terms to support the learning of students with severe forms of autism is a specialist approach and structured support (Autism Education Trust/CRAE, 2011). The Treatment and Education of Autistic and related Communication Handicapped Children programme (TEACCH, 1998), for example, combines cultivating individual strengths and interests with structured teaching. The TEACCH approach does not just look for environmental stimuli that trigger particular behaviours, but it considers the way the child 'reads' his or her environment. The principles guiding TEACCH include improving skills through education and modifying the environment to accommodate individual autistic students, structured teaching rather than more informal approaches, and parents collaborating with professionals as co-therapists so that techniques can be continued at home.

In classrooms, to take account of the challenges facing autistic students, teachers can address the learning and behavioural needs of children on the autistic spectrum in a number of ways:

- paying close attention to clarity and order, reducing extraneous and unnecessary material in order that children know where their attention needs to be directed, and maintaining a predictable physical environment with very predictable and regular routines, ensuring that everything is kept in the same place;
- teaching children agreed signals to be quiet or to call for attention;
- providing specific low-arousal work areas free from visual distractions (headphones might be made available to reduce sound);
- using alternative and augmentative communication (see above), for example, by providing a visual timetable with clear symbols to represent the various activities for the day, and a simple visual timer with, for example, an arrow that is moved across a simple timeline to show how much time has passed and how much is left.

In order to develop greater understanding of personal emotions, children might be taught in a very deliberate, overt and structured way:

- to name their feelings and relate these to their own experiences, predict how they are likely to feel at particular times and in particular circumstances, and recognise the signs of extreme emotions, such as anger. A visual gauge showing graduated degrees of anger in different shades of colour can often be helpful here;
- to identify and name others' feelings and link these to possible causes, and identify appropriate responses to others' emotions. They might, for example, keep a feelings diary in which they record times when they feel happy, sad or frightened, and what they can do about this. Teachers might use art, drama and social stories to identify the different kinds of emotions and explore their physical aspects and talk through situations that need to be resolved.

Above all, it is really important to get to know the pupil really well and to understand his or her individuality, strengths, weakness, likes and dislikes, and so on.

An individual behaviour support plan for an autistic student is included as Appendix B10 on pp. 256-9.

Reflection 4.1: Teaching communication skills

In a recent interview (Wearmouth, unpublished), Martha, the mother of an 8-year-old autistic child, N, described how she and her husband taught N to communicate with them at home, using PECS (see above) and other strategies. The hardest thing for them was how long every aspect of development in his ability to communicate took. They started with teaching him the purpose of communication because up till then he had not seen the purpose of it. His mother had done everything for him. To teach him, they used the technique of object exchange. To begin, his mother stuck a picture of a chocolate biscuit to a fridge magnet, put his hand on to the magnet, removed it from the fridge and put it into her own hand saying, 'Chocolate biscuit, please.' Then she gave him the biscuit, saying, 'Chocolate biscuit', to make the link between the picture and the sound symbols of the words. Finally, she helped him to put the magnet back on the fridge as an end to that routine. Suddenly there was strong motivation for the child to want to use the object exchange and a purpose in communication and he quickly learned to do it for himself. A 'stop' sign was put on the fridge to symbolise 'no more', also.

Signing in order to communicate was also important at this point. Mother and child together learned Makaton signing from the CBBC programme *Something Special* which has an actor signing all the way through. They found Makaton simple and fun to use together. Signing was also used at a special pre-school group to teach him to transition between tasks – when to stop an activity, and so on. For many autistic children, the stream of language, in words, makes little sense, but as soon as signs and pictures are used as well, the child can understand.

The mother taught the boy what the signs meant when she quite deliberately gave him the verbal equivalent every time she used one. 'Every time you sign, you also say at the same time, and he makes the connection.'

At this point the boy was therefore using object exchange, and also the mother was 'signing and saying' simultaneously. She spoke in very short, punctuated sentences when she commented on what was going on, and did not expect him to understand what was going on in her mind.

The speech therapist advised that he might become very anxious if activities were sprung on him without any warning. Next, therefore, in developing his communication skills, came pictures to forewarn him what was about to happen, for example, pictures of a car and the local supermarket to show that they were about to go shopping. (A picture of a timer to indicate 'time to go' was no use, probably because the concept of time itself was too complex.)

Following this, his mother made line drawings on the pictures to make the link between pictures of the real thing and symbols to represent them. For example, a line drawing of a red door represented the supermarket. The line drawings made the instigation of simple communication, through PECS, possible for him. This was always around requests for food and drink.

Signing continued, accompanied by a running commentary from his mother on what was happening.

Subsequently, the use of PECS made scheduling possible. 'There is so much safety in schedules for an autistic child because one thing leads to the next.' After a while, words can be written underneath the drawings to encourage literacy. N's mother described the family's use of scheduling as follows:

> We regularly use scheduling with picture cards at home. The cards have pictures of what we do during the day, places we visit, and tasks to be completed. At the beginning of the day, we choose pictures that represent what will happen that day. We stick the cards on a velcro strip, and as we complete activities through the day we unstick each card and 'post' it in a 'completed' box. The benefit is that my son can see the whole day's happenings and can predict what will happen next. I have found that using schedules has reduced my son's stress, and built his confidence and, over time, has increased his flexibility. If the schedule needs to change, it can be discussed and my son can see that the rest of the schedule remains unaltered, which can be reassuring to him.

It is essential that an autistic child knows that he or she can communicate with others, so learning to sign was important for other members of the family and friends.

By the time he went to school at the age of nearly 5, N spoke only three words: hippo, purple and ten. On entry, a very sensitive TA supported him very successfully through his first year. She set out to understand N as a person and how to communicate with him. At times he still ran into problems, however. For example, his schedule for going to the toilet included washing his hands and turning off the tap, but one day the tap was stuck on, and he would not leave the washroom because he could not complete the expected activities.

By the end of Year One, his vocabulary had increased considerably. The target on his IEP was to learn how to ask for help and, to assist him with this, he was given a card that said: 'Help me'. Now N is about to move to a middle school, so the concern for his parents is how to liaise effectively with the SENCO and other staff, and hope that they are all prepared to get to know, communicate with, and understand their son.

The use of ICT to support communication

Many assistive devices are available to enable students to communicate: electronic language boards, voice synthesisers and voice recognition software. Screen magnifiers, with or without a speech facility, are intended to support students who experience visual difficulties, to access on-screen text, graphics, tool bars, icons through magnification, colour-changing options, speech, Braille output, and so on (http://www.inclusive.co.uk/product-list?Text=screen%20magnifier, accessed 1 June 2015).

The standard computer keyboard favours right-handed people with the numeric keypad on the right. It is also sensitive and strings of letters may appear on the screen if a key is held down for slightly too long. The way the keyboard behaves can be changed, however, by using some of the accessibility in, for example, Windows. The use of 'StickyKeys' enables one finger to be used to operate shift, control and alt keys (http://windows.microsoft.com/en-GB/windows-xp/help/using-stickykeys, accessed 1 June 2015). 'FilterKeys' allow adjustment to the length of time a key needs to be held down before it appears or on the screen (https://www.microsoft.com/resources/documentation/windows/xp/all/proddocs/en-us/access_filterkeys_turnon.mspx?mfr=true, accessed 1 June 2015). 'MouseKeys' enable the mouse pointer to be moved around using the numeric keypad keys. Keyguards with holes positioned over each key can make it impossible to press two keys at once while it is possible to rest hands and arms on the guard without pressing keys (http://www.bltt.org/quicktips/foakeyguards.htm, accessed 1 June 2015). They can be removed and fitted for use only when required. 'IntelliKeys' can be used as a programmable alternative keyboard that plugs into the keyboard or USB port to enable users with physical, visual or cognitive disabilities, to type, enter numbers, navigate on-screen displays and carry out menu commands (http://www.inclusive.co.uk/intellikeys-usb-keyboard-p2392#, accessed 1 June 2015).

Different sizes and shapes of keyboards can also replace the standard keyboard, and the position of the keyboard can be changed to accommodate individual needs. Retractable lap trays bolted under the desk can hold the keyboard to enable a lower typing position if needed. Keyboards can be tilted, and switches and pointers can be fixed in specific positions where they can be handled more easily. Alternatively, on-screen keyboards enabling letters to be selected by a mouse or trackball can be used to make the selection. Some on-screen keyboards also have a facility for word prediction to make typing quicker (http://windows.microsoft.com/en-us/windows/type-without-keyboard#type-without-keyboard=windows-7, accessed 1 June 2015).

It is also possible to adjust the way the mouse operates, for example, the speed, and the amount of time needed for double clicking. The buttons can be swapped over for left-handed use. Mice also come in different sizes and shapes; and require varying amounts of pressure on buttons. A trackball is like an upturned mouse but it is a static device with the ball on the top which is moved with fingers, thumbs and palms (http://www.trackballmouse.org/, accessed 1 June 2015). Larger trackballs can be moved with one's feet.

Voice recognition is an alternative to typing on a keyboard. There can be a difficulty in the use of voice recognition software to support the writing of text, however, where students' words are not sufficiently clear to be encoded into text. With screen-based devices such as touch screens and a light pen, which is a light-sensitive stylus wired to a video terminal that is used to draw pictures or choose an option from a menu, selections and movements can be made by pointing at the screen surface. However, where a user is physically or cognitively unable to use any keyboard or pointing device, then a starting point can be to use a switch, a button which sends a signal to the computer to drive the software. Switches can be operated by any controlled movement of the body.

An example of a writing support and multimedia tool for children of all abilities is 'Clicker Writer' (http://www.cricksoft.com/uk/products/clicker/home/writer.aspx, accessed 1 June 2015). At the top of the screen is a word processor. At the bottom of the screen is the 'Clicker Grid'. This has 'cells' containing letters, words or phrases that teachers can click on, to send them into Clicker Writer so that students can write sentences without actually writing or using the keyboard.

In Chapter 5, we consider issues related to difficulties in cognition and learning, and some of the ways in which these might be addressed.

5

Understanding cognition and learning needs

Introduction

The Latin root of the word 'cognition' is 'cognoscere', which means 'to get to know', or 'to recognise'. In general terms, the way in which 'cognition' is used in the Code of Practice relates largely to information-processing associated with problem-solving, language, perception and memory and the development of concepts. The cognitive difficulties experienced by some students clearly extend to the area of communication and interaction discussed above. It is obvious, for example, that language acquisition and use are integral to the development of thinking, problem-solving and communication (Wearmouth, 2009).

In this chapter, we examine:

- the issue of difficulties in cognition within a framework of understanding learning as a developmental process;
- some of the areas in schools where young people might experience particular problems, for example, in the comprehension of written text, and in learning mathematical concepts;
- the implications of profound difficulties in cognition and learning;
- the effects of cognitive difficulties in two particular areas:
  - Down's syndrome;
  - dyslexia.

Understanding children's modes of learning

As discussed in Chapter 2, and despite criticisms made of them, Piaget's four universal stages of learning and Bruner's (1966) model of three modes of representation of reality might be seen as useful frameworks within which to think about the level of learning at which young people are operating as they develop their conceptual understanding of the world. Those who experience cognitive difficulties are likely to need more time to understand and absorb new concepts and to need support for their learning through concrete objects for a longer period than their peers if necessary.

Although movement through the four stages, or three modes, above can be seen as developmental, it must be said that they are not necessarily age-dependent, or invariant. As adults, we habitually use all three modes of representation, for example (Bruner, 1966).

Moderate difficulties in learning

Children who experience difficulty in understanding more abstract concepts might learn effectively from teachers who understand that children learn by doing first, and some children need longer than others. The Primary National Strategy (2005, ref 1235/2005) suggested that, whenever possible, pupils should have direct experience of a concept before it is used. To ensure that all students understand what is said, as Wearmouth (2009) notes, it is important to ensure that students realise they are being spoken to, and when they are being asked a question. Teachers should check that they speak calmly and evenly, and their faces are clearly visible. They might use visual aids related to the topics being discussed, and explain something several different ways if they have not been understood the first time.

Understanding written text

Commonly, difficulties in learning may include barriers relating to reading comprehension. At an early stage, the use of symbols on some computer programs acts as scaffolding for reading. Symbols can be used with one student and gradually withdrawn until he or she can read without them. The left–right directionality of reading can be reinforced through the Clicker programme (http://www.cricksoft.com/uk/products/clicker/home/writer.aspx, accessed 1 June 2015). Sound to support reading and writing can be used in many different ways. Word-processors with speech synthesis can be very powerful. Learners can hear what they have written, either as they are writing, or hear the whole text after they have finished. Sound can be introduced to text by dropping it into a standard text-to-speech utility or talking word processor. The text may also be dropped into a program such as Writing with Symbols (Widgit computing) which gives a symbolic version that can be printed out and spoken aloud. Talking word-processors may be particularly useful tools to enable students to decode text downloaded from the Internet.

An example of a program to develop switch-accessible stories and slide shows is 'SwitchIt! Maker 2' (http://www.switchitmaker2.com/, accessed 1 June 2015). Each activity has a sequence of on-screen pages which can have a picture, video or text-based material, music or recorded speech. Pages can be turned by a simple switch, the computer's spacebar, the mouse buttons or IntelliKeys.

Using ICT can also facilitate writing for some pupils. Word-processing can offer:

> a means of drafting and re-drafting that is easy, efficient and accessible and so is a great equaliser in presentation... Pupils can work more quickly and demonstrate different types of writing exercise and have the opportunity to experiment... and thus demonstrate their true ability.
>
> (Lilley, 2004: 89)

Chapter 4 contains discussion of the use of ICT to address children's difficulties in communication which may well be applicable in relation to cognitive difficulties also.

Memory problems

In the area of moderate learning difficulties, very poor memory is a problem for a number of students. Students may not have grasped the information clearly in the first place. They may not have sufficiently linked the new information to previous knowledge (Wearmouth, 2009).

Memory is quite often seen as having two distinctive parts: long-term memory and short-term or 'working' memory. Many students with short-term memory difficulties have problems absorbing and recalling information or responding to and carrying out instructions within a busy classroom situation. They may find it difficult to copy from the blackboard as they are unable to memorise what they have seen and transpose it to the paper on the desk. As well as this, they are required to rotate this visual image through 90 degrees from the vertical to the horizontal and also to transpose the size of the letters involved.

Difficulties in mathematics

Much teaching and assessment in the area of mathematics takes place in the context of a symbolic representation of mathematics, that is, through written text and pictures (Rogers, 2007: 2). Many children appear to adopt mathematical symbols and algorithms without having grasped the concepts that underpin them (Borthwick and Harcourt-Heath, 2007). Learning to use number symbols is likely to occur simultaneously with acquiring the alphabetic principle and sound-symbol correspondence in literacy acquisition and, as Grauberg (2002) comments, 'Where is the "f" in 5?' Learners' ability to understand symbolic representation depends on an understanding of the first-hand experience to which the symbolic representation refers. In the case of younger learners, this may involve, for example, the handling and counting of everyday items.

Pictorial symbols or icons are clearly different from abstract symbols used at the formal operational (Piaget, 1969) of symbolic representational stage (Bruner, 1966). Lack of symbolic understanding in mathematics can lead to difficulties in the written recording of number work, relational signs: 'plus', 'minus', 'equal(s)', place value and 'zero', money and time, as Grauberg (2002: 5) notes.

Adding and subtracting both imply actions. Without an understanding of what the action is there is little point in trying to encourage the use of the symbol. '=' is often interpreted by children as 'makes', but it is obvious that a child's notion of 'makes' is clearly not what the symbol '=' means, mathematically.

Difficulties with the concept of place value and 'zero' can be experienced by students right to the end of their secondary education. Without understanding the whole concept of place value, the use of zero as a place holder in a multi-digit line is difficult to comprehend for some students. Addressing problems with place value might mean continuing to use concrete equipment such as Dienes materials – unit cubes, 'longs' of 10 cm cubes, and 'flats' of 100 cm cubes – for much longer than generally anticipated, providing that this can be done without embarrassing the child. For example, 54 might be written down at first as 50 with the 4 superimposed over the 0. And 504 would be written down as 500 with the 4 superimposed over the last 0 (Wearmouth, 2009).

It requires a lot of concrete activities in a variety of different contexts before a child with cognitive difficulties understands the concept of 'numberness'. In some countries in Europe and the Far East, for example, Japan, the preference in teaching numbers in the early years seems to be to emphasise recognition of small quantities without counting. Recognising a small number, for example, 4, as a quantity involves one operation of matching a sound symbol or visual symbol to an amount. This seems, logically, easier than recognising 4 from a number sequence, as seems to be common practice in the UK and the USA (Grauberg, 2002). This latter involves remembering that 4 comes after 3 and before 5, and simultaneously counting up to the total amount.

Time

'Time' is a complex concept for children. As Piaget (1969) notes, it includes points in time, duration and sequence of events, frequency of events, and intervals between them. Bruner's three modes of representation again offer a framework for thinking about activities and approaches for students who experience difficulties in the acquisition of time-related concepts. Using a timer or some sort of clock might help in the initial stages to enact the representation of time passing. Concentrating on the sounds emitted on striking a percussion instrument can encourage a sense of the frequency of events. These days the concept of a visual timetable for use in schools with young children and older children who experience cognitive difficulties is quite common (Selikowitz, 2008).

Addressing moderate difficulties in cognition and learning

Stages of learning and modes of representation

One way to begin to conceptualise a plan for addressing cognitive difficulties may be to reflect on the young person's stage of learning (Piaget, 1969) or the mode of representation habitually used (Bruner, 1966). For some children in mathematics, for example, it might be important to use concrete aids to establish number learning, for example, Cuisenaire rods and an abacus, for much longer than for other children. A major question is how to move from the act of adding, taking away or balancing to competent use of the abstract symbols. One way to do this might be to encourage children to devise their own symbols for the actions first so that the icon visibly represents their own understandings.

Precision teaching

Behaviourist principles can be applied when devising programmes for learning new material. A learning sequence using behaviourist principles might be structured by, first, breaking down the new information into a series of small steps, then teaching this information separately and sequentially. The difficulty level of the questions has to be graded so the learner's response is always correct. The learner responds to every question and receives immediate feedback and reinforcement of positive learning behaviour and the correctness of the response. Good performance in the lesson, in other words the desired behaviour of effort and achievement, is reinforced by verbal praise, prizes and good grades.

Thinking clearly about the next steps in learning can be very useful where a child experiences difficulties in conceptual understanding. Behaviourist approaches to learning in what we might call the basic skills can be very powerful in their effectiveness. Spelling programmes and basic numeracy programmes using the four rules of number have been devised along these lines, reinforcing the learning through repetitive drill and practice with rewards (reinforcers) for correct responses. However, these approaches cannot apply to all new learning. For example, the requirement for information to be broken down into small steps and for each response to be reinforced immediately restricts what can be learned through this approach. Further, not everything can be broken down into a clear sequence of stages that are the same for all learners. There is also the criticism of these approaches that they can be rigid and mechanical. Although it is useful in learning repetitive tasks like multiplication tables and those word skills that require a great deal of practice, higher-order learning is another matter. Furthermore, it is not possible, or desirable, that all new learning should be preprogrammed and that the outcomes should be known in advance because that would deny the importance of, for example, individual critical thinking, personal research and analysis and individual responses to art, drama, music, and so on. Also, some educators, for example, Hanko (1994), feel that behavioural approaches also fail to address students' ability to reflect on their own learning and achievement adequately.

Even so, behaviourist approaches have been very commonly adopted in schools and can still be identified in many software programs that are intended, for example, to encourage awareness of the four rules of number in mathematics, and teach phonics in decoding text and reading, and are designed to provide immediate feedback and reinforcement of learning.

Scaffolding learning

One of the ideas that has been developed from a sociocultural view is that of 'scaffolding' to support learning (Wood et al., 1976). Rogoff (1990) identifies six elements in scaffolding learning. First, engage the learners' interest in the task, and then demonstrate how to do it. Next, if possible, reduce the number of steps needed for the task so learners can recognise their own progress. Then, control frustration, and offer feedback so that learners can see their own progress. Finally, find a way to motivate the learners so they continue with the task.

To be successful, the interaction must be collaborative between student and the more knowledgeable other. The scaffolding must operate within the learner's zone of proximal development (ZPD). The scaffolder must access the learner's current level of understanding and then work at slightly beyond that level, drawing the learner into new areas of learning. The scaffold should be withdrawn in stages as the learner becomes more competent. In schools, the final goal is for the learner to become autonomous, secure enough in the knowledge required to complete the task.

Not all learning requires the physical presence of an adult. Learners need scaffolding from more knowledgeable others, but not too much. Learning is also about participating, for example, having the chance to behave as a reader, writer, and so on, alongside other readers and writers. Learning is often highly charged with emotion. Feelings accompanying success can be very pleasant and exciting. The sense of failure can be very upsetting and disturbing, especially when it is a frequent occurrence. Feelings are therefore very powerful in supporting or preventing learning. Getting the balance right is crucial. This is often especially difficult in school where there is a tendency in most classrooms for the adults to talk too much and for the learners to talk too little. Other resources, apart from adults, can scaffold learning also: IT, peers, books, materials, pop music, and so on.

Profound and multiple learning disabilities

Some children with profound and multiple learning disabilities may have autism or Down's syndrome. Others may have Rett syndrome, Tuberous Sclerosis, Batten's Disease or another disorder. One common factor for everyone is that they experience great difficulty communicating. Mencap (undated: 4) notes how many people with profound and multiple learning disabilities 'rely on facial expressions, vocal sounds, body language and behaviour to communicate'. Some people may only 'use a small range of formal communication, such as speech, symbols or signs'. Another factor is that learning is likely to be very slow. 'Short-term memory may well be very limited and children may need frequent repetition of the same concepts in the same situations' (Mencap, undated). Some may not reach the stage where they can communicate intentionally. Many may find it hard to understand what others are trying to communicate to them. It is very important, therefore, that those people who support people with profound and multiple learning disabilities 'spend time getting to know their means of communication and finding effective ways to interact with them' (Mencap, undated).

For very many years there was a general assumption that children with multiple and profound difficulties were ineducable. However, since the 1970 Education Act, the right of all children to an appropriate education, irrespective of the degree of difficulty in learning, has been acknowledged.

Down's syndrome

Down's syndrome is another condition often associated with some impairment of cognitive ability. A small number have severe to profound difficulties in learning, but children with Down's tend to have difficulties ranging from mild to moderate difficulties. The average IQ is around 50 (Dykens and Kasari, 1997).

Language skills show the difference between understanding speech and expressing speech, and commonly individuals with Down's syndrome have a speech delay (Bird and Thomas, 2002). Fine motor skills are delayed and often lag behind gross motor skills and can interfere with cognitive development. Delays in the development of gross motor skills are variable. Some children will begin walking at around 2 years of age, while others will not walk until age 4. Physiotherapy and participation in other specially adapted programmes of physical education may promote enhanced development of gross motor skills.

A 'syndrome' is a group of recognisable characteristics occurring together. Down's syndrome was first described by an English doctor, John Langdon Down, in 1866. It is a congenital condition – one present at birth. Down's is chromosomal. It occurs because each of the body's cells contains an extra copy of chromosome 21, and this can be identified in a foetus through amniocentesis during pregnancy, or in a baby at birth. In the United Kingdom, around one baby in every thousand, around 775 per year (http://www.nhs.uk/conditions/downs-syndrome/pages/introduction.aspx, accessed 1 June 2015), is born with Down's syndrome, although it is statistically much more common with older mothers. At maternal age 20, the probability is one in 1450 and at age 45 it is one in 35 (Morris et al., 2003). There is also data to suggest that paternal age, especially beyond 42, increases the risk of having a child with Down's syndrome (Fisch et al., 2003).

The medical consequences of the extra genetic material are highly variable and may affect the function of any organ system or bodily process. Health concerns for individuals with Down's syndrome include a higher risk of congenital heart defects, recurrent ear infections, obstructive sleep apnea and thyroid dysfunctions (Selikowitz, 2008). The incidence of congenital heart disease in children with Down's syndrome is up to 50 per cent (Freeman et al., 1998). Eye disorders are relatively common. For example, almost half have strabismus, in which the two eyes do not move in tandem (Yurdakul et al., 2006). In the past, prior to current treatment, there was also a high incidence of hearing loss in children with Down's syndrome. These days, however, with more systematic diagnosis and treatment of ear disease, for example, 'glue-ear' (see below) almost all children have normal hearing levels.

Individuals with Down's syndrome differ considerably in their language and communication skills. It is common for receptive language skills to exceed expressive skills. Overall cognitive development in children with Down's syndrome is quite variable, which underlines the importance of evaluating children individually (Selikowitz, 2008). Down's syndrome cannot be cured, but the learning and other difficulties associated with it can be addressed if appropriate help is offered and other people accept and include. Above all, it is important to stress that children with Down's syndrome are all individuals and will vary in their abilities and achievements.

Dyslexia

Some young people experience difficulties in learning in specific areas that appear to be unrelated to their overall ability. One of these areas of difficulty is dyslexia.

'Dyslexia' is a concept about which there is much controversy, for example, whether or not there is an identifiable entity that we might term 'dyslexia' and, if so, what its precise nature, causes and explanations might be (Stanovich, 2000). 'Dyslexia' is most commonly understood as a psychological explanation of difficulties in learning. The information-processing system of 'dyslexic' individuals is seen as different from that of non-dyslexics in ways which have an impact on a number of areas of performance. Some definitions relate only to difficulty in acquiring literacy as reflected by its derivation from Classical Greek: δυσ (dys), meaning 'bad' or 'difficult', and λεξίς (lexis), meaning 'word', or 'speech'. The British Psychological Society (BPS) Working Party adopted this narrower view of dyslexia related solely to literacy:

> Dyslexia is evident when accurate and fluent reading and/or spelling develops very incompletely or with great difficulty. This focuses on literacy learning at the 'word level' and implies that the problem is severe and persistent despite appropriate learning opportunities. It provides the basis for a staged process of assessment through teaching.
>
> (British Psychological Society, 1999: 18)

In terms of literacy acquisition, the difficulties experienced by dyslexic students are usually related to difficulties in processing either visual and auditory information and making the connections between the visual symbols and the sounds they represent, commonly called 'decoding'. In relation to visual factors, learners may experience difficulty in any of the following areas (Wearmouth, 2009): recognition of the visual cues of letters and words; familiarity with left–right orientation; recognition of word patterns; and recognition of letter and word shapes. Or they may encounter problems with any of the following auditory factors: recognition of letter sounds; recognition of sounds and letter groups or patterns; sequencing of sounds; corresponding sounds to visual stimuli; discriminating sounds from other sounds; and discriminating sounds within words.

Other definitions are wider and include reference to difficulties in co-ordination, personal organisation, balance, patterning, directionality (right/left confusion), sequencing, rhythm, orientation, memory, and so on. The wider definition espoused by the British Dyslexia Association includes difficulty in the development of literacy and language-related skills, particularly in phonological processing, and also in working memory, the speed of processing information and the automatic development of skills that may not reflect the level of other cognitive abilities. 'Conventional' teaching methods may not be sufficient to address such difficulties but information technology and individual counselling may lessen the effects (http://www.bdadyslexia.org.uk/dyslexic, accessed 1 June 2015).

The Rose Review, in its report on identifying and teaching dyslexic children, concurs with this wider view (Rose, 2009: 30) and identifies dyslexia as a learning difficulty associated with 'difficulties in phonological awareness, verbal memory and verbal processing speed' that 'affects the skills involved in accurate and fluent word reading and spelling', but also acknowledges a wider range of information-processing difficulties in various 'aspects of language, motor co-ordination, mental calculation, concentration and personal organisation'. However, these aspects alone are not markers of dyslexia. A 'good indication' is the extent to which 'the individual responds or has responded to well-founded intervention'. In other words, as the BPS (1999) also implies, if a child experiences difficulties but has not received good teaching, then it cannot be assumed that he or she is dyslexic.

Theories explaining dyslexia

There are a number of theories that attempt to explain the difficulties experienced by dyslexic learners.

Visual-based theories

As Everatt (2002) explains, there are visual-based theories which propose that dyslexia may be the consequence of an abnormality in the neural pathways of the visual system. There are others suggesting a lower level of activity in the areas of the visual cortex thought to be responsible for identifying the direction of movement (Eden et al., 1996). There is also a view that visual difficulties may be caused by over-sensitivity to certain wavelengths (or colours) of light. This is sometimes referred to as scotopic sensitivity syndrome (Irlen, 1991). The significance of this is that coloured filters, overlays or lenses which are said to alleviate reading problems for some learners (Wilkins et al., 1994) have increasingly been incorporated into teachers' practice, with variable results.

Phonological deficit hypothesis

Since the 1980s the dominant theory used to explain dyslexia has been the phonological deficit hypothesis (Bradley and Bryant, 1983; Snowling, 2000; Stanovich, 2000). Phonological processing is strongly related to the development of reading. Difficulties experienced at the level of phonological representation and the relationships between symbols and the sounds they represent constrain reading development (Hatcher and Snowling, 2002). Activities such as non-word reading are problematic because of the difficulties associated with sound–symbol relationships. Dyslexic children with poorer phonological representations will have fewer compensatory word attack strategies to draw on and this will further undermine their reading performance.

Effects on performance

At the pre-school level, dyslexic children may experience a delay in spoken language, including difficulty in learning nursery rhymes and verbal sequencing, for example, days of the week and letters of the alphabet (Riddick et al., 2002: 12–13). There may also be poor gross motor co-ordination, for example, in learning to ride a bicycle or swim, poor fine motor skills, for example, in copying shapes and letters, and poor short-term memory, such as remembering a sequence of instructions and names. At primary age, a child is likely to experience difficulties in reading, writing, spelling and number work. The child may be unable to identify rhythm and alliteration, or read single words accurately. He or she may reverse some words, for example, 'pot' and 'top', miss out whole lines and read some sections of text twice without realising it, and have better understanding of text than word accuracy. Reading age for fluency and accuracy is likely to be below chronological age. Children who begin school with poor letter knowledge and poor rhythmic ability may be at risk of developing difficulties in reading. Snowling (2000: 213–14) says that difficulties in encoding the phonological features of words (that is, the sound system of a language) are core to dyslexic children's difficulties. A child may spell the same word different ways in the same text, spell incorrectly words learnt for spelling tests, make several attempts to spell words with frequent crossings out, spell phonetically but incorrectly, use what look like bizarre spellings, for example, 'bidar' for 'because', leave out syllables, for example, 'onge' for 'orange, or part of a letter blend especially when there is a blend of three letters, for example, 'sred' for 'shred', reverse letters, especially 'b' and 'd', 'p' and 'q'. He or she may experience difficulty copying from the board, produce work that is chaotic or very untidy, begin writing anywhere on the page, confuse upper and lower case letters, produce very little output, and what there is may be unintelligible, even to the child.

Dyslexic children experience a number of difficulties in mathematics, including the learning of number bonds and multiplication tables, the understanding of concepts involving directionality (Weavers, 2003), sequencing activities and orientation of both numbers and processes. Confusion can arise through having to process different operations in different directions, for example, the conventional right to left calculation of addition and subtraction, and left to right of division. There may be limited spatial awareness and visual discrimination, resulting in confusion of signs and reversal of digits. Children may also have very poor mental arithmetic (mental manipulation of number/symbols in short-term memory) (Wearmouth, 2009).

Addressing dyslexic difficulties

Teaching approaches for dyslexic students can be grouped into those that are designed to enable the child to overcome the difficulties that are experienced as far as possible – almost to train the personal information-processing system to become more organised in a deliberately systematic and focused way (personal reflections) – and those that enable to child to cope (Wearmouth, 2009).

Training to overcome difficulties

Hatcher and Snowling (2002) outline examples of phonological awareness training: playing rhyming games, making up nonsense rhymes, repeating rhyming strings, and playing other games which require the manipulation of sounds such as identifying words as units within sentences, syllable awareness and blending tasks. Interventions that rely exclusively on training in phonological awareness are less effective than those that combine phonological training with print and meaning in the context of sentences in text, however.

At almost any age, paired reading arrangements can enable dyslexic individuals to gain more experience in reading ('reading mileage', Clay, 1993; 1998) and in visual tracking of the text in order to increase word identification, knowledge of letter/sound combinations and use of contextual information and inference. Students might be encouraged to choose reading material of high interest to themselves, irrespective of its readability level, and both children might read out loud together, with the reading partner modulating his or her speed to match that of the dyslexic pupil. Or children might be encouraged to use recordings of books that they really want to read, tracking through the text with their eyes while listening to the CD.

Allowing students to dictate their thoughts onto a digital recorder and then transcribing them for them, or allowing them to dictate thoughts to the teacher, an older child or parent may be the first step in writing. Subsequently listening to the recording of his or her own thoughts and then writing the text from this is one way to separate out the conceptual thinking around content and the mechanical aspects of writing with which the young person experiences difficulty.

Providing writing frames can support extended writing and encourage logical sequencing (Wray, 2002).

Multi-sensory approaches that introduce visual, tactile, auditory and kinaesthetic modes to teaching and learning enable students who need extra reinforcement in their learning to see, touch, hear and move, sometimes simultaneously, in their learning activities. The principles of multi-sensory teaching which apply to language work also apply to the mathematics field, for example, introducing new mathematical concepts and processes using concrete materials, diagrams, pictures and verbal explanations. Progress should be carefully monitored at each stage, checking that a particular concept has been thoroughly mastered and understood before moving on to the next step.

'Metacognitive' strategies can also help dyslexic and other students to reflect on their own thinking processes to build on their own strengths. 'Mind-mapping' (Buzan, 2000), for example, encourages learners first to produce a visual representation of all those areas to be covered in the text to develop a structure for producing extended text.

Coping strategies

Research (Florian and Hegarty, 2004) stresses the motivational value of computer-assisted learning, for example, word-processing which can increase the time that students are willing to practise writing. Spell-checkers can remove much of a pupil's inhibition about writing that comes from poor spelling. Drafting and correcting become less laborious and the printed copy can be corrected away from the machine by the student or the teacher and improved versions created without difficulty. Everything can be saved and re-used easily, allowing work to be done in small amounts. Presentation is improved; when the final version is printed, it is legible and well presented. Optical comfort is also important. A choice of screen colours can be helpful to students.

'Reasonable adjustments': examination concessions

Where a young person has a formal assessment of severe dyslexia, it may be the case that this is interpreted as a disability under the terms of the 2010 Equality Act. If this is the case, then, as discussed in Chapter 3, he or she is entitled to 'reasonable adjustments' to enable access to the school or college curriculum, including internal and external examinations. The school might give internal examination concessions (extra time, answers in note form, an oral test to support written examination, the use of a word processor in course work, examinations, etc.) and 25 per cent additional time. Examination papers might be duplicated so that the pupil can see both sides of a page at the same time, enlarged or printed on coloured paper, along with the use of highlighting pens to help with the analysis of questions. Guidelines for access arrangement during external examinations have been issued by some qualifications bodies to ensure compliance with the 2010 Equality Act, for example, the Joint Council for Qualifications (JCQ) (2014) in relation to secondary students.

In Table 5.1 we illustrate the first part of a learning plan designed to take account of the learning needs of a dyslexic student at secondary level. This plan is not complete because it does not contain all the information that should be expected, for example, dates for evaluation of progress and so on. The planning process is discussed in much greater detail in Chapter 9.

Table 5.1 Extract from sample individual learning plan

Name: ______________

Area of concern: Dyslexia which is linked to poor literacy skills, poor short-term memory, low self confidence

Start date: ___________

Review date: __________

Targets	Success criteria	Resources	Strategies	Support from teaching assistant
Progress in reading accuracy	Minimum of 6 months progress on standardised test of reading accuracy	High interest reading books and CDs	Paired reading, access to digital recorder	Organisation of paired reading activities, records of books read and progress made
Measurable improvement in accuracy of spelling in written work	Minimum of 10 new spellings learned weekly	Record of personal spellings, spelling books, corrected written work	Multi-sensory techniques to learn spellings from own written work	Support to teach technique and keep record of progress
Improve confidence in producing more extended written work	Measurable termly increase in quantity of written work produced	Digital recorder, word processor and printer	Dictate written work on to digital recorder, transcription provided, access to word processor with spell checking facility	Transcription of recorded written work. Monitoring of extent of written work produced
Improved short-term memory skills	Remember five random items in a list and five daily activities	Pictures, word lists, memory games	Discuss mnemonics; examples of, and practice in, visualisation techniques	Explain principles of mnemonics and visualisation techniques; memory games, monitor progress
Learn 5x and 6x tables in mathematics	Accuracy in tables tests	Tables patterns, auditory recordings, tables cards	Search for patterns, chant along to recordings, practise with cards, use ‘finger’ method	TA to give practice in reciting tables, teach multi-sensory strategies

Source: Adapted from Wearmouth (2009: 124).

6

Understanding social, emotional and mental health needs

Introduction

Interpretations of, and responses to, behaviour perceived as challenging at home and in schools often generate a great deal of heated debate. Schools play a critical part in shaping a child's identity as a learner (Bruner, 1996). Effectively addressing difficult student behaviour associated with social, emotional and mental health difficulties must relate to the consideration of the learning environment in which that behaviour occurs as well as the way that students make sense of their own worlds (Wearmouth et al., 2005), even if this may be experienced as uncomfortable at times.

In this chapter we look at some of the issues associated with:

- the use of terminology in this area;
- the concept of 'nurture' in the education of young children, and its origins;
- attention deficit/hyperactivity disorder (AD/HD);
- physical restraint in schools;
- Tourette syndrome;
- emotional upset associated with bereavement.

Use of terms

The terms 'emotional and behavioural difficulties' (EBD), first formally used by the Warnock Report (DES, 1978), or 'social, emotional and behavioural difficulties' (SEBD), or, as now in England, 'social, emotional and mental health' difficulties are ill-defined. Use of these terms to explain why some students behave badly or inappropriately is not always helpful to parents and teachers. Poulou and Norwich found from a review of international studies that the more teachers thought student behaviour stemmed from problems within the students themselves, such as the 'child wants to attract attention' or the 'child's innate personality', 'the more they experienced feelings of "stress", "offence" and even "helplessness", especially for conduct and mixed behaviour difficulties' (Poulou and Norwich, 2002: 112, 125).

Young people's behaviour does not occur in a vacuum (Watkins and Wagner, 2000). Teachers see themselves as able to deal with a student's problematic behaviour if they consider that students' problems generally are caused by 'factors originating from teachers themselves, like their personality, manners towards the child with EBD, or teaching style' (Watkins and Wagner, 2000). In other words, if they think they can control the cause of a difficulty, they believe 'that they can also sufficiently treat it. In addition, they perceived themselves in such cases as even more responsible for finding an effective solution for the child's problem' (Poulou and Norwich, 2002: 112).

Most commonly, understandings and strategies in classroom management are based on principles from a behaviourist psychology frame of reference (Skinner, 1938; Baer et al., 1968). Behavioural methodologies hold that all (mis)behaviour is learned and, therefore, that learning and (mis)behaviour can be modified through intervening in a systematic, consistent, predictable way in the environment. In Rogers' view, we should not excuse students from 'taking ownership for their disruptive behaviour', or 'facing accountability for such behaviour by facing appropriate consequences' or 'learning that behaviour is not an accident of birth or location', and that 'one can learn to make better and more conscious choices about behaviour' (Rogers, 1994c: 167). Classroom and school rules are examples of antecedent conditions (or setting events) that are intended to signify behaviour that is acceptable or appropriate. Such rules can also provide punitive consequences for behaviour that is unacceptable.

Nurturing young children in schools

One psychological theory of human development that has had considerable influence on educational provision for young children whose behaviour is of concern to teachers is that of attachment theory (Bowlby, 1952). Babies quickly attach themselves emotionally to their adult carers and progress through well-recognised stages of development towards maturity. Successful development depends on needs being adequately met at an earlier stage. Where this is not the case, then children will persist in inappropriate attachment behaviour, being over-anxious, avoidant or aggressive, or becoming incapable of warm attachment and positive human relationships (Harris et al., 1995; Bennathan, 2000).

Attachment theory has influenced education in the early years through the development of 'nurture groups' in some infant schools, originally in the Inner London Education Authority in 1970–71 by Marjorie Boxall, an educational psychologist, and re-established more recently by some local authorities. The Boxall Profile is an observational tool that was developed as a way of assessing the level of skills that children possessed to access learning and of identifying their developmental needs to support the work being done in nurture groups. It was originally standardised for children aged 3–8 years but has recently been developed for use in secondary schools. Boxall (2002) argues that learning, personality and behaviour difficulties, which are more likely in the young children of families experiencing disadvantage and deprivation, can be the result of inadequate early care and support from parents who struggle with poverty, damaged relationships and harsh and stressful living conditions. The underlying assumption of the nurture group means recreating in school the total experience of a normally developing child from babyhood onwards and planning the routine of the nurture group day to provide a predictable, reliable structure in which children can go on to interact and learn in regular settings (Bennathan, 2000).

Provision in a nurture group

Nurture groups attempt to create features of adequate parenting within school to provide the opportunity to develop trust, security, positive mood and identity through attachment to a reliable attentive and caring adult, as well as autonomy through the provision of controlled and graduated experiences in familiar surroundings.

Some features of such groups include:

- easy physical contact between adult and child;
- warmth, intimacy and a family atmosphere;
- good-humoured acceptance of children and their behaviour;
- familiar regular routines;
- a focus on tidying up and putting away;
- the provision of food in structured contexts;
- opportunities to play and the appropriate participation of the adults;
- adults talking about, and encouraging reflection by children on, trouble-provoking situations and their own feelings;
- opportunities for children to develop increasing autonomy. These opportunities incorporate visits outside the nurture group, participation in games, visits to regular classrooms and children's eventual full-time inclusion in a mainstream class.

(Wearmouth, 2009: 167)

Attention Deficit/Hyperactivity Disorder (AD/HD)

One of the conditions that is sometimes attributed to a physical condition is Attention Deficit/Hyperactivity Disorder (AD/HD), described by Norwich et al. (2002: 182) as

> a medical diagnosis of the American Psychiatric Association... characterised by chronic and pervasive (to home and school) problems of inattention, impulsiveness, and excessive motor activity which have seriously debilitating effects on individuals' social, emotional and educational development, and are sometimes disruptive to the home and school environment.

According to the British Psychological Society (1996), 2–5 per cent of British school students are believed to experience this condition. Defining AD/HD as a mental disorder is problematic. There is a strict requirement for 'pervasiveness and persistence' across a range of contexts. This means that behaviour which is seen largely in one context only does not constitute grounds for a diagnosis. 'We have evidence that children given the diagnosis ADHD don't attend, don't wait and don't sit still. But just because they don't do all these things does not mean that they cannot do them' (BPS, 1996: 23).

In some cases, a medical diagnosis may result in a prescription for particular kinds of medication. The use of psychostimulants is based on a theory of biochemical imbalance:

> The medication stimulates areas of the brain regulating arousal and alertness and can result in immediate short-term improvements in concentration and impulse control. The precise mechanism is poorly understood and the specific locus of action within the central nervous system remains speculative.
>
> (BPS, 1996: 50–1)

Of the most commonly used stimulants, methylphenidate (Ritalin) is most widely prescribed. It is usually administered in the form of tablets to be taken regularly. See Chapter 11 for a discussion of teachers' responsibilities for administering medication to students.

Although the prescription of a chemical psychostimulant is fairly common, as noted by the British Psychological Society, apart from all the ethical considerations, prescribing a drug provides an insufficient response. 'Medication must not become the first, and definitely not the only, line of treatment' (BPS, 1996: 2). Students' core values associated with self-identity, self-esteem and a sense of purpose as a functioning member of a social and cultural group must also be considered in addressing their overall well-being. Rogers (1994c) argues that effective approaches should focus on the effects of consequences through positive reinforcement, response cost and training in the reduction of behaviour viewed as problematic. Individualised behaviour management strategies should make it clear to pupils what kind of behaviour is unacceptable and also provide opportunities for modelling, rehearsing and reinforcing behaviour that is acceptable (Rogers, 1994c: 167–9).

Some evidence exists that a few students experience intolerance to particular foods and there is the suggestion of a link between this and difficult behaviour. 'Common allergens included additives, chocolate, dairy products, wheat, oranges and other fruit. These particular substances are found in many commercially produced foods and medicines' (BPS, 1996: 52). The area of the influence of diet over behaviour is largely under-researched and controversial.

Reflection 6.1: The issue of physical restraint

On occasions, students may be aggressive, out of control and a danger to themselves and others. It is very important to minimise the risk of physical confrontation in the first instance, rather than having to take action after the event. It seems sensible for teachers to avoid confrontations with students where these can be avoided and use physical restraint only as a last resort to manage a dangerous situation.

In a non-statutory advisory document on the use of 'reasonable' force in schools (DfE, 2013b: 4), school staff are advised that reasonable in this context means 'using no more force than is needed' to control or restrain young people:

- Control means either passive physical contact, such as standing between pupils or blocking a pupil's path, or active physical contact such as leading a pupil by the arm out of a classroom.

- Restraint means to hold back physically or to bring a pupil under control. It is typically used in more extreme circumstances, for example, when two pupils are fighting and refuse to separate without physical intervention.

'School staff are urged always to try not to cause injury, but it is acknowledged that in extreme cases it may not always be possible to avoid injuring the pupil.' All members of a school staff have the power to use such 'reasonable' force, and this includes searching pupils for 'prohibited items' such as knives or illegal drugs.

Addressing behavioural concerns

Using behavioural methodology

Behavioural methodology is a scientifically based technology, so the first requirement is a clear definition of the target behaviour. For instance, if a child is thought to be 'hyperactive', Merrett (1985) suggests an operational definition of behaviours such as 'out of seat' will be required. Once the behaviour has been operationally defined, there should be systemic observational sampling across times of day, situations, nature of activity, person in charge, and so on. Such observations need to be taken over a period of about five days to establish the baseline level of responding. Once the baseline can be clearly seen, an analysis detailing the following three stages should be carried out:

> **A** – the antecedent event(s), that is, whatever starts off or prompts
> **B** – the behaviour, which is followed in turn by
> **C** – the consequence(s).
>
> (Merrett, 1985: 8)

Merrett advises that where a consequence of a behaviour 'is shown to be maintaining [the] behaviour at a high level, then that consequence is, by definition, and regardless of its nature, reinforcing it positively'. Telling children off can temporarily choke off certain behaviours, but these may recur after a very short time. This can be 'very frustrating for the teacher'. However, it may be the teacher's scolding that is maintaining the child's behaviour. 'By definition, "ticking off" is positively reinforcing the child's "attention-seeking" behaviour. If that positive reinforcement is removed, then the rate of occurrence of the behaviour will be reduced. It will eventually become extinguished' (Merrett, 1985: 9).

Strategies to maximise students' learning of new behaviours include 'shaping', which breaks complex tasks down into a series of steps, and ensures that each step is reinforced in a particular sequence. Other procedures include modelling, where students are rewarded for matching the behaviour being displayed for them.

From a behaviourist perspective, then, and as Rogers (2013) comments, a child's background is no excuse for poor behaviour. Socially acceptable behaviour is learned and can, therefore, be taught. Key to motivating pupils to choose appropriate behaviour are 'positive reinforcers': teacher praise, rewards of various sorts and positive communications with parents. If children disrupt the lesson, they should take ownership of this and be given a reminder what the rules are: 'Jayson... you're calling out... Remember our class rules for asking questions, thanks' (Rogers, 2013: 238). In classrooms, younger children can be given a non-verbal cue to appropriate behaviour and shown clearly what is expected.

Adults' behaviour is very important in modelling and reinforcing specific ways of behaving in particular situations. In doing so, it is really important not to allow oneself to be drawn into a power struggle that some young people find rewarding and that is likely to reinforce the way they are behaving. Students may imitate negative as well as positive behaviour, however, so, for example, the use of abusive or sarcastic language should be avoided at all costs. This might entail modelling ways of resolving conflict that respect the rights of students to learn and feel safe, and do the following:

- meet the needs of both parties, that is, provide win-win outcomes wherever possible;
- bring an end to the conflict, or at least reduce it;
- do not leave either party 'wounded'.

(Sproson, 2004: 319)

There are a number of techniques that can enable teachers to avoid power struggles with students:

- Some young people may take pleasure in not doing what they are asked immediately, especially if they have an audience of peers. In this situation Rogers (2013: 240), among others, advocates that, in the classroom, teachers build in a brief 'take-up' period for pupils to respond. Make the request, walk away so as to imply compliance, and acknowledge compliance when it happens.
- The 'broken record' approach (Rogers, 2013) also encourages teachers to repeat a request a number of times, calmly, without being drawn into an argument.
- Pupils bringing inappropriate objects into classrooms, or engaging in inappropriate activities might be given what Rogers (2013: 242) calls 'directed choices'. As a newly appointed teacher, my own sister was once in a situation where teenage girls brought long sticks into her mathematics lesson in a class where every student had been suspended the previous term – to test her out, as they later admitted. She simply responded by directing their choices: 'Shall I put them in this cupboard or that one? I'll keep them safe for you till the end of the day.' They never asked for them back.

Multi-Element Planning (MEP)

The design and development of effective individual intervention programmes based on behavioural principles require clear assessment of both student performance and the learning environment. One practical approach currently used in parts of the UK as well as in other areas of the world is that of Multi-Element Planning (MEP). This approach takes account of the following:

- potential causes of difficulties experienced by the child;
- factors that appear to maintain the behaviour seen as challenging or otherwise of concern;

- strategies related to improving the learning environment and the teaching skills that will be useful to the child;
- strategies that will prevent the recurrence of the problematic behaviour or provide a way of safeguarding the child, peers and staff when the behaviour does recur.

One of the issues to be considered in MEP is that of ethics. Where teachers deliberately set out to change students' behaviour, then there is always a question of how that teacher's power is exercised, which behaviour is seen as preferable and why, and in whose interest it is that the behaviour should be changed in this way. Pitchford (2004) poses the following questions before any assessment or intervention is devised:

> What gives us the right to manipulate or change someone's behaviour?
> How certain are we that the problem behaviour is not a perfectly reasonable response to unreasonable circumstances?
> If we do intervene, how ethically sound are our techniques and what is their record of effectiveness?
>
> (Pitchford, 2004: 311)

In his work, Pitchford references the MEP described by LaVigna and Donnellan (1986) which has four main components:

1 *Change strategies* that 'examine whether there are mismatches between the child and his or her environment that require a change in the environment not a change in the child' (Pitchford, 2004: 312). Change strategies should be considered in relation to interpersonal, physical, and instructional contexts in which the behaviour occurs.
2 *Positive Programming* which involves 'teaching children skills that will have a positive impact on their lives', working on the assumption that 'learning is empowering, gives dignity to the individual, helps them get their needs met and helps them cope with an imperfect world' (Pitchford, 2004: 313). Three areas of skill development are addressed: general, functionally-equivalent and coping:
   (a) *general*: 'academic or life skills that the child has not mastered that are having a negative impact on his or her quality of life' (Pitchford, 2004: 313);
   (b) *functionally-equivalent*: that is, socially acceptable skills or behaviour that will serve the same purpose for the student as that which is seen as unacceptable. 'No matter how strange, behaviour always has a purpose or a function (LaVigna and Donnellan, 1986). If we understand that purpose or function, we are more likely to be able to channel it in a constructive way' (Pitchford, 2004: 314). Pitchford provides examples of 'problem behaviours' and their functionally-equivalent skills that could be included in an MEP.
   (c) *coping* skills designed to help students 'manage and tolerate the frustrations and difficulties in their lives'.

3 *Preventive strategies*, comprising the antecedent control strategy and the use of reward strategies (LaVigna and Donnellan, 1986):

(a) antecedent control strategies include removing those events that act as a direct trigger to problem behaviours (Glynn, 1982);

(b) 'reward strategies only work well when they are used in the context of the types of positive programming and ecological strategies described earlier. Rewards can be artificial. The teacher will not always be there to reward the child and since our aim is to teach the child to be independent, rewards may only be a short term expedient... From a behavioural perspective, basically there are three ways of rewarding children' (LaVigna and Donnellan, 1986): (i) rewarding children for being 'good'; (ii) rewarding children for not being 'naughty'; and (iii) rewarding children for being 'naughty' less often than they were before. However, as Pitchford comments, this technique may be inappropriate for behaviour seen as dangerous.

4 *Reactive strategies* which 'are included in the plan in order to safeguard the child, his or her peers and staff when things go wrong... In particular we should know what safe non-punitive techniques will be used if the problem behaviour occurs and what support will be given to the child. Just as important is consideration of the practical and emotional help or support that should be given to the member of staff' (Pitchford, 2004: 321).

Pitchford (2004: 314) offers the following example of 'problem behaviours and their functions together with the functionally-equivalent skills that could be included in an MEP to help the child achieve the same end (Table 6.1).

Table 6.1 Identifying functionally-equivalent skills

Problem	*Function*	*Functionally-Equivalent Skill*
Shouting out	Initiate social contact	Teach hand up and waiting quietly. Teach hand up and saying, 'Excuse me, Miss, I've finished my work.'
Aggression (bullying)	Obtain things or events (children are made to share or give sweets unwillingly)	Teach play skills, turn-taking skills and negotiation skills.
Tantrums	Express emotion	Teach child to express emotions in writing or art or small world play.
Tantrums	Avoid situations (e.g. repeated failure in maths)	Teach key maths skills. Teach how to ask for help.
Makes silly noises	To gain excitement (children laugh)	Teach child • how to tell jokes • right and wrong time and place to tell jokes.

We discuss the issue of functional assessment of behaviour further on p. 92

Tourette syndrome

Tourette syndrome is a neurological disorder characterized by motor and vocal tics: repetitive, stereotyped, involuntary movements and vocalisations. As NINDS (2005) outlines, motor tics are–commonly–sudden, brief, repetitive movements that may include eye blinking and other vision irregularities, facial grimacing, shoulder shrugging, and head or shoulder jerking, or, more dramatically, touching objects, hopping, jumping, bending, twisting, or motor movements that result in self-harm such as punching oneself in the face. Vocalisations often include repetitive throat-clearing, sniffing, or grunting sounds – or, at the extreme, coprolalia (uttering swear words) or 'echolalia' (repeating the words or phrases of others). People with Tourette syndrome often report that tics are preceded by an urge or sensation in the affected muscles, commonly called a 'premonitory urge' that builds up to the point where it is expressed. Excitement, anxiety or particular physical experiences can trigger or worsen tics.

Across the world the prevalence of the condition among school children 'range[s] from 1 to 10 per 1000, with a rate of 6 per 1000 replicated in several countries' (Piacenti et al., 2010: 1929). Tics tend to start in early childhood, peak before the mid-teen years, and improve subsequently (NINDS, 2005). Medication can be prescribed for young people whose tics are severe enough to interfere with their functioning. However, as Piacenti et al. (2010: 1930) comment, this 'rarely eliminates tics and are often associated with unacceptable sedation, weight gain, cognitive dulling, and motor adverse effects', such as tremors. Particular interventions based on a behaviourist approach have been developed that seem, from small controlled trials, to be effective in reducing tic severity (NINDS, 2005).

Young people with Tourette syndrome often cope well in mainstream classrooms. However, frequent tics can interfere with academic performance or disrupt social relationships with peers. My own experience is that, in a well-managed classroom, other young people can be very understanding and supportive. All young people with Tourette syndrome, as with any other kind of special educational need, benefit from a learning environment that is supportive and flexible enough to accommodate their individual learning needs. This may mean making special arrangements if the tics disrupt the pupil's ability to write, or problem-solving with the pupil on ways to reduce stress in the classroom or during examinations.

Addressing behaviour associated with Tourette

A number of approaches have been advocated to support individuals with Tourette to manage their behaviour themselves. 'Habit reversal training', for example, acknowledges that tics have a neurological basis and also, in its design, takes into account the context in which the individual lives and works as well as the internal experience of premonitory urges. Piacenti et al. (2010: 1930) describe the main components of habit reversal as tic-awareness and 'competing-response training':

- Awareness training comprises self-monitoring of tics and the early signs that a tic is about to occur.

- Competing-response training involves deliberately engaging in a behaviour that is not physically compatible with the tic as soon as the premonitory urge is felt. Tics are not suppressed; the individual is taught to manage the urge and initiate an alternative socially acceptable behaviour that replaces the tic. The competing response can be initiated when the individual notices that a tic is about to occur, during the tic, or after the tic has occurred. For vocal tics, the most commonly competing response that is taught is slow rhythmic breathing from the diaphragm. With practice, patients are able to complete the competing response without disengaging from routine activities.

Bereavement in childhood

One of the events in childhood that is likely to affect children's behaviour very profoundly, and, indeed, may have resonances later on in life, is that of the death of the primary caregiver, most often the mother, or of close family members. According to Cruse (2015), 1 in 29 children aged 5–16 in the UK has been bereaved of a parent or sibling, and 1 in 16 has lost a close friend (http://www.cruse.org.uk/, accessed 1 June 2015). The deep distress that results from a child's bereavement may create a special educational need of a short- or long-term nature.

Some people may assume that a young person who loses a parent, caregiver, sibling or grandparent will not be affected too deeply as he or she is too young. However, emotional disturbances that are not immediately obvious may become apparent later and last for several years (Rutter, 1966). Cruse (2015) states that it is common for 'some bereaved children and young people to delay their grief for months or sometimes years'. Subsequently, 'Other life changing incidents such as moving home, acquiring a step parent or experiencing a further bereavement can serve to release the bereaved child or young person's delayed or unresolved grief.' There seems to be no way to divert grief: '[U]ltimately, regardless of how long the child or young person has managed to deny their grief, they will have to go through the grieving process eventually' (Cruse, 2015, http://www.cruse.org.uk/for-schools/symptoms, accessed 1 June 2015).

As Cruse notes, above all, young people need to be given the opportunity to grieve. Ignoring or averting the child's grief is not supportive, and can prove extremely damaging as the child becomes an adult. Young people need to be allowed to talk about their feelings. Everyone has their own way of grieving. Not all young people will experience the same emotions, behave the same way or respond similarly to other people who have lost close friends or relations.

7

Understanding sensory and physical difficulties and needs

Introduction

The greatest challenge for a child with a sensory impairment is communication (Spencer and Marschark, 2010). A child who can see and hear will reach out and explore his or her surroundings naturally. A child with a sensory impairment will not necessarily do this and may need encouragement to explore and interact with others. For a deaf child, normal progress in language may be hard. Intensive education and support may be needed throughout the child's life. Early intervention in the child's life is clearly very important. Assessing difficulties in this area is generally through the identification and assessment of the extent of a child's sensory or physical impairment.

In this chapter we outline some of the issues associated with including young people who experience:

- hearing impairment;
- visual impairment;
- multi-sensory impairment;
- physical difficulties, with a focus on muscular dystrophy.

In doing so, we adopt the view that, however much is known about a child's sensory or physical difficulties, as Miller and Ockleford (2005) aptly comment, that child is still an individual with his or her own personal strengths and needs, interests, experiences, background, and so on, that, together with his or her own views, must all be taken into account when drawing up any intervention plan.

Hearing impairment

There are different degrees of deafness, most often classified as mild, moderate, severe or profound (Spencer and Marschark, 2010). Few children are totally deaf. Deafness can be:

- *conductive*, when sound cannot pass efficiently through the outer and middle ear to the cochlea and auditory nerve. The most common type in children is caused by 'glue ear' (NDCS, 2010), a build-up of fluid in the middle ear which affects about 1 in 5 children at any time. For most children, the glue ear clears up by itself. A few need surgery to insert 'grommets' into the eardrums, tiny plastic tubes that allow air to circulate in the middle ear and help to prevent the build-up of fluid.
- *sensori-neural*, which is permanent and occurs when there is a fault in the inner ear or auditory (hearing) nerve.

A delay in late identification of deafness can mean a delay in establishing effective communication with the child (Goldberg and Richberg, 2004; Moeller et al., 2007). Children who do not hear clearly or whose hearing varies may be late to start talking, have difficulties with speech sounds, or fail to develop good listening skills (Yoshinaga-Itano, 2003). They may also have poor memory and language-processing skills, poor basic vocabularies as a result, reading and spelling problems, difficulty with sentence structure and comprehension, and achieve lower attainments in reading and mathematics. Pupils with a conductive hearing loss have a higher tendency to behavioural problems, poor motivation and attention, shyness and withdrawal (Spencer and Marschark, 2010), especially those whose conductive deafness started in early infancy and persisted undiagnosed for long periods.

Including children with hearing impairments in mainstream schools

These days, many children with sensory impairments are in mainstream schools. It is essential, therefore, that non-specialist as well as specialist teachers understand how to include them most effectively.

There are three major 'types' of approach: Auditory-Oral (or 'Oral/Aural'), Sign-Bilingual, or Total Communication. 'Generally the evidence for any one method working better than another for deaf children as a whole is unclear, and all the approaches can point to some evidence which shows successful outcomes for children' (NDCS, 2010: 45).

> The 'best' communication approach for any child and family is the one which works for them, both fitting in with the family's culture and values and most importantly, allowing the child to develop good self-esteem, a positive self-image, successful relationships... in all aspects of her life.
>
> (NDCS, 2010: 50)

Auditory-Oral approaches emphasise the use of amplification such as hearing aids, cochlear implants and radio aids to maximise the use of the child's 'residual' hearing (Spencer and Marschark, 2006). The aim is that deaf children should learn to use whatever residual hearing they may have to develop good listening and speaking skills, which will enable them to communicate and mix with hearing people as part of the wider hearing community (Beattie, 2006). The most widely used of these approaches is the Natural Aural Approach. Here no sign language is used and children are not encouraged to rely on lip-reading (Lewis, 1996).

Sign Bilingualism in the UK uses British Sign Language (or Irish Sign Language in Ireland) and whatever is the spoken language of the home (Moores, 2008). A sign bilingual approach is rooted in the belief that a visual language is essential for deaf children to have full access to language learning, education, information and the world around them, together with a strong positive deaf identity.

British Sign Language (BSL) is a complete language in its own right with its own grammar and linguistic rules which are different from English, so it is not used simultaneously with spoken language. BSL has developed as a visual language which uses body language, head position, facial expressions and gesture as well as the hands. It also uses finger-spelling for some words which have no signs, such as names. Use of BSL can therefore bring with it a connection with Deaf culture and the opportunity and expectation of taking part in the Deaf community as well as the hearing world (Burman et al., 2006). Where a child uses BSL, it is useful if the rest of the family, classmates and teachers learn to sign also.

Total Communication is based on the principle that deaf children can learn to communicate effectively by using any and all means that they can, in whatever combination works best: sign, speech and hearing, finger-spelling, gesture, facial expression, lip-reading and cued speech. Signed/Signs Supported English (SSE) is a sign support system which uses signs taken from BSL, together with finger-spelling (Moores, 2001). It is used in the word order of English to supplement what is being spoken. Signed English, similarly, uses signs taken from BSL together with some specially developed 'markers' made with the hands, and finger-spelling, to give an exact representation of the word order and the grammar of English through sign. It is mainly used to support the teaching of reading and writing. In finger-spelling, each letter of the alphabet is indicated by using the fingers and palm of the hand (Padden and Gunsals, 2003). It is used to support Sign Language to spell names and places and for words that do not have an established BSL sign. Lip-reading is the process of reading words from the lip patterns of the person speaking (Spencer and Marschark, 2010). For a number of reasons, lip-reading is never enough on its own. Many speech sounds are not visible on the lips. Lip patterns also vary from person to person. Further, lack of clarity around the face, for example, poor lighting conditions, beards or moustaches that obscure the mouth, or eating while talking can make lip-reading difficult. Lip-reading therefore is used to support other communication approaches. Cued Speech is a sound-based system that accompanies natural speech and uses eight hand shapes in four different positions (cues) to represent the sounds of English visually (Hage and Leybaert, 2006). Some spoken sounds cannot be fully lip-read: 'p', 'm' and 'b' all look the same on the lips; sounds like 'd', 'k' and 'g' cannot be seen on the lips. Hand shapes are 'cued' near to the mouth to make clear the sounds of English which look the same when lip-read. It is intended to make every sound and word clear to deaf children and therefore enable them to have full access to spoken language. The association between the sounds and letters of spoken English is intended to help develop literacy skills as well as spoken language.

Assistive devices

As the NDCS (2008: 31) comments, deaf children often use assistive listening devices to help them to hear what a speaker is saying, particularly in noisy listening conditions.

Personal FM systems (often known as radio aids) are very useful, especially at school, college or at home. 'They can help reduce effects of background noise in, for example, a school classroom, and help a child to concentrate on one person's voice, often their teacher.' Radio aids have a transmitter with a microphone and a receiver. The person talking wears the transmitter and the sounds are transmitted by radio waves to the receiver. The deaf child wears the receiver which picks up the signal from the transmitter and converts it back to sound. The child's hearing aids or implants amplify the sound so that the child can hear what is said.

Classroom soundfield systems are designed for similar reasons as radio aids, but are not the same. A soundfield system includes a microphone worn by the speaker that is linked to an amplifier by either an FM radio transmitter or an infra-red transmitter so that the speaker can walk around a room with no need for wires. Loudspeakers are fitted around the room. The soundfield system amplifies the speaker's voice to produce a clear, consistent level of sound above the background noise (NDCS, 2008). Most children with hearing aids or cochlear implants will still need to use a radio aid in a classroom with a soundfield system.

Sound waves reverberate and increase the amount of background noise in rooms with hard surfaces (Moeller et al., 2007). Soundfield systems and the acoustic treatment of teaching spaces can improve the listening environment for all students. It is important for class teachers to think carefully about the clarity of their spoken language (Wilkins and Ertmer, 2002). Teachers should use natural speech patterns and not exaggerate lip movements or shout, highlight key terms and key concepts and place themselves in a position appropriate for students to lip-read or benefit from a hearing aid where the maximum range is often 2 metres. Deaf students may also need to be encouraged to see the faces of peers who are speaking. To acquire spoken and written English, students may also need the support of visual and written forms of language, as well as lip-reading or multi-sensory clues (Harris and Moreno, 2006). For example, with video materials, deaf students might benefit with advanced access to a summary of the programme and new vocabulary and concepts explained, as well as sub-titles.

Visual Impairment

Visual impairment (VI) is a general term that indicates a continuum of sight loss (Mason et al., 1997). It is estimated to affect around 25,000 children between the ages of 0 and 16 years in the UK (Tate et al., 2005), and 15,000 between the ages of 17 and 25 years.,

Working with students with a visual impairment in the classroom

As a result of their visual difficulties, before going to school, children with a visual impairment may well have had less opportunity to explore their environment and learn through observing and copying the actions of others (Douglas and McLinden, 2005). Both academic progress and children's social skills may be influenced by this. Children may therefore need teaching of literacy development through specialist

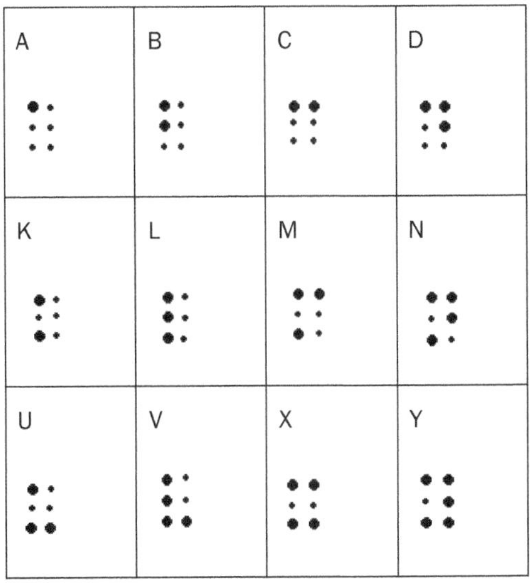

A	B	C	D
K	L	M	N
U	V	X	Y

Figure 7.1 Braille alphabet

codes such as Braille or Moon or through print/modified print Braille, and specialist teaching of mobility, tactile and keyboard skills, as well as social and life skills generally. It is important to consider whether and when to withdraw the child from the mainstream classroom for specialist or additional teaching so that the pupil does not become socially isolated and the mainstream teacher maintains full responsibility for the pupil.

Braille is the alphabet and numbers, designed to be read by fingers rather than eyes through a series of raised dots on a page. A blind French schoolboy, Louis Braille, devised the code more than 200 years ago. This code is based on six dots arranged in two columns of three (Figure 7.1). Different types of Braille codes use combinations of these dots, 63 in all, to represent letters of the alphabet, numbers, punctuation marks and common letter groups.

There are two grades of Braille: uncontracted (previously Grade 1) and contracted (previously Grade 2). Uncontracted includes a letter-for-letter and number-for-number translation from print. Contracted has special signs for common words and letter combinations. This usually increases the speed of reading. Particular subject areas, for example, music, mathematics, science and foreign languages, have their own specialist codes.

As Mason (2001) also comments, in order to plan appropriate support for pupils with VI, teachers and support staff need to consider whether the child has a preferred or dominant eye or a defect in field or colour vision. This is important for both seating and using appropriate teaching strategies. There may well be restrictions on physical activities which may constrain the child's participation with peers. Low vision aids may have been prescribed, so it is important to know when they should be used and whether the child has been trained to use them. Also, a consideration of lighting levels as well as size and contrast of print is important to maximise the child's vision.

Multi-sensory impairment

Multi-sensory impairment means difficulty with both vision and hearing. The reduced and possibly distorted visual and auditory information that pupils with multi-sensory impairment receive means that they have a limited and possibly confused experience of the world (Aitken, 2000). Some children become skilled at using touch as a means of learning about the world and a means of communicating. Others may become skilled in using the sense of smell. Others may sense movement around them from differences in air pressure. Taylor (2007: 205) notes the difficulties experienced by many of these children in communicating:

> These include: a reduced and confused experience of the world, becoming passive and isolated, and the tendency to be echolalic or repeating the last word said to them, all of which limit their ability to make choices. Aitken and Millar (2002) also highlight the effects of hearing impairment on individuals' communication, including isolation from information and from other people. A physical impairment in association with communication difficulties will also present additional challenges. The child with MSI has all these difficulties compounded.

For those young people whose visual and vocal ability is severely affected, many assistive devices are available to enable students to communicate: electronic language boards, voice synthesisers and voice recognition software.

Multi-sensory teaching

Multi-sensory teaching is simultaneous use of visual, auditory and kinesthetic-tactile senses to enhance memory and learning. The use of such an approach for children whose senses are compromised or greatly reduced could be effective if careful planning takes account of their individual sensory needs. Helen Keller is, perhaps, the best known deaf-blind child in history. The breakthrough to communicating with her came when her teacher, Anne, pumped water over one of Helen's hands and spelled out the word 'water' in the other. Something about this made the connection between the word and its meaning. Helen made rapid progress after that. Anne taught her to read, first with raised letters and later with Braille, and to write with both ordinary and Braille typewriters.

Addressing hearing and visual difficulties

A summary of the advice given by the National Deaf Children's Society (NDCS) (2010: 10–12) to teachers of children with hearing impairments that might well be included in an individual learning plan is presented in Reflection 7.1.

Reflection 7.1: Communicating with deaf children: Advice from the RNID

When teaching young people with a hearing impairment in a mainstream classroom, the RNID advises:

- avoiding competing noise in the background that makes hearing difficult;
- bringing everyday sounds to the child's conscious attention;
- helping the child make the connection between the object and the sound it is making by looking at it. In the home, it might be a vacuum cleaner. At school, it might be the bell.
- using carpets, curtains and soft furnishings that do not reflect sound because they are more 'acoustically friendly' than wooden or ceramic flooring and blinds;
- staying within the child's vision, as much as possible to enable the child to use visual clues from body language, including facial expressions and lip-reading, and not placing the child facing the window so that he or she is looking into bright light. Wearing plain rather than patterned clothes means that the child can see the signed communication more easily.
- using visual supports, such as objects, books, toys or pictures, to help children to understand unfamiliar concepts;
- drawing deaf children's attention to the variety of interactions and forms of communication going on around them;
- encouraging everyone around deaf children to use signing with each other as well as with the children so they can interpret verbal interactions between everyone around;
- facing deaf children when speaking to them, and repeating and re-phrasing if they do not understand;
- encouraging adults and peers to respond to deaf children's attempts to communicate and not speak for them.

The kind of materials that support staff might help to develop for students who, for example, experience visual difficulties, might well be checked in relation to advice from the Royal National Institute for the Blind (RNIB) (https://www.rnib.org.uk/services-we-offer-advice-professionals-education-professionals/guidance-teaching-and-learning, accessed 1 June 2015).

Muscular dystrophy

Individual children with severe motor difficulties 'may have difficulties affecting some or all of their limbs, limited hand function, fine and gross motor difficulties and sometimes difficulties with speech and language. Most, though not all pupils will have a medical diagnosis' (Pickles, 2001: 290).

An estimated 8,000–10,000 people in the UK have a form of muscular dystrophy (Pohlschmidt and Meadowcroft, 2010). The term is used to refer to a group of genetic muscle diseases associated with progressive weakness and wasting of muscles owing to the degeneration of muscle cells. Most of these involve a defect in a protein that plays a vital role in muscle cell function or repair. To take one example, Duchenne muscular dystrophy affects only boys, with very rare exceptions, about 100 boys born in the UK each year. A problem in the genes results in a defect in dystrophin, which is an important protein in muscle fibres. Most boys with this condition develop the first signs of difficulty in walking at the age of 1–3 years and are usually unable to run or jump like their peers. By about 8–11 years, boys become unable to walk. By their late teens or early twenties the muscle-wasting is severe enough to shorten life expectancy (Pohlschmidt and Meadowcroft, 2010). Regular supervision from a clinic is very important to manage the condition as effectively as possible.

Summary

Four areas of need are outlined in the new Code of Practice (DfE, 2014a), although it is clearly acknowledged that there is potentially a lot of overlap between them in terms of the difficulties individual students may experience. For all students, it is essential that solutions to learning difficulties are sought, first, in the learning environment and quality of differentiated teaching, and only then, if the individual continues to make progress that is less than satisfactory, should assessment and planning for individuals take place through the assess→plan→do→review cycle.

8

Assessment of learning, behaviour, physical and sensory needs

Introduction

All pupils have a statutory right to have their special educational needs and disabilities identified and met. Identification of the barriers to pupils' learning and assessment of special learning requirements is crucial to the role of the special needs co-ordinator. In many schools it will be the special needs co-ordinator who plays the major role in information gathering and assessment, and in planning intervention aimed at reducing the barriers to learning experienced by such pupils. It is obviously very important that SENCOs have a firm grasp of the stages of assessment outlined in the Code of Practice (DfE, 2014a), because, as discussed already, this is used as a shared text during school inspections. However, a clear understanding of broader issues particularly relevant to assessment of individual learning needs is essential because approaches to identification and assessment have an important influence on how a school constructs its special needs policies and provision.

This chapter starts by explaining how some children can be supported to make huge learning gains and, consequently, will feel much more positively about themselves as learners if teachers, parents and others clearly understand the power of some forms of assessment, monitoring and focused feedback. It will continue by discussing the following topics:

- principles of different kinds of assessment of difficulties in learning:
  - summative and standardised;
  - on-going formative assessment and constructive feedback to students;
  - criterion-referenced assessment.
- ways of assessing behaviour experienced as problematic or challenging, including assessments from a biological or medical perspective;
- assessment of sensory impairments;
- the significance of understanding the barriers to learning from the student's and family's perspective;
- a framework for planning;
- developing, implementing, monitoring and evaluating an individual plan to address different experiences of difficulties at different ages and stages.

Assessment of the learning environment

It is very clear from the new Code of Practice (DfE, 2014a) that additional intervention and support for individuals in schools and colleges should not be expected to compensate for the lack of good teaching. High quality teaching, appropriately differentiated for individuals, is the first step in responding to possible special educational needs (SEN). The new system, SEN support, recommended for schools and colleges should be designed to ensure support is focused on individual need and outcomes, not on the amount of support that is available, or classifications.

Ysseldyke and Christenson (1987; 1993) argue that it is important to assess the characteristics of the classroom learning environments in which students are placed because these can be changed to support more effective learning. They identified a number of instructional factors in the classroom environment that influence student outcomes and used these to design 'The Instructional Environment Scale' (TIES) as a framework for the systematic collection of data to analyse contextual barriers to students' learning. Data are gathered through classroom observation and interviews with both student and teacher on 12 components of teaching: Instructional presentation, Classroom environment, Teacher expectations, Cognitive emphasis, Motivational strategies, Relevant practice, Academic engaged time, Informed feedback, Adaptive instruction, Progress evaluation, Instructional planning and Student understanding (Ysseldyke and Christenson, 1987: 21).

In a different context, the authors of the Primary Strategy (QCA, 2005) developed an inclusive teaching checklist to evaluate the extent to which pedagogy in classrooms can be evaluated as inclusive of all learners. This checklist has been adapted as Table 8.1.

The Code (DfE, 2014a, §6.44) recommends a graduated approach to assessing, planning and intervening to support students' learning, that is '[a] cycle through which earlier decisions and actions are revisited, refined and revised with the growing understanding of pupils' needs and of what supports the pupil in making good progress and securing good outcomes'.

Assessment of need starts with a whole school and college approach to monitoring all students' progress that can quickly identify where a young person is not making adequate progress. Schools should assess each pupil's current skills and levels of attainment on entry. Class and subject teachers, supported by the senior leadership team, should make regular assessments of progress for all students. Where individuals are falling behind or making inadequate progress given their age and starting point, they should be given extra support. Adequate progress can include that which:

- is similar to that of peers starting from the same baseline;
- matches or betters the child's previous rate of progress;
- closes the attainment gap between the child and their peers;
- prevents the attainment gap growing wider.

The assess→plan→do→review cycle recommended in the Code (DfE, 2014a: §6.45–6.56) assumes that a clear understanding of a child's needs is a critical precondition to planning effective provision and adjustments to teaching that will lead to good progress and

Table 8.1 Inclusive teaching observation checklist

	Yes/No	*Evidence*
Has the teacher identified appropriate and differentiated learning goal for all the students?		
Is there use of multi-sensory teaching approaches and/or approaches that enable some students to use more concrete learning aids?		
Is there use of interactive strategies, for example, students being invited to come to the front to take a role, or having their own whiteboards to support their learning?		
Is there use of visual and tangible aids for all students: real objects, signs or symbols, photographs, and so on?		
Does the teacher find ways of making abstract concepts concrete, for example, using pictures to illustrate word problems in mathematics modelling with concrete resources?		
Does the teacher use both simplified tasks for some groups (e.g. with shorter concrete texts) and extended more abstract tasks for others?		
Are tasks made closed or more open to suit students' current learning levels?		
Over time, does the teacher employ a variety of pupil groupings?		
Can all students see and hear the teacher clearly, and any resources in use?		
Is new or difficult vocabulary discussed and clarified, displayed, and returned to?		
Does the teacher check for understanding of instructions?		
Does the teacher ask students to explain them in their own words?		
Are questions pitched so as to challenge pupils at all levels?		
Is this a secure and supportive learning environment where there is safety to have a go and make mistakes?		

(continued)

Table 8.1 Inclusive teaching observation checklist *(continued)*

	Yes/No	*Evidence*
Does the teacher give personal thinking time before responses are required? Is progressively more scaffolding offered until a student can answer correctly?		
Is extra adult support for lower-achieving students used in ways that promote autonomy, encourage self-esteem and increase students' inclusion within the group?		
Do the adults who provide support in the classroom clearly know what the students are to learn?		
Does the teacher work directly with lower-attaining groups as well as the more able?		
Does the teacher explain, or model, tasks clearly? Does he or she check students have understood what they should do?		
Are pupils provided with, and regularly reminded of, resources to help them be autonomous (e.g. word lists or mats, dictionaries of terms, glossaries, number lines, tables squares)?		
Does the teacher use scaffolding (e.g. writing frames) to support learners to complete the required activities?		
Has the teacher made arrangements where necessary to ensure that all students have access to written texts?		
Has the teacher planned alternatives to written tasks, where appropriate?		
Does the teacher make effective use of ICT as an access strategy for some students where appropriate?		
Is desired behaviour noticed and praised, rewarded or encouraged?		
Are all students involved in setting their own targets and monitoring their own progress?		

improved outcomes. Where pupils continue to make inadequate progress, despite high quality teaching targeted at their areas of weakness, the class or subject teacher, working with the SENCO, should assess whether the child has a significant learning difficulty. Assessment should draw on:

- teachers' assessments/experience of the student;
- information from the school's core approach to student progress, attainment and behaviour;
- the individual's development in comparison to peers;
- the views and experience of parents, the child's own views and, if relevant, advice from external support services.

Information gathering should include the use of high quality formative assessment, effective tools and early assessment materials. For higher levels of need, schools should have arrangements in place to draw on more specialised assessments from external agencies and professionals. Arrangements should be agreed and set out as part of the local offer. The individual school's approach to identifying and assessing SEN should be published in accordance with the *Special Educational Needs and Disability Regulations* (see Chapter 11).

Where there has been an individual assessment of need, there should be agreement about the SEN support that is required for the young person. Any concerns raised by a parent should be recorded. Assessment should be regularly reviewed.

The place of assessment in supporting learning and behavioural needs

By law, a child or young person has special educational needs if he or she has a learning difficulty or disability which calls for special educational provision to be made for him or her (Children and Families Act, 2014, Part 3, §20 (1)) and the educational provision that is required to meet the needs is 'special'. Deciding whether a child's need is 'special' by definition, therefore, means using a form of assessment, often very formal, summative by nature and standardised against national norms, that enables comparison with the learning achievement and behaviour patterns of peers, or norms for sight, hearing, movement, and so on. There are some obvious questions raised here, however, for example:

- how to gauge whether what is already provided in the learning context is insufficient so that 'special' provision is therefore required; and
- how to ensure that a child whose attainment levels are demonstrated to be very poor in comparison with peers does not feel so demoralised that he or she will not try any more (Murphy, 2002).

We do not always wish to compare one child with others, however. It is always important to have a sense of children's on-going progress in learning through on-going continuous formative assessment that can provide teachers and others with opportunities to notice what is happening during learning activities, recognise the level and direction of the learning of individuals and see how they can help to take that learning further.

Sometimes we also need to know whether a child has reached a particular threshold or level in his or her learning. What is called criterion-referencing means comparing a child's achievements with clearly stated criteria for learning outcomes and clear descriptors of particular levels of performance within them. Setting out criteria for an assessment clarifies both what is required of learners but also assists teachers or others in deciding what they need to teach. Criterion-referencing can also improve the quality of feedback offered to learners as the descriptors of levels of performance and the overall criteria should be clear enough to serve as indicators of what learners have to do to succeed (Wearmouth, 2009).

Formal, norm-referenced (standardised) tests

Identification of the students who are eligible for special educational provision may depend on the results of norm-referenced assessment that is designed to indicate a learner's achievement in comparison with others. Whatever is assessed here has to be measurable, otherwise it is not possible to compare one child's score with another. For example, it is very common to use norm-referenced tests in the area of reading accuracy and comprehension.

To understand the use, and potential misuse, of standardised testing it is important to understand the test standardisation process, as well as a number of important concepts related to standardised tests and test procedures: 'measure of spread' of scores, validity and reliability, the usefulness of standardised scores and interpretations of percentile ranks, confidence bands and reading ages.

The standardisation process

One way to make test scores more readily understandable and comparable with other test scores would be to convert them to percentages. However, these percentages on their own do not tell us either the average score of all children taking the same tests and therefore how well or badly children are doing in comparison with peers, or how spread out the scores are around the mean (average). Standardising a test score involves assessing a large, nationally representative sample using a particular test and then adjusting the mean (average) to a score of 100. It is straightforward to compare a child's result with this score of 100.

An important concept associated with standardised tests is that of the 'measure of the spread' of scores, what is called the 'standard deviation'. This is usually set to 15 for a test of educational attainment. Irrespective of the difficulty of the test, about 68 per cent of students in a national sample will have a standardised score within one standard deviation (15 points) of the mean (that is, between 85 and 115), and about 95 per cent will have a standardised score within two standard deviations (30 points) of the mean. These examples come from a frequency distribution, known as the 'normal distribution', which is shown in Figure 8.1.

Validity and reliability

The terms 'validity' and 'reliability' are often associated with formal and informal tests. In general, the 'validity' of a test is the degree to which that test assesses what it is intended to test. We might ask, for example:

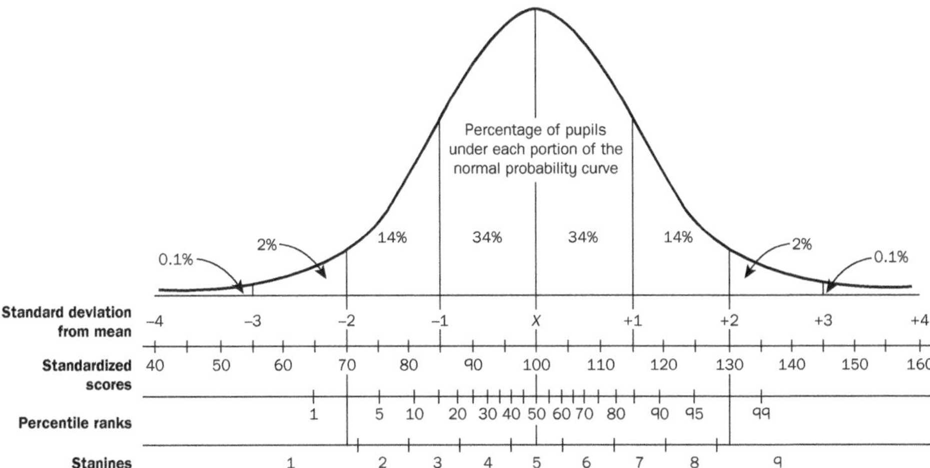

Figure 8.1 The relationship between standardised scores, percentile ranks and stanines under a normal distribution curve

- whether a test of cognitive ability or reading that has been developed and standardised in Britain would be valid for young people from a completely different culture and new to the UK;
- how valid the concept of 'reading age' is as it relates to adults;
- whether the test has 'context validity', that is, whether it tests what we expect it to test in the context in which it is being used.

'Reliability', on the other hand, generally means asking whether we would obtain the same result on the same test with the same cohort of individuals if we did the test procedure again.

Reflection 8.1: The usefulness of standardised scores

Standardised scores are often thought to be useful for a number of reasons. To what extent do you agree with this view?

- Standardised scores produce a scale that enables a comparison of results so that we can see whether a child is above or below the national average. The date when the test was standardised is important here, however. An old test might well be out of date in terms of comparisons of individuals with national norms. Re-standardisation of an old test might well give different norms in relation to the current generation.
- Scores are standardised so that the ages of the children are taken into account. We can therefore tell whether a child's test result is above or below that of other children of the same age.
- We can compare a child's performance on a standardised test in one area of the curriculum, for example, reading, with that in another, for example, mathematics. Or we can compare performance in two different aspects of the same area, for example, reading comprehension and reading accuracy, which might be important in assessing whether a child is dyslexic.

Percentile ranks

There is a constant relationship between percentile ranks and standardised scores when the same average score and standard deviation are used. The percentile rank is the percentage of students of the same age who gained a score at the same level or below that of the child's score. So performance at the 50th percentile indicates that the child performed as well as, or better than 50 per cent of the sample when age is taken into account.

Confidence band

The 'confidence band' indicates the range of scores within which an accurate assessment of attainment is likely to fall. It is not possible to obtain the hypothetically perfect measurement of ability. Tests of the sort discussed here measure attainment, that is, the level of the student's work, not 'ability'. Also, however carefully tests are constructed and administered, errors can result from factors such as a child's state of health, tiredness, unfamiliarity with formal assessments, and so on.

Reading age

Reading age is a commonly used concept in relation to norm-referenced assessments of literacy learning. It is obtained by working out for each age group the average raw score of the whole sample and then smoothing out any irregularities in the resulting graph. Increases in performance with age are smaller for older age groups. Hence the concept of reading age for older students is problematic because the accuracy and rate of reading would show no improvement beyond a certain point.

Reflection 8.2: Issues associated with norm-referencing

Anyone considering assessing a child needs to be fully conversant with test procedures, their aims and rationale as well as wider cultural and social factors, the school, the area of the curriculum concerned, and also the attributes of the individual child. Standardised tests alone are not designed to diagnose the root of difficulties in learning. Additionally, there are a number of issues associated with normative assessment, including equity and the link between achievement norms and teacher expectations of particular learners. To what extent would you need to take these into consideration in your own context?

- *In relation to equity*, some students may be allocated additional resources after achieving only very low scores on norm-referenced tests. However, there is a very grey area around the cut-off point above which other students will receive no additional provision.
- *Regarding reading age*, these represent snapshots of a progression in literacy development, not fixed and exact measures of reading attainment. Reading is a learned behaviour that is closely aligned with access to good teaching and resources, development and age. Thus, a low reading score does not

necessarily suggest general low ability, slow developmental growth, and so on. However, if we use the measured score while taking account of the confidence band, we can then view reading ages as estimates of reading ability at the time of testing.

- *With regard to teacher expectations*, when an individual student's test score lies within the bottom 'tail' of a normal distribution curve, there is often an assumption that the student's innate ability is very low. However, poor scores on normative tests can also mean that students' failure to achieve in school is automatically 'blamed' on poor ability, or the family, or the ethnic group. Sometimes this is known as the 'deficit' view of children who experience difficulties. This view can limit teachers' expectations of what to expect of certain students and, therefore, can lead to continued poor achievement (Rosenthal and Jacobson, 1968). It also absolves schools from responsibility for that learner's progress in school rather than opening up discussion of how classroom teaching practices and the school curriculum generally can be adapted to suit students' learning and behaviour better. 'Success' and 'failure' on norm-referenced tests are not just the result of children's natural ability, however (Tomlinson, 1988). Some families cannot support their own children adequately as a result of the circumstances in which they find themselves and the way that schools are structured, as much as of a lack of innate ability in the child.

Formative assessment

As the Assessment Reform Group (1999: 2) comment: 'There is no evidence that increasing the amount of testing will enhance learning' on its own. Results from externally-imposed summative tests, especially where there are very high stakes attached to these results, can have a very negative effect on students (Wearmouth, 2009).

Assessment can be a powerful educational tool for promoting learning but it depends on the kind of assessment that is used. In a seminal piece of work, Black and Wiliam (1998) demonstrated clearly that student achievement, particularly that of lower achievers, can be raised through formative assessment in the classroom. They found that improving learning through assessment depends on five 'deceptively simple' factors: (1) providing effective feedback; (2) actively involving students in their own learning; (3) modifying teaching in response to the results of assessment; (4) recognising the influence of assessment on students' motivation and self-esteem; and (5) enabling students to assess themselves and understand what they need to do to improve (Assessment Reform Group, 1999: 5). Assessment that supports learning must therefore involve students so that they are informed about how well they are doing in order to guide subsequent learning in a constructive way that shows them what they need to do, and can do, to make progress.

The shift in emphasis in the purpose of day-to-day assessment in classrooms has resulted in a focus in many places on 'Assessment for Learning' (AfL), that is, on-going day-to-day formative assessment to collect information on what children do or do not understand and the adaptation of teaching in response to this. On-going day-to-day assessments include questioning and discussions with children, observations of children while they are working, analysing children's work and giving quick feedback. Feedback that connects directly to specific and challenging goals related to students' prior knowledge and experience helps those students to focus more productively on new goals and the next learning steps (Ministry of Education, 2005: 16).

Criterion-referencing

Criterion-referencing is different from norm-referencing. The level of achievement is evaluated by how well the individual learner has performed in relation to specific criteria that specify key features of learning, achievement, and quality at different stages of children's development (Dunn et al., 2002). In order to enable teachers to gauge levels of achievement and to moderate marking across different assessors, some schools use authentic examples of students' work that illustrate what these criteria look like in practice. Teachers can compare a student's work sample with the exemplars in order to identify specific strengths and weaknesses, identify individual teaching and learning needs and prioritise new learning goals. By discussing and exemplifying a child's achievement and progress in relation to selected samples of work, parents and caregivers can be better informed about the quality of work at a particular curriculum level and how they too can better support future steps in learning.

Assessment of behaviour

Students' behaviour in schools does not occur in a vacuum (Watkins and Wagner, 1995; 2000). Students are members of classrooms which function as aspects of the school system within particular neighbourhoods. Students also fulfil roles within their own families and communities. Difficult behaviour which seems to relate to a particular student may be indicative of a range of contextual issues associated with society, the family, the ethnic or community group, school, classroom, peer group or teacher, as well as the individual student (Wearmouth et al., 2005).

Interventions designed to improve student behaviour can be centred on the child, on the environment, on the child and the environment or on the interface between the child and their environment. There are a number of ways of conceptualising the interactional relationship between the learning environment and the learner.

Collecting evidence of individual children's behaviour

Observing children and young people in the environment of the classroom or school is something that is a part of teachers' everyday practice. It is rare, however, for teachers to have the opportunity to stand back and closely observe the processes, relationships and behaviours involved in teaching and learning. For the purposes of assessment of individual students' behaviour, this process might need to be formalised. If so, it should be systematic and there should be an effective means of recording and interpreting what is seen.

Reflection 8.3: Problem-solving worrying behaviour

In order to develop effective problem-solving to identify when the challenges presented by an individual student's behaviour require special consideration, Watkins and Wagner (1995: 59) as cited by Wearmouth (2009: 70–1) pose a number of questions:

- What specific behaviour is causing concern?
- In what situations does the behaviour occur or not occur?
- What, specifically, happens before and after the behaviour? That is, what triggers it and what maintains it?
- What skills does the person demonstrate or not demonstrate?
- What does the person's behaviour mean to him or her?
- How does the person consider himself or herself, and what do others think?
- Who is most affected by this behaviour?

The last question often turns attention from the behaviour causing concern to the way the concern is being handled by others.

Observation of behaviour

As Fisher et al. (2004) comment, there are a number of different formats that can be adopted to observe students' behaviour. The first step is to make decisions about exactly *what* will be the focus of the observation: people, activities or events, or a combination of these. It might be important to observe an individual, a group, or a whole class in particular lessons or playground activities. If the problem-solving approach recommended by Watkins and Wagner (1995) is adopted, observations may take place in specific, pre-selected lessons or locations where individual students' behaviour has been identified as particularly problematic. Then, as Fisher et al. (2004) go on to note, there is a question about the time frames to be used: whether to sample what goes on during short pre-determined time periods or whether an individual student will be 'shadowed' for a longer period of time. The answers to these questions will, to a large extent, be dictated by the kinds of concerns raised in relation to the behaviour of individual students, the kind of reflection that has already taken place in relation to the evidence already collected, and the extent of an audit of the learning environment.

Birmingham Local Education Authority's three-level approach outlined in its strategy document *Behaviour in Schools: Framework for Intervention* (Birmingham City Council Education Department, 1998) begins with an audit of behaviour and of the learning environment. This is followed by reflection on how to alter that environment to make a positive impact on behaviour and learning.

Reflection 8.4: Assessing behaviour in context

The teacher first takes a baseline of behaviour by recording:

- frequency;
- place;
- time;
- social situation;
- setting events;
- description of problem behaviour;
- duration of problem behaviour;
- severity of behaviour (if appropriate);
- consequences to exhibiting child;
- consequences to others.

(Williams, 2004: 285)

The teacher then audits the changeable factors in the general learning environment that may influence the learner's behaviour:

- classroom physical environment, organisation and equipment;
- classroom management;
- classroom rules and routines;
- environment, routines and rules outside class;
- whole school policies and support for staff;
- roles of parents and governors.

(Williams, 2004: 285–6)

Next, the teacher considers information relating to the individual student:

- possible sensory difficulty – particularly with hearing;
- significant medical factors affecting the child;
- significant life events which may affect the child.

(Williams, 2004: 285)

We might add to this list other difficulties in learning, for example, in reading, writing and spelling, that might influence behaviour.

The next step is to think about what changes in the environment and teaching approaches might influence behaviour in a positive way, and then implement these changes and monitor the consequences. After this has been done, responses continue if necessary with a greater focus on the individual student within the learning environment. The teacher then goes on to involve external agencies if necessary.

Sometimes it might be appropriate to use a pre-set list of behaviours as a checklist for classroom teachers, against which the seriousness of particular kinds of behaviour can be assessed across different contexts. An example of such a checklist is included as Table 8.2. This checklist can be amended to suit your own context.

Table 8.2 Checklist of behaviours

Please tick the appropriate box	*Always*	*Frequently*	*Sometimes*	*Never*
Interrupts teacher, or responds inappropriately				
Shouts out in class				
Overly demanding of teacher attention				
Inappropriate talking to adults in classroom				
Annoys other children				
Has difficulty sitting still				
Leaves seat to wander about the classroom				
Very short attention span				
Makes inappropriate noises				
Displays excessive or inappropriate physical behaviour				
Damages or steals other pupils' property				
Damages or steals school property				
Damages own property				
Is verbally bullied				
Is physically bullied				
Verbally bullies or intimidates peers				
Physically bullies or intimidates peers				
Uses abusive language to other pupils				
Uses abusive language to adults				
Tells lies				
Verbally threatens teachers or other adults				
Can make and keep friends				
Can co-operate with peers				
Adapts to new situations/adults				
Tells the truth				
Copes with stress well				
Completes tasks				
Considerate to other children				
Can read well with understanding				
Can write well				

When conducting observations, it is usually more helpful to make notes at the time, even if systematic time sampling or event recording procedures are being implemented. These notes might be open-ended, where general points of interest are recorded, or can be focused on targeted events as and when they happen. A useful format is to write down what happened, and then to add a brief comment or interpretation later.

If the observer is looking for particular events or behaviours which can easily be categorised, they could devise an 'observation schedule'. Systematic observation procedures might involve the construction of an open grid in which instances of specified learner, peer and adult behaviours can be recorded as they occur.

Functional assessment of individual behaviour

One of the questions posed by Watkins and Wagner above relates to the gain for the individual (that is, the function that is served) by behaving in a particular way. Functional analysis can be seen as an experimental approach to behavioural assessment in which variables hypothesised to precede or to maintain the target behaviour are systematically examined in order to isolate their individual effects (Moore, 2004). Functional assessment therefore aims to discover the antecedents, setting events and consequences that cause or maintain challenging behaviours. The analysis can then be used as a means of identifying the functional relationships between particular behaviours and specific antecedent or consequent events.

One practical approach currently used in parts of the UK as well as in other areas of the world is that of 'Multi-Element Planning' (MEP) (Pitchford, 2004) as discussed on pp. 66-8. This takes account of a range of potential causes of the problems experienced by the child and considers the factors that appear to maintain the problematic behaviour. It then focuses on strategies related to improving the learning environment and teaching skills that will prevent the recurrence of the problematic behaviour or provide a way of safeguarding the child, peers and staff when the behaviour does recur.

Three practical steps need to be taken before drawing up the plan. First, should be an identification of the frequency, seriousness and the contexts in which the behavioural problems occur. Next, the problems should be prioritised. Finally, baseline data should be collected against which progress can be assessed. All data collected should be used to support the setting of targets for the MEP, reviewing progress and establishing appropriate criteria for rewards.

The issue of ethics is a very important consideration in MEP. Where teachers deliberately set out to change students' behaviour, then there is always a question of how that teacher's power is exercised, what kind of behaviour is seen as preferable and why, and in whose interest it is that the behaviour should be changed.

Biological and medical assessments of behaviour

Biological and medical explanations of behaviour theorise problems as emanating from within the individuals themselves. Difficult or challenging behaviour, from a medical perspective, is the result of an underlying condition, disease or dysfunction of the individual, which requires treatment. Two biologically- and medically-based understandings of behaviour are Attention Deficit/Hyperactivity Disorder (AD/HD) and autism.

Attention Deficit/Hyperactivity Disorder (AD/HD)

As Norwich et al. (2002) note, there are differences in the reported incidence of AD/HD internationally. In particular regions of the USA, up to 9 per cent of children have been identified as having AD/HD, while only 0.007 per cent have been identified in the UK. In Britain and Europe, the tradition has been 'to use the diagnostic systems of the International Classification of Diseases (ICD) published by the World Health Organisation' (Norwich et al., 2002: 13) and to assume a 'hyperkinetic disorder'. There is a strict requirement for 'pervasiveness and persistence'. This means that behaviour which is seen largely in one context only does not constitute grounds for a diagnosis. The criteria for diagnosis in the ICD-10 manual, for example, are that the child should have demonstrated abnormality of attention and activity at home and at school or nursery, for the age and developmental level of the child. The 'directly observed abnormalities of attention or activity' must be 'excessive for the child's age and developmental level'. The child should 'not meet criteria for pervasive development disorder, mania, depressive or anxiety', the difficulties should have begun 'before the age of 6 years' and should last 'at least 6 months'. The child should have a measured 'IQ above 50' (World Health Organisation, 1992).

While checklists of behaviour are an expedient way to classify adult perception of students' behaviour, behaviour assessment which is intended to lead to intervention in the context of a student's education needs to take account of a comprehensive range of factors that influence the student's behaviour in the context of school. Defining AD/HD as a mental disorder is problematic. The British Psychological Society (1996: 23) comments: 'The pattern of ADHD-type behaviour might be maladaptive to environmental requirements, but it is not necessarily the result of psychological dysfunction.'

Assessment of autism

Autism is also a medical explanation of individual behaviour. Some 80 per cent of individuals with autism score below 70 on norm-referenced intelligence tests (Roth, 2002), and severe general learning difficulties are correlated with an increasing occurrence of autism (Jordan, 1999). Sheehy (2004), therefore, notes difficulty in separating out the effects of autism from those of profound difficulties in learning. As Klin et al. (2000: 163) comment: 'There are no biological markers in the identification of autism, despite advances in neuroscience.' Hence a profile of symptoms and characteristics of autistic behaviour with agreed diagnostic criteria is used to identify autism in young people. The *International Statistical Classification of Diseases – ICD-10* (World Health Organisation, 1992) is commonly used in Europe.

In the ICD-10 (1992: F84.0), autism is described as a disorder that is 'pervasive' and 'developmental', and that is identified through 'abnormal and/or impaired development' that is evident before 3 years of age and by particular 'abnormal functioning' in social interaction, communication and 'restricted, repetitive behaviour'. Boys are affected three to four times more often than girls. Impairments 'in reciprocal social interaction' which manifest as 'an inadequate appreciation of socio-emotional cues' are always present. Impairments in communications include a 'lack of social usage of whatever language skills are present', as well as poorly developed 'make-believe and social imitative play'. During conversations, the ability to synchronise personal responses to the utterances of others is impaired as well as the ability to respond with feeling to other people's overtures. Autism is also said to be characterised by 'restricted, repetitive, and stereotyped patterns of behaviour, interests, and activities' that are demonstrated by 'a tendency to impose rigidity and routine on a wide range of aspects of day-to-day functioning'.

Assessment of visual impairment (VI)

Visual impairment (VI) is a general term that indicates a continuum of sight loss (Mason et al., 1997). Total blindness is extremely rare.

A standard eye chart is used to test visual acuity. One eye is covered at a time and the vision of each eye is recorded separately, as well as both eyes together. The most common chart is the Snellen eye chart, originally devised by a Dutch ophthalmologist, Dr Hermann Snellen, in 1862. This chart has a series of letters or letters and numbers, with the largest at the top. As the person being tested reads down the chart, the letters gradually become smaller. Many other versions of this chart are used for people who cannot read the alphabet.

In the Snellen fraction 20/20, the top number represents the test distance, 20 feet. The lower number represents the distance that the average eye can see the letters on a particular line of the eye chart. So, 20/20 means that the eye being tested can read a certain size letter when it is 20 feet away. If a person sees 20/40, at 20 feet from the chart he or she can read letters that a person with 20/20 vision could read from 40 feet away. Originally Snellen worked in feet but later (in 1875) he changed from using feet to metres (from 20/20 to 6/6 respectively). Currently, the 20-foot distance continues to be used in the United States, but 6 metres is used in Britain.

Although the Snellen fractions are measures of sharpness of sight in relation to identifying letters or symbols with high contrast at a specified distance, they tell us nothing about the quality of vision in general, for example, the ability to see larger objects and objects with poor contrast – or, indeed, whether vision is more or less efficient when using both eyes together (Strouse Watt, 2003).

A clinical assessment of vision usually focuses on four aspects: distance, near, field and colour vision (Mason, 2001). However, this clinical assessment identifies only what a child can or cannot see. As in other areas of special educational needs in schools, a whole range of information is needed to ensure that support for an individual is appropriate (Miller and Ockleford, 2005). This includes the views of the child and the parents/family, medical and school records as well as the clinical assessment of vision.

Assessment of auditory impairment

A decibel (dB) is a measure of sound pressure level. Normal voice measures 60 dB at a distance of 1 metre, a raised voice 70 dB at 1 metre, and shouting 80 dB at 1 metre.

The severity of a hearing impairment is measured in decibels of hearing loss and is ranked according to the additional intensity above a nominal threshold that a sound must be before being detected by an individual. In schools or colleges, for educational purposes, young people with hearing impairments will probably require hearing aids, adaptations to their environment or particular teaching strategies in order to access the curriculum.

Assessment of hearing

There is a variety of tests that can be used to find out how much hearing a child has. The tests used will depend on the child's age and stage of development. It is possible to test the hearing of all children from birth onwards. Screening tests are normally done first to see if it is likely that there is a hearing loss and the child needs to be referred to an audiologist. The audiologist will then perform more detailed tests to build up an accurate picture of the child's hearing.

Since 2006, babies have been screened to test their hearing within a few days of their birth. Babies 'begin to develop language and communication from their earliest months', so early screening means that 'much can be done to positively support and encourage that development... when early identification of deafness is combined with effective early intervention, with parents and professionals working together, language outcomes for deaf children can be similar to those for hearing children' (NDCS, 2010: 6).

For children of school age, hearing is usually measured with behavioural tests using pure tones. The sounds come through headphones and each time a child hears a sound they respond by moving an object, pressing a button or saying 'yes'.

Quantification of hearing loss

Hearing sensitivity varies according to the frequency of sounds. To take this into account, hearing sensitivity can be measured for a range of frequencies and plotted on an audiogram. Hearing sensitivity is indicated by the quietest sound that an animal can detect, called the hearing threshold, in other words, the quietest sound to which the person responds. The test is carried out for sounds of different frequencies.

In humans, the term hearing impairment is usually reserved for people who have relative insensitivity to sound in the speech frequencies. The severity of a hearing loss is categorised according to the increase in volume that must be made above the usual level before the listener can detect it. In profound deafness, even the loudest sounds that can be produced by an audiometer (an instrument used to measure hearing) may not be detected. Normal hearing thresholds within any given species are not the same for all frequencies. If different frequencies of sound are played at the same amplitude, some will be perceived as loud, and others quiet or even completely inaudible.

Four categories of hearing impairment are generally used: mild, moderate, severe and profound. As noted by NHS Choices (2015) (www.nhs.uk, accessed 1 June 2015):

- With 'mild deafness: 20–40 dB' a child could hear a baby crying but may be unable to hear whispered conversation. Mild deafness can sometimes make hearing speech difficult, particularly in noisy situations.
- With 'moderate deafness: 41–70 dB', a child could hear a dog barking but not a baby crying. A young person may have difficulty following speech without using a hearing aid.
- With 'severe deafness: 71–90 dB', a child would hear drums being played but not a dog barking. He or she would usually need to lip-read or use sign language, even with the use of a hearing aid.
- With 'profound deafness: >90 dB', a child might hear a large lorry but not drums being playing. People who are profoundly deaf can often benefit from a cochlear implant. Other forms of communication include lip-reading and sign language.

What suits the child best may depend on the degree of hearing loss, the extent of the delay in language acquisition and what the child and the family feel about the situation.

Taking students' views into account

In terms of eliciting students' perceptions of, and feelings about, their own behaviour and learning, it is important to recognise that 'children will make decisions about people they can talk to and trust, and those they cannot' (Gersch, 1995: 48). Some young people find it much more difficult to communicate than others. Difficulties in accessing information, communication, sensory impairment, mobility and relationship-building might make meaningful discussion with some young people problematic. For example, the communication of students with profound and multiple learning disabilities which may depend on reflexes, actions, sounds and facial expression needs to be carefully observed and interpreted by the various people who know those pupils best (Porter et al., 2001). For those young people who cannot express themselves verbally, but for whom pictures and symbols are meaningful and who can understand what is going on, a variety of powerful and useful tools have been developed to attempt to elicit their views. These include the use of cue cards (Lewis, 2002: 114) that can act 'as prompts for ideas about... people, talk, setting (indoor/outdoor variants), feelings and consequences about the particular event under discussion... that can convey meaning in a neutral way'. In a similar way, 'Talking Mats' (Cameron and Murphy, 2002) can enable children who experience difficulties in verbal expression to express their views by moving symbols about on mats.

Issues of confidentiality

There are many instances in schools where students disclose very sensitive information about themselves to teachers. Before engaging in any activity where this is likely to happen, teachers need to familiarise themselves very well with any guidelines that may exist in their own schools about handling information that may emerge from students' self-disclosure, for example, information relating to abuse of various kinds.

Reflection 8.5: Sensitive issues in eliciting students' views. An example of an interview technique: 'Talking Stones'

Wearmouth (2009: 73) discusses the practical and ethical issues involved in using a powerful interview technique, 'Talking Stones', to help students to represent problematic relationships and learning contexts as they see them.

> During an individual interview, a student is given a pile of stones of varying shapes, sizes, colours and textures. The student is encouraged to project on to them thoughts and feelings about him/herself in relation to school, and about his/her relationships with other students and teachers. The individual selects one stone to represent him/herself as a student in school and discusses his/her choice. Subsequently s/he selects more stones to represent significant others in the school and/or classroom context, describes why they have been chosen, and then places them on a rectangular white cloth or large sheet of paper. The edges of the rectangle form a boundary to the positioning of the stones. Stones, their attributes and their positions and distance in relation to each other can be understood as a student's representation of his/her world of school and his/her place within it.

One way in which a procedure such as 'Talking Stones' can contribute to the process of assessment in schools is in the manner in which it can open up problematic relationships between, typically, teenagers and staff members, and facilitate dialogue between them.

'Talking Stones' is a powerful procedure. Teachers using 'Talking Stones' should be aware of ethical principles associated with techniques of a counselling nature, for example, the principle of not doing any harm (McLeod, 1998). The use of the technique is ethically questionable unless there is a clear benefit for the student. Asking personal questions may be interpreted as prying into a student's privacy. However, addressing difficult student behaviour can be very difficult if teachers are not aware of major factors driving that behaviour. Reflecting on the ethics of the situation also raises the question of who should decide whether the risks of using a technique such as this outweigh the benefits.

Summary

Assessment should be viewed as a tool that supports learning and not simply as a politically expedient solution to perceived concerns about standards and ways to make schools accountable to parents, families and society as a whole (Assessment Reform Group, 1999). A constructive and positive approach to assessment begins with an evaluation of the learning environment and considerations of how to modify to enhance behaviour and learning. The approach then continues if necessary with a greater focus on understanding the individual student and his or her learning needs.

The awareness of learning and ability of learners to direct it for themselves is of increasing importance in the context of encouraging lifelong learning. Assessment can therefore serve to either reinforce or undermine the motivation to strive for future achievement. Students' sense of themselves as having the potential to learn and achieve alongside peers may be constructed and constrained by the forms of assessment that are used with them. Assessment therefore must aim to build on students' experiences and identities and look for strengths as well as weaknesses. (Wearmouth, 2009). Assessment that is on-going, continuous and formative and provides teachers with formal and informal opportunities to notice what is happening during learning activities, recognise where the learning of individuals and groups of students is going and how they as the teacher can help take that learning further, is likely to lead to positive learning gains (Assessment Reform Group, 1999).

9

Planning provision for individual needs

Introduction

In this chapter we adopt the view that planning provision to address the assessed needs of individuals should take place within the process of planning the whole class/ whole subject curriculum. We therefore focus on:

- planning for differentiation in the classroom;
- the assess→plan→do→review cycle;
- issues related to consulting or liaising with parents and families. These issues will be considered more fully in Chapter 12;
- development of individual learning and behaviour plans mapped to assessment of needs, with examples;
- the example of pupil 'passports';
- formal Education, Health and Care plans:
    - legal requirements;
    - process.

A differentiated approach for all

Before turning to the question of the planning process for individual students, we should stress that teaching and learning for all students are expected to be framed within the National Curriculum inclusion statement (DfE, 2014g).

Setting suitable challenges

4.1 Teachers should set high expectations for every pupil. They should plan stretching work for pupils whose attainment is significantly above the expected standard. They have an even greater obligation to plan lessons for pupils who have low levels of prior attainment or come from disadvantaged backgrounds. Teachers should use appropriate assessment to set targets which are deliberately ambitious.

Responding to pupils' needs and overcoming potential barriers for individuals and groups of pupils

> 4.2 Teachers should take account of their duties under equal opportunities legislation that covers race, disability, sex, religion or belief, sexual orientation, pregnancy and maternity, and gender reassignment.
>
> 4.3 A wide range of pupils have special educational needs, many of whom also have disabilities. Lessons should be planned to ensure that there are no barriers to every pupil achieving. In many cases, such planning will mean that these pupils will be able to study the full National Curriculum...
>
> 4.4 With the right teaching, that recognises their individual needs, many disabled pupils may have little need for additional resources beyond the aids which they use as part of their daily life. Teachers must plan lessons so that these pupils can study every National Curriculum subject. Potential areas of difficulty should be identified and addressed at the outset of work.

It might therefore be sensible for teachers to concentrate at first on 'Quality First Teaching', strategies which improve the learning environment and increase the range of teaching approaches, rather than assuming that something different has to be organised for every individual. Inclusive teaching in this context means adjusting learning objectives to suit individual students' needs. It also means teaching that draws on a variety of approaches, for example, open and closed tasks, short and long tasks, visual, auditory or kinaesthetic activities. It implies, too, understanding that the learning context itself can support, or hinder, learning. For example, science laboratories with high benches and stools, or art rooms with little rooms between tables, chairs and easels may be very difficult for students with restricted movement. The acoustic environment is important for the attainment of all students, but particularly for those who experience auditory difficulties.

Some students who experience difficulties in learning can work on the same learning objectives as others in the class, as long as the teacher plans appropriate access strategies. For example, a teacher might build in alternatives to written recording, and provision of appropriate age and culturally-related resources. Disability legislation calls modifications to learning and teaching programmes 'reasonable adjustments'. For example, if a barrier to a mathematics lesson on problem-solving is a dyslexic student's lack of fluent knowledge of number facts, he or she may need to use a calculator. If, however, the barrier is a motor coordination difficulty that prevents accurate drawing of shapes and graphs, the student may need the use of appropriate software which is programmed to draw shapes and graphs. If it is difficulty with use of abstract symbols he or she may benefit from the use of concrete materials of some kind. Teachers might try out ideas and assess results to develop their own practice. Strategies that do not result in improved learning and behaviour can then be seen as experiments leading teachers towards solutions, not failures.

Reflection 9.1: Auditing differentiation in the classroom

- At this point you might choose to look back at Table 8.1 and audit the extent to which you feel that a classroom in your school or college is inclusive of all students' needs.
- When you have done this, if the classroom is your own, what changes will you make as a result?
- If it is a colleague's, how will you approach supporting him or her to make changes?

Individual plans need to be embedded in the regular cycle of classroom activity integrated with the learning experience offered to the student through the curriculum. In lesson planning, teachers and classroom assistants need to be aware of which pupils have plans and be conversant with their content so that they can take adequate account of individual pupils' needs.

Reflection 9.2: Planning for differentiation

As Cowne (2000) advises, teachers must have a very clear grasp of eight issues when planning lessons that take plans for individual pupils into account. You might choose to look at these now and consider whether you might take account of them in your own lesson planning, and in CPD for other colleagues, or in some other way:

- how the principal curriculum objectives and key concepts for the lesson relate to the overall schemes for the school;
- the way in which the principal objectives and key concepts are to be assessed, the criteria which indicate a satisfactory level of skills and understanding of key concepts, ways in which the assessment process might be differentiated and the means by which the outcome of the assessment is to be recorded as part of the IEP;
- the prerequisite skills for the principal objectives, and the prior level of knowledge required to understand key concepts;
- the extent to which all pupils in the classroom, including those identified as having special learning needs, have the prerequisite skills and prior knowledge in order that any 'pre-teaching', or a different resource to assist access to information, might be arranged;
- relevant skills and knowledge that might be cross-referenced from another curriculum area;
- ways in which various kinds of group work, with or without additional assistance from adults, might assist learning in the particular lesson;
- the extent those pupils with the greatest needs might be expected to fulfil the principal objectives and grasp all key concepts;
- whether an alternative set of objectives will be needed for any children.

Cowne's views imply a flexibility of approach which demands a thorough grasp of, and familiarity with, the National Curriculum structure and its underlying principles in addition to the strengths and needs of individual pupils.

Differentiation to enable all students to access the curriculum remains of prior importance in any teacher's planning activity.

Reflection 9.3: Creating a plan for access to learning for a whole class

One of the SENCOs on a recent National Award for SEN Co-ordination course at the University of Bedfordshire created what she called an 'Access to Learning Plan' (Mythen, unpublished) to differentiate teaching approaches according to the range of students in her classes, and their particular learning and behaviour needs. We have reproduced this as Appendix B1 on p. 212-20. You might choose to have a look at this now and reflect on whether and how it might be suitable for use in your own school or college.

We already discussed issues related to literacy difficulties in Chapter 5. There are many ways of differentiating support offered to students who experience difficulties in written expression and it is worth outlining how this differentiated support might be integrated into a mainstream lesson.

Reflection 9.4: Differentiating classroom writing activities

The National Literacy Strategy offered a really clear example of differentiation in literacy learning lessons at primary level. You might wish to consider ways in which you might use this.

Examples of structural support strategies during a sequence of lessons intended to facilitate children's written story-telling skills might include some of the following.

- *A story hand*. Individuals draw around their hands and represent in key words, simple icons or pictures the key events in the beginning (thumb), middle (middle three fingers), and end (little finger) of the story. The themes of the tale can also be shown as rings on the hand or a bracelet encapsulating the narrative.
- *A physical story board.* Groups of children freeze-frame a key element in the story/chapter so that the whole structure is physically represented by the class in several tableaux. If titles are given to these tableaux, a summary or resume of the tale/chapter is effectively created.
- *Story maps*. These can be varied to suit the narrative, but could include the geographical settings in the story, the main movements of the protagonists and antagonists, the sequence of events and the key phrases from the tale.
- *Story mountains*. These suit climactic stories and clearly demarcate the climax of the tale at the apex of the mountain range. Made out of sugar paper with small pictures or keywords to denote the sections of the story, mountains are very versatile and can be cut to suit the number of significant episodes in the narrative.
- *Flow charts*. These show the development of the story, scene by scene. They can be used as a planning device.
- *Paragraph/scene charts*. These provide a series of boxes in which each scene is drawn or notes are made. They can be flexible if Post-its are used, as this means

that scenes can be moved around. For instance, instead of beginning a story at the beginning, a writer might start with the dramatic event and then have a flash-back to the opening.

- *Enacting the tale*. If children have just acted out a scene or improvised an event, then they will find writing easier because the key sequence of events can be more firmly fixed in the mind.
- *Telling (or retelling) the tale*. With children working in pairs, or as a story circle, stories can be retold or invented. Oral rehearsing of a story means that some refining and revision can take place before the act of writing.
- *Mind mapping*. The more children internalise a range of basic structures, the more they are able to write successfully. This is because they know the direction in which the tale must move. This allows them to be imaginative to allow unexpected events to creep into the tale.

(adapted from PNS, 2005, cited in Wearmouth, 2009: 88–9)

Table 9.1 presents an example of a daily lesson plan format designed to incorporate provision for differentiated learning.

The planning process

Where students continue to make inadequate progress, despite effective differentiated teaching in the classroom, current legislation and guidance across the UK refer to

Table 9.1 Daily lesson plan

Year Group: **Class:** **Set (if appropriate):**	**Time of Session:** **Length of Session:**	**Date:**	**No. of children:**
Target(s):			
Students' subject knowledge: (Write in bullet points the essential knowledge students need)			
Learning Objectives: (including reference to NC where appropriate).			
Key Vocabulary:			

(continued)

Table 9.1 Daily lesson plan (*Continued*)

Year Group: **Class:** **Set (if appropriate):**	**Time of Session:** **Length of Session:**	**Date:**	**No. of children:**

Resources and materials required:

Organisation & Management: Who will introduce the activity? How will the children be organised during lesson (e.g. whole class for the introduction, then work as groups or individuals for the activity) Whom will you work with? How will teaching assistants or other adults be used? How will you manage transitions within the lesson, e.g. children moving from one area to the next?

Whole Class Input: What is the stimulus? How will you capture the students' attention? Include key questions you will ask.

Activity, Independent or Adult-Led (e.g. collaborative groups):
What will the students be doing? How will the activity be differentiated? How will you use other adults? What will be your role in the teaching activity?

Students with additional access needs:

Students with no additional access needs:

Higher attainers:

Extension Activities: What will children who finish the activities do next? How will this develop their learning further?

Conclusion/evaluation:

(Adapted from Wearmouth, 2009, pp. 90-2)

individual plans to record the nature of a student's difficulties and how they are going to be addressed. It is expected that both parents and students will be actively involved in creating and assessing the effectiveness of the individual. Effective planning, as outlined in the Code (DfE, 2014a: §9.22) is that which:

- focuses on the child or young person as an individual, not the SEN label;
- uses clear ordinary language and images, not professional jargon, so it is easy for children, young people and their parents to understand;
- highlights the young person's strengths;
- enables the young person, and his or her family to say what they have done, what they are interested in and what outcomes they are seeking in the future;
- tailors support to the needs of the individual;
- organises assessments to minimise demands on families;
- brings together professionals to agree overall approach.

The class teacher, the SENCO, any teaching assistants, the student, parents or carers, and outside agencies, if appropriate, should all be involved in the planning process. It is imperative, for example, that:

- teachers work closely with TAs or specialist staff to plan and assess the impact of targeted interventions;
- planning and review time are explicitly planned for and regularly take place;
- there is joint planning time with support staff, which might necessitate:
  - paying support staff to join planning/department meetings;
  - quick and concise communication tools to convey outcomes of targeted provision;
  - targeted provision work carried out in pupil's class or on the subject books so teachers can see what work has been carried out and to what standard, and pick up emerging issues.
- The effectiveness/impact of support should be reviewed in line with the agreed date so that:
  - impact on progress and pupil's/parents' views feed back into the analysis of the young person's needs;
  - the SENCO and teacher revise support in light of progress;
  - involvement of external specialists is considered where the young person continues to make little progress. This involvement should be shared with parents and recorded.

Statutory advice in the Code (DfE, 2014a) advises that the teacher and SENCO should negotiate with parents and the student and agree:

- interventions and support, together with expected impact on progress;
- a date for review.

The plan should then be recorded on the school's information system.

The student's class teacher should remain responsible for working with the child on a daily basis and for planning and delivering an individualised programme. The SENCO, however, should take the lead in:

- further assessment of the child's particular strengths and weaknesses;
- planning future support for the child in discussion with colleagues;
- monitoring and subsequently reviewing the action taken.

Schools must provide an annual report for parents. If the student 'receives' SEN support, the teacher 'with good knowledge of child' and the needs (usually the class teacher or tutor supported by the SENCO) should meet parents each term. This should be an opportunity for the parents to share concerns and aspirations, and to plan. The views of the young person must be included and his or her record must be updated. Appropriate school staff must be informed of the outcomes of any review meeting, and revised targets.

Reflection 9.5: Involving the young person

You might like to carry out the following activity to assess the extent to which young people in your school or college with individual plans are aware of them. Some questions to ask:

- Does every young person know he or she has an individual plan?
- Does he or she know his or her current targets?
- Does he or she contribute to targets?
- Does he or she know arrangements to support him or her?
- Does he or she have regular feedback on and recognition of progress made?
- Does he or she feel that his or her views are considered?
- How is he or she involved directly or indirectly in the review?

Parental/family engagement with the planning process

Not all families feel comfortable in formal school or college settings particularly if, for example, their own educational experiences were difficult. Suggestions for professionals dealing with parents in schools, adapted from Friend and Cook (1996: 232) include:

- Create an environment that is welcoming.
- Schedule the meeting at the convenience of the parent.
- Provide an advance summary of the topics to be covered and a list of questions that the parent might want to ask.
- Suggest the parent brings to school copies of work the child has done at home.
- Let the parent be seated at the meeting table first.
- Provide the parent with a file folder containing copies of the information that the professionals have in their folders.
- Use your communication skills to structure the meeting so the parent has opportunities to provide input throughout the meeting.

Reflection 9.6: Supporting family engagement in formal meetings

In a recent discussion with a group of SENCOs from schools and colleges across the sectors, the following principles were agreed as important in establishing effective partnership-working with parents and families. How far would you agree with these from your own experience?

- Building trust and rapport.
- Keeping parents up to date.
- Transparency – under-promise and over-deliver.
- Communication with all involved that enables everyone to be heard.
- Note differences between primary and secondary.
- Mutual respect – ground rules.
- Listening without talking.
- Establish understanding of the three-way partnership.
- The meeting must be 'going somewhere'.
- Consistent approach between home and school.
- Consistent personnel – single point of contact for families.
- Clear channel of communication and process within the school and with other agencies.
- Child needs-led.
- Clear communication.
- Openness in a safe environment.
- Trust and shared realistic expectations.
- Accessibility of information.
- Positive and collaborative working relationship.
- Resourcing.
- Consistency.

Planning for the long, medium and short term

Curriculum planning for any learner or group needs to incorporate an overall long-term plan based on a global view of the learner and an awareness of the context within which the plan must take effect. From this long-term plan, it is possible to draw up medium- and short-term plans. A flowchart can show how both an initial assessment of the difficulties experienced by the learner and the context of the whole-school curriculum might, together, lead to long-term, medium- and short-term planning. This chart takes into account some of the principles described in the work of Tod, Castle and Blamires (1998) (see Figure 9.1).

Planning for the long term implies taking a view about the pupil's future over the next few years. A longer-term vision of a range of possibilities for a learner that can be shared between the learner, the parent/carer and the professionals is important to give a sense of direction to the whole planning process. At the meeting to review the student's progress, a considerable amount of revision and amendment to a pupil's programme might be needed in the light of current achievement and personal development, changes in the learning environment and the stage reached in the National Curriculum.

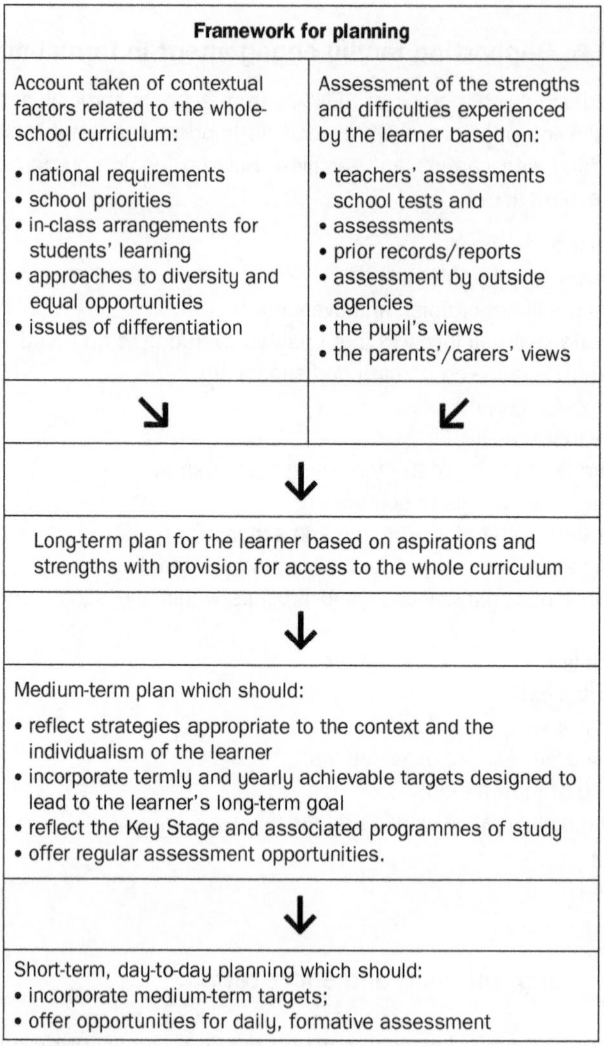

<table>
<tr><th colspan="2">Framework for planning</th></tr>
<tr><td>Account taken of contextual factors related to the whole-school curriculum:
• national requirements
• school priorities
• in-class arrangements for students' learning
• approaches to diversity and equal opportunities
• issues of differentiation</td><td>Assessment of the strengths and difficulties experienced by the learner based on:
• teachers' assessments school tests and
• assessments
• prior records/reports
• assessment by outside agencies
• the pupil's views
• the parents'/carers' views</td></tr>
<tr><td>↘</td><td>↙</td></tr>
<tr><td colspan="2">↓</td></tr>
<tr><td colspan="2">Long-term plan for the learner based on aspirations and strengths with provision for access to the whole curriculum</td></tr>
<tr><td colspan="2">↓</td></tr>
<tr><td colspan="2">Medium-term plan which should:
• reflect strategies appropriate to the context and the individualism of the learner
• incorporate termly and yearly achievable targets designed to lead to the learner's long-term goal
• reflect the Key Stage and associated programmes of study
• offer regular assessment opportunities.</td></tr>
<tr><td colspan="2">↓</td></tr>
<tr><td colspan="2">Short-term, day-to-day planning which should:
• incorporate medium-term targets;
• offer opportunities for daily, formative assessment</td></tr>
</table>

Figure 9.1 Long-, medium- and short-term planning
Source: Adapted from Wearmouth (2009: 75).

Reflection 9.7: Planning for needs over the long term

The review cycle does not detract from the need to think about possible routes for learners over a much longer period than this. Individuals' needs change over time. It is very important to retain flexibility of thinking so that the planning process is facilitative of learning rather than restrictive.

How far do the comments of Pickles reflect concerns with any of the students for whom you have some responsibility? In the case of pupils with severe motor difficulties, for example, individual children:

> may have difficulties affecting some or all of their limbs, limited hand function, fine and gross motor difficulties and sometimes difficulties with speech and language. Most, though not all, pupils will have a medical diagnosis. A diagnosis may have been given at birth, at about the age of two or a later date, though deteriorating conditions such as muscular dystrophy may not be diagnosed until the child attends school. Some children may have physical difficulties as a result of an accident or illness, which can happen at any age. It must be remembered that, in the same way as other children, they may also have learning difficulties, dyslexia, dyspraxia, asthma, epilepsy, vision and hearing difficulties or hidden handicaps affecting their visual/auditory perception or eye/hand co-ordination, etc.
>
> (Pickles, 2001: 290)

A long-term plan for these pupils would take into account 'dignity and emotional needs . . . especially in positioning, toileting and transfers . . . to enable pupils to be as independent as possible . . . recognising that teaching methods may need to vary as needs change is all part of inclusion' (Pickles, 2001: 292). It would also need to include:

- views of the student as a person, with the same hopes, expectations and rights as every other student;
- considerations of physical access to the school environment;
- ways in which the needs of the family and the student's place within it can be taken into account by the school;
- in-school factors that support, or militate against, the student's inclusion;
- the role of the support assistant(s) and the kind of relationship that might be established with the student and the family, and any issues this raises;
- the role and function of information and communications technology;
- the role and function of any other appropriate technological aids;
- professional development and awareness raising of teachers and other staff in the school;
- awareness-raising among peers, if appropriate;
- the place of therapy in the student's curriculum.

Medium- and short-term planning should be seen to flow logically from the long-term plan for the learner. For example, as in the case of pupils with severe motor difficulties described by Pickles (2001):

> A life skill, long-term physical target might be for the pupil to stand and walk with a walker. The long-term target might be for the pupil to stand and weight bear. The short-term target might be for the pupil to use a prone stander in a low angle position, twice daily for 20-minute sessions, in class, taking some weight on the body and raising the angle of the stander by a few degrees with success.

Any specific equipment should also be noted at this point, detailing where, when, how and why it should be used.

Making effective use of individual learning plans

Planning to address individuals' learning needs effectively means setting out to work from strengths and interests. Staff attitudes and students' view of themselves as able to learn (or not!) make for potent interactions for good or ill. When planning for students who experience difficulties in learning, we first need to know whether the student or group can, with appropriate access strategies, work on the same learning objectives as the rest of the class. Getting this right will depend on accurate assessment of what the student knows, understands and can do.

If a student cannot work on the same objectives as the class as a whole, the teacher might want to choose learning objectives that are linked to the topic on which the whole class is working, but earlier in a learning progression. It will often be possible to 'track back' to locate earlier learning objectives.

Planning will also need to be informed by the individual priorities for students. Normally it will be appropriate for them to work on objectives that are similar and related to the whole class topic. However, at other times, teachers will also have to consider whether the students have other priority needs that are central to their learning, for example, a need to concentrate on some key skills such as communication, problem-solving, working with others, managing their own emotions, and so on. These needs may be detailed in the student's individual plan. They can often be met within the whole class learning, for example, relating physiotherapy objectives to the PE curriculum, communication to literacy lessons, problem-solving to mathematics, history or geography.

Some students may have additional therapeutic or other needs which cannot easily be met through class activities. For these students, alternative objectives may be needed to meet specific needs for identified periods of time as long as they are in the context of ensuring that, over time, all students receive a broad and balanced curriculum.

This process begins by ensuring students receive appropriate learning goals related to the appropriate stage of learning with the National Curriculum guidelines, and are engaged in interactive learning conversations throughout their learning activities within a well-informed understanding of what constitutes an appropriate curriculum for the age group and the students' peers in the first place. Learning conversations are based on evidence from assessments and observations carried out in authentic learning contexts. Learning conversations include responsive feedback that connects to the student's own experience of difficulties in learning and feed forward to help the student identify their next most appropriate learning steps.

Target setting

Individual plans, profiles or records can only be as effective as the rigour of the thinking underlying their design. Similar issues arise in relation to target setting for individual plans or profiles as those relating to target setting within the national context. The strength of targets may be that they provide a focus for the combined efforts of all those concerned to support a learner's progress and highlight the need to link planning and provision. However, there are specific areas of the curriculum where it may be problematic to conceptualise measurable targets. These areas involve behaviour, the emotions and creativity.

Setting measurable targets is closely associated with behavioural approaches. A school and a national curriculum can be seen as a ladder of progression which children are expected to climb, with specific assessment learning goals at each rung. An inherent difficulty in this view, however, is that not all children learn the same way, so setting targets which follow in a similar sequence for all students is not necessarily appropriate. Dockrell and McShane (1993) highlight problems associated with this approach and note that one important criticism of task analysis and setting learning objectives is the conceptualisation of the learning process that this approach reflects. They comment that, instead of a single instructional hierarchy common to all children, there may be a number of different routes by which a child can master the skill. They note that a task analysis analyses the task and not the learning processes or the learning context, hence it assumes that each child will learn the components of the task in the same order. There is also the possibility that too much reliance on task components can lead to a rigid prescription of what is to be taught which takes little account of the knowledge a child brings to a task or the particular strategies that a child might otherwise use. In addition, some areas lend themselves to this approach more easily than others.

Reflection 9.8: Ways to address needs across the four areas

In Chapters 4–7 we discussed the four areas of need. In doing so we outlined possible ways to address needs in each of these areas under the headings below. You might choose to look back through these chapters to see whether you might consider any of these possibilities in the individual planning process:

- communication and interaction:
  - pragmatic language impairment (PLI)
  - autism
  - use of ICT to facilitate communication.
- cognition and learning:
  - precision teaching
  - scaffolding learning through the zone of proximal development (ZPD)
  - dyslexic difficulties.
- social, emotional and mental health
  - using behavioural methodology:
    - 'Multi-element planning'
    - planning a nurture group
    - Tourette syndrome
- sensory and/or physical needs:
  - hearing and visual difficulties.

Individual provision maps

These days some SENCOs have dispensed with individual plans for some children and use group plans instead. Some may rely on 'provision maps' which can be either documents that identify provision for individual children, or whole-school provision with analyses of student outcomes and value for money, or both. We have included an example of an individual provision map for a young man with autistic tendencies in Appendix B2 on p. 221-3.

'Pupil passports'

In order to ensure that all staff are aware of students' needs, some schools have adopted 'pupil passports' which the young person carries with him or her to each lesson. These comprise a one-page summary document that is often compiled with the student and written in the first person. There is no formal requirement or set format, but as a general guide they contain the student's name and photograph together with the following, written in the first person:

- 'I would like you to know that...';
- 'This means that...';
- 'I find it difficult to...';
- 'It would help me if you could...';
- 'I will help myself by...' (self-help strategies agreed with the student);
- additional support, e.g. interventions in place;
- important data, e.g. reading age.

(www.pupilpassport.co.uk, accessed 28 May 2015)

Education, Health and Care plans

There are specific requirements for the contents of an EHC plan. An EHC plan specifies:

- the child's or young person's special educational needs;
- the outcomes sought for him or her;
- the special educational provision required by him or her;
- any health care provision reasonably required by the learning difficulties and disabilities which result in him or her having special educational needs;
- social care provision which is being made for the child/young person under the Chronically Sick and Disabled Persons Act 1970 and any social care provision reasonably required by the learning difficulties and disabilities which result in the child or young person having special educational needs, to the extent that the provision is not already specified in the plan.

If an EHC plan does not contain all of the sections which are needed, it will not be legally compliant.

The statutory assessment process and development and review of EHC plans require co-operation between schools and LAs. Where the child or young person has not made expected progress despite a school having taken appropriate action to identify, assess and meet the SEN, an EHC needs assessment might be requested. During the course of an assessment, the LA must gather advice from relevant professionals about the young person's education, health and care needs and special educational, health and care provision that may be required to achieve desired outcomes. The child's parent or the young person has the right to request a particular school be named in their EHC plan. The LA must consult the governing body of that school about admitting the child or young person and to name the school in the EHC plan, unless it would be unsuitable for the age, ability, aptitude or SEN of the child or young person, or the attendance of the child or young person would be incompatible with the efficient education of their peers or the efficient use of resources. The school is involved in the development or review of the EHC plan to determine what can be provided from within the school's own resources and what will require additional external expertise or further funding from the LA which must then make sure the support identified in the plan is provided.

Some of the provision specified may be procured by the child's parent or the young person using a Personal Budget. Where a direct payment is to be used to deliver provision on the school premises, the LA must seek the written agreement of the school for this arrangement. Local authorities have a duty to review EHC plans as a minimum every twelve months, and can require schools or other educational institutions to convene and hold the review meeting on their behalf. In most cases, reviews are held at, and led by, the young person's educational institution. The child's parents or the young person, a representative of the school or other institution, a local authority SEN officer, a health service representative and a local authority social care representative must be invited and given at least two weeks' notice of the date of the meeting. Other individuals relevant to the review should also be invited.

The school should seek information about the child or young person prior to the meeting from all participants, and send any information gathered to all those invited at least two weeks before the meeting. Subsequently, and within two weeks of the meeting, the school should send a report to everyone invited with recommendations on any amendments required to the EHC plan, and should refer to any difference between the school or other institution's recommendations and those of others.

Summary

To summarise, there really is no golden formula for addressing the special learning needs of every student who experiences difficulties of some sort in schools. There are some general principles (Wearmouth, 2009), however. For example:

- Every student who experiences difficulties in learning is different;
- Every situation is different.

Addressing difficulties is a question of problem-solving:

- Find out about the learner and the expectations of the particular curriculum area.
- Find out about the difficulties he or she experiences.
- Think about the barriers to learning in the classroom environment.
- Reflect on what will best address those barriers to help the learner to achieve in the classroom.

10

Achieving coherence and cost-effectiveness in provision

Introduction

A number of issues related to the use of additional provision to meet a young person's special educational needs and disability have continued to echo down the years. Among these there are issues of equity and also of the (in)effectiveness of the provision that has been made. Whenever there is a question of resourcing or allocating additional, alternative or 'special' resources to particular pupils, inevitably the issue of fairness arises. In a climate of increasing accountability and recourse to litigation, it is vital that those responsible for requesting, or overseeing the allocation of, additional or special resources are very clear in their procedures and practice which must be open to scrutiny. The issue of effectiveness is also a recurring theme throughout much of the recently published guidance on provision for special educational needs and disability in schools. The Ofsted review team (2010) found that, for students identified as having the most severe degree of need during the process of statutory assessment, the statutory provision that was made as a result often did not meet their needs effectively and did not lead to significantly better outcomes for the child or young person. In the *Schools' Guide to the 0 to 25 SEND Code of Practice* (DfE, 2014b: 16), schools are reminded of the requirement to 'take action to remove barriers to learning and put effective special educational provision in place'. Coordinating provision for pupils to meet special educational needs therefore requires a flexibility of approach in incorporating and embedding additional and unfamiliar resources into the curriculum in ways that address identified needs and are demonstrably both effective and cost-effective.

In this chapter the focus is on discussion and examples of ways to achieve coherence and cost-effectiveness in provision across the school or college, such as:

- the management role of SENCOs, and ways to achieve time-efficiency;
- the purpose and function of provision-mapping;
- discussion of a range of approaches to provision mapping: whole school, year group, individual, and so on:

  - examples of good clear coherent provision maps and the process by which they were developed in practice (taken from practising SENDCOs' development work in schools);
  - checklists of effective interventions to audit cost-effectiveness.
- achieving good communication across the school and college in relation to meeting the needs of young people with SEND:
  - examples of effective practice in developing good communication;
  - communication at stages of transition between institutions;
  - examples of good practice.
- CPD for school/college staff:
  - examples in practice: process and evaluation.

Management role of the SENCO

In England, Wales and Northern Ireland, the role of special educational needs co-ordinator (SENCO) was first formalised in a Code of Practice (DfE, 1994) in response to the introduction of legislation related to the identification of children with SEN and a statutory requirement to meet their needs in schools. Since that time, changes in the law have been mirrored by developments in the SENCO role.

Cole (2005) notes how the ethos of the school and the values of individual head teachers have a direct impact on the role, status and, therefore, power of the SENCO to work towards an inclusive culture in the school. Without the support of the senior management team, SENCOs can face a very heavy workload with vulnerable children who are not particularly popular in schools in competition with each other for position on league tables of pupil outcomes.

In many places the role of the SENCO has developed considerably since the publication of the (1994) Code. In relation to the current law, the strategic nature of the role in policy development is clear. The *Code of Practice* (DfE, 2014a: §6.87), for example, states:

> The SENCO has an important role to play with the headteacher and governing body, in determining the strategic development of SEN policy and provision in the school. They will be most effective in that role if they are part of the school leadership team.

There is also clear indication of the managerial function (DfE, 2014a: §6.88):

> The SENCO has day-to-day responsibility for the operation of SEN policy and co-ordination of specific provision made to support individual pupils with SEN, including those who have an EHC plan.

The role may be allocated to members of the school senior management team or class teachers. SENCOs may have responsibilities both at the level of the individual children and the whole school. They may take charge of budgeting, resource allocation, timetabling and other managerial and administrative roles. They may also work with individual students, as well as advising, appraising and training staff, and liaising with outside agencies, professionals and parents.

Reflection 10.1: The management role of a SENCO

You might like to check through the list of key responsibilities of the SENCO as outlined below (DfE, 2014a: §6.90) and ask yourself:

- Which roles do you carry out now?
- Which roles do others carry out?
- Which others do these?
- Are there any gaps?

Key responsibilities of the role may include:

- overseeing day-to-day operation of the school's SEN policy;
- co-ordinating provision for children with SEN;
- liaising with the relevant Designated Teacher where a looked-after pupil has SEN;
- advising on the graduated approach to providing SEN support;
- advising on the deployment of the school's delegated budget and other resources to meet pupils' needs effectively;
- liaising with parents of pupils with SEN;
- liaising with early years providers, other schools, educational psychologists, health and social care professionals, and independent or voluntary bodies;
- being a key point of contact with external agencies, especially the local authority and its support services;
- liaising with potential next providers of education to ensure a pupil and their parents are informed about options and a smooth transition is planned;
- working with the head teacher and school governors to ensure that the school meets its responsibilities under the Equality Act (2010) with regard to reasonable adjustments and access arrangements;
- ensuring that the school keeps the records of all pupils with SEN up to date.

One of the issues for many SENCOs is how to cope with the time demands of the role and, in particular, of the bureaucratic demands of assessment and planning for individual young people, evaluation of progress and the requirement for record-keeping that accompanies this. These days some SENCOs have dispensed with individual plans for some children and use group plans instead. Some may rely on 'provision maps' which can be either documents that identify provision for individual children, or whole-school provision with analyses of student outcomes and value for money, or both.

In order to ensure that the SENCO is in a position to carry out this role, schools and colleges are advised:

> [to] ensure that the SENCO has sufficient time and resources to carry out these functions. This should include providing the SENCO with sufficient administrative support and time away from teaching to enable them to fulfil their responsibilities in a similar way to other important strategic roles within a school.
>
> (DfE, 2014a: §6.90)

Table 10.1 is an example of a year planner developed by one SENCO in the course of her work to ensure that she set aside time to complete all her duties.

Provision mapping

In recent years, drawing up a map of the special educational or additional provision in a school or college, what is called 'provision-mapping', has assumed increasing popularity and significance as a strategic management tool that allows SENCOs and school leadership teams to analyse outcomes for interventions and show how they are raising attainment and providing value for money. Provision maps can enable an institution

> [to] take into account the full scope of provision, including high quality whole class teaching, guided and group work and individual interventions in order to identify and overcome potential barriers to learning and meet the needs of all pupils within and beyond the school setting.
>
> (DfE, 2012)

A transparent approach to provision mapping can also ensure equitable use of resources. All children are eligible for help when they need it.

> Provision maps are a powerful way of showing all the provision that the school makes which is additional to and different from that which is offered through the school's differentiated curriculum...The use of provision maps helps SENCOs to maintain an overview of the collective programmes of individual children and young people and provides a basis for monitoring the levels of intervention and assessing their impact on progress.
>
> (DfE, 2014a: 105)

Teachers can start to organise support and intervention more creatively. Help can be provided for high fliers as well as struggling children. This is to the benefit of all pupils as teachers may stop seeing their classes as two distinct groups of those with special needs and 'the rest'. Instead they will look at their classes and identify which children need help in accessing the curriculum for some or all subjects, who is not progressing and who is capable of even more. Thus, the teaching and learning of all children can be improved.

Massey's (2014) focus on provision mapping as evaluative as well as a way of maintaining records can be seen as a particularly useful system. The year-long process with reviews ideally six times a year means that provision maps are working documents with the potential to lead to improvements in the areas of accountability, teaching and learning, evaluation of assessment and identification of need, target setting, self-evaluation, resourcing, staff training and school self-evaluation.

Table 10.1 School SEND tasks for 2014/2015

Day-to-day operations		*Management*	*Monitoring and evaluation of provision*	*Comment*
Key priorities for year		Individual plans, provision and support Provision mapping	Effectiveness of in-class differentiation and interventions	
		• Draft Code INSET- Sharing with staff assess⟶plan⟶do⟶review cycle / ongoing monitoring sheet • Develop guidelines on entrance and exit criteria for support [in line with LA criteria]		
Autumn term	• Teachers Day - Staff Meeting: - Timetables for support go over with staff + TAs - Go over SEN Procedures - Discuss individual review dates for Year - Discuss individual plan date- when they must be in to SENCO - Discuss SEN record • Planning meeting with EPS • Year 6 Annual Review	• Devise tracking sheet to track progress of pupils on intervention programmes • STS advise on other resources/ support approaches • Training for TAs + Literacy teachers on supporting pupils with literacy difficulties	• Audit of SEN materials/ programmes being used in classroom – evaluate effectiveness of support	

Spring term	• Completion of records – for LA/Given updated SEN • Record to office/Check information entered correctly • Monitoring new individual plans • Deadline for individual plans sent out to parents and relevant staff • Targets discussed with pupils and written in planners	• Advise about Provision Mapping – Learning Support Advisory Teacher	• Lesson observations as prioritised in School Development Plan • Monitoring of Teachers' planning and effective use of Teaching Assistants in the classroom. • Review of individual plan monitoring sheets
Summer term	• Alternative QCAs – support needed/ marking of papers SEN group did • Transfer meetings for Year 8 pupils to Upper School • Transfer of SEN Files to High Schools	• Complete tracking sheet • Complete audit of pupil needs • Drawing up provision map for 2014/2015 • TA Timetables- Discuss with TAs/days to work [with Bursar TA hours] • Support provision at Wave 2 and 3 discuss at SMT	• Analysis of pupils' progress data- Information using baseline, SEN assessments + Teacher assessments in line with IEP reviews. • Analyse of progress made by pupils on specific intervention programmes

Reflection 10.2: Prerequisites for developing provision maps

Provision mapping cannot be carried out effectively unless particular features are in place in a school, however. The Department for Education (2013a) has identified some essential prerequisites. You might like to read through the text below and reflect on the extent to which these features are evident in your school/college:

The first relates to the school or college system for assessment and tracking of student progress. Without an effective system which is updated on a regular basis with assessment data that is reliable and valid, the information that is uploaded on to the provision map may threaten the trustworthiness and, hence, the usefulness of the whole provision map.

- Schools with effective provision mapping have rigorous on-going assessment and pupil tracking throughout the Key Stages.
- A range of performance and engagement data (e.g. attendance and behaviour, feedback from pupil voice) is used to assess and track the progress of individuals/groups through, for example, termly pupil progress meetings.
- Teacher assessment is regular, robust and consistent.
- Progress data is shared with and understood by staff, pupils, parents/carers and governors.

The second relates to monitoring and evaluation of impact and analysis of data. Monitoring the effectiveness of interventions, for example, is essential. In relation to analysis of available data the DfE recommends that underachievement is less likely among students if:

- Staff use both historical and current data analysis to identify current and future needs. By predicting future cohort needs and planning provision the school is proactive in preventing underachievement.
- A range of performance and engagement data is collected and analysed to inform the school about the current and historic performance of vulnerable groups.
- Analysis identifies the pupils who are at risk of underachieving/under-attaining and those who are making good progress.
- Data is analysed by all staff, including senior leadership team, subject leaders, year group leaders, classroom teachers and support staff and shared with governors.
- Schools identify what is working well and what adaptations need to be made to whole class teaching, curriculum, schemes of work, pupil groupings and interventions.

Schools and, now, colleges are expected to get to know about what the DfE (2014a) calls the 'vulnerabilities' of the young people in their care. Institutions are likely to be more effective in their provision mapping and overall provision for SEND if:

- there is a shared agreement among all staff about what counts as vulnerable in their school's context. Staff are aware that all pupils are likely to experience risk of underachievement. By identifying and removing potential barriers to learning for vulnerable pupils, staff can help prevent underachievement and ensure success;

- [all staff recognise] current patterns of vulnerability, how these have changed in recent years and likely changes in the future, have all been identified including within and across phases.
- the potential vulnerabilities of all pupils are identified and reviewed by staff at senior leadership, department, year group and class level;
- all staff are aware of the potential barriers to learning posed by different vulnerabilities and address these in whole class teaching, guided work and group/individual intervention.

Evaluating the effectiveness of interventions

Schools that regularly review the impact of provision in relation to their impact on student learning and progress, including whole class teaching, are more able to target the most effective provision at individual pupils. Table 10.2 contains a suggested intervention monitoring tool to assist in this process. The suggested pro-forma (Table 10.3) enables tracking of progress across three skill areas. This template can be adapted as required.

Table 10.4 comprises a further checklist that you might wish to consider to ensure the effectiveness of interventions.

Types of provision maps

Provision maps can be drawn up in a variety of ways, depending on the suitability and appropriateness to the individual school or college. They can map special and

Table 10.2 Intervention monitoring for <name of intervention>

Need addressed
Criteria for inclusion in intervention
Target by end of intervention
Length of intervention in weeks
Hours per week
Number of pupils in group
Cost of intervention per pupil in hours and £s
Total cost of intervention in hours and £s

Table 10.3 Impact of intervention on pupil progress

Name	Baseline Assessment Date:			Interim Assessment Date:			End Results Date:			Details of progress/ Outcome [+/−/=]		
	Skill area 1	Skill area 2	Skill area 3	Skill area 1	Skill area 2	Skill area 3	Skill area 1	Skill area 2	Skill area 3	Skill area 1	Skill area 2	Skill area 3

Evaluation of Impact: [Name of intervention]	
Greatest individual student learning/behaviour gain over time	
Further needs	
Lowest individual student learning/behaviour gain over time	
Further needs	
Average/mean student progress across time	
Evaluation of overall effectiveness of intervention	Comments

additional provision made for an individual student, or for students in an individual class or subject area, or for the students in a year group or, very commonly, for the whole school or college. Provision maps contain details of the range of additional provision, staffing and support and consider the following:

- whole-school inclusion, special educational needs or additional needs;
- the SEND Code of Practice's (DfE, 2014a) graduated response strands of action: school action, school action plus and statement;
- the four areas of need identified in the Code;
- the three 'waves' of support as identified in the National Strategies currently:
    - inclusive Quality-First teaching for all;
    - additional interventions to enable children to work at age-related expectations or above;
    - additional highly personalised interventions.
- costs, either termly or annually.

Table 10.4 Checklist for a quality intervention

Management in school	
Is care taken that the intervention is not used as a substitute for properly differentiated Quality First Teaching?	
Do the effective features of the intervention feed back into QFT, so that QFT continually improves?	
Are the appropriate children identified through data, targeted and their progress carefully tracked?	
Are there clear entry and exit criteria for the intervention?	
Is regular review of children's progress incorporated as an intrinsic part of the programme?	
Are children involved, so that they understand the purpose and intended outcomes of the intervention?	
Are parents/carers involved, both in the decision that their child will take part and in knowing how they can support at home what the child is learning through the intervention?	
Is the intervention time limited?	
Has there been good training for the person delivering the intervention?	
Is there on-going support and training for the person delivering the intervention?	
Is the quality of the teaching monitored regularly?	
Has there been good training for the class teacher involved?	
Is there joint planning between the class teacher and the person delivering the intervention? Does the class teacher know what the child is learning and how to support this in everyday teaching?	
Do the class teacher and person delivering the intervention have time to meet to review children's progress?	
Is the impact of the intervention on the group of children who have received it evaluated systematically using measures of progress – both short-term (at the end of the intervention), and long-term by monitoring outcomes in National Curriculum tests, optional tests, etc.?	
Is the use of the intervention reassessed regularly in the light of this evaluation, to identify whether it should continue to be run?	
Is the use of the intervention reassessed regularly in the light of data on the profile of need in the school?	
Teaching	
Does the intervention programme include strategies to enable children to identify their own learning targets and to assess their own progress?	
Does it help them become independent learners?	

(Adapted from DfES, 2006 03817-2006PCK)

As noted above, robust and consistent assessment and tracking underpin this whole process.

Individual provision maps

At the level of the individual student, provision maps may well be used in place of individual education or learning plans. An individual provision map (IPM) for a student should include the following information:

- name of student;
- background information on the student;
- student's current class, or teaching groups in secondary schools;
- entry data relating to areas of difficulty for which special provision is being made;
- interventions accessed;
- review for each half term, including outcome comments (whether the student needs continued intervention/different intervention/no intervention);
- exit data relating to the same areas as above;
- progress made within the half term.

We included an example of an IPM negotiated for a young man who experienced autistic-type difficulties in Chapter 8.

Mapping by area of need

Provision maps may also be organised by area of need. This has the advantage that it indicates where there are strengths in provision, and where there may be gaps. Table 10.5 is an example of such a whole-school map.

Developing provision mapping in a middle school: two worked examples

Example 1

'Susan' (not her real name) decided to create class provision maps as well as a whole school provision map with the following aims:

- The class provision maps become working documents that are updated each half term and track pupil progress to ensure quality and effectiveness of provision that supports learning and progress.
- The class provision maps show provision is being regularly reassessed for effectiveness and prompts teachers to evaluate the effectiveness of strategies and whether children's needs have changed.
- The SENCO has a clear understanding of the interventions being used and the effects they are having.
- Where teachers do not have the skill or resources to support a child's needs, training and support will be provided quickly to enable the child to move on in their learning.

Table 10.5 Provision map by area of need

Area of need	*All pupils, where appropriate*	*Plus for some pupils – Catch up*	*Plus for a few pupils*
Cognition and Learning	• Differentiated curriculum planning, activities, delivery and outcome • Increased visual aids/ modelling, etc. • Visual timetables • Illustrated dictionaries • Use of writing frames • Access to ICT • Progress Files	• Catch-up programmes – literacy and numeracy, e.g. Springboard 7, FLS Further Literacy Support • In-class support from TA • Multi-sensory spelling practice groups • Reading Groups – Units of Sounds • Reduced/increasingly individualised timetable at KS4	• Intense literacy/numeracy support • Exam concessions • Alternative accreditation/vocational courses, e.g. Certificate of Achievement • Advice from EP/STS • Access to Connexions LDD PA • Highly differentiated work
Communication and Interaction	• Differentiated curriculum planning, activities, delivery and outcome, e.g. simplified language, Key words • Increased visual aids/ modelling, etc. • Visual timetables • Use of symbols • Structured school and class routines	• In-class support with focus on supporting speech and language • ICT – Clicker 4, N* (phonics) Fingers • Communication skills	• Speech and Language Therapist • Nurture Group 'The Zone' • Advice/Input from Autism Outreach • Visual organiser – Viewtech • ICT – Writing with Symbols, enlarged letters on keyboards • Hearing Impairment Team

(continued)

Table 10.5 Provision map by area of need *(continued)*

Area of need	*All pupils, where appropriate*	*Plus for some pupils – Catch up*	*Plus for a few pupils*
Social, emotional and mental health	• Whole school behaviour policy • Whole school/class rules • Whole school/class rewards and sanctions systems • Circle Time	• Small group Circle Time • Social Skills group training • Anger management • KS4 – Work-related learning • In-class support for behaviour targets, access, safety • Involvement of EWO, Access to Connexions LDD PA	• Individual counselling and support – Well - Being Coordinator • Individual reward system • Re-integration programme • Advice from EP • Home-school record • Peer mentoring (as appropriate) • Emotional literacy programme • Music therapy • PAT dog
Sensory and Physical	• Flexible teaching arrangements • Staff aware of implications of physical impairment • Writing slopes • Pencil grips • Medical support/advice	• Brain gym exercises • Keyboard skills training • Additional fine motor skills practice • In-class support for access, safety	• Individual support in class during appropriate subjects, e.g. Science, lunchtime • Physiotherapy programme • Occupational therapy • Exam concessions • Environmental adaptations to playground • Advice Input from STS • Use of appropriate resources, e.g. Access to Connexions LDD PA

- When concerns are raised about children during pupil progress meetings (PPMs), assessments and observations will be put into place quickly to plan support for children. The PPM is important because it forces accountability and identifies errors or missing information and detail. Teachers have to be prepared in advance for them. As Massey (2014) comments, it is important to give time within the school day and staff meetings to evaluate and write provision maps to give status to the process.
- The school has a provision mapping system, including class and whole school provision maps, that is dynamic and enables on-going evaluation and revision of provision for children with special needs.

Susan achieved her aims in leading the development, first, of class provision maps and, subsequently, of a whole school by taking the following steps. She first introduced provision mapping to the senior leadership team. Susan explained that:

- It should lead to better progress and engagement for every child within the school, raising standards throughout.
- The staff would develop a better understanding of inclusion and it would therefore improve provision for all of the children.
- Teachers will make the most appropriate provision to meet the needs of the pupils.
- This would lead to more effective self-evaluation and planning for future development.

She explained her concern that provision mapping, although useful for planning provision and supporting learning, should turn not into a desperate 'fudging' game if the primary concern became meeting targets rather than passing on accurate data to inform teaching and learning. She said the school should do the following:

- lead staff training on the purpose, usefulness and approaches to class provision mapping;
- provide staff with an exemplar provision map;
- set aside staff meeting time for year groups to produce class provision maps and be available to give support;
- introduce intervention evaluation sheets. There is always the question, of course, of who should carry out such an evaluation. Susan felt that training for a teaching assistant to carry out a particular intervention should include completing a template such as Table 10.6, at the end of the intervention period. It is, of course, important for records to be kept of group interventions carried out in any year groups. Table 10.7 is a copy of the intervention group record log she developed, to be maintained by all those, mostly teaching assistants, who carried out the interventions.
- Share the class provision map with governors and give them the opportunity to offer suggestions and ask for clarification.
- Collate information from class provision maps onto a whole school provision map and cost the intervention.

Table 10.6 TAs' record sheet for evaluating student progress in interventions

Name of TA:

Focus of intervention:

Time in hours per week:

Length of intervention in weeks:

Name of student	Gender	Baseline measurement	Target measurement	Actual measurement	Details of progress

Comments and/or personal observations

Table 10.7 Intervention Group Record Log

Group: ____________________

Date and time	Children	Activities completed and comments

- Arrange staff meeting time to input data and prepare for PPMs where groups of teachers would discuss the progress, barriers to learning and achievement, and approaches to overcoming these barriers. Given the responsibility of class teachers for all the young people in their classrooms, it seems to be the most obvious course of action that the member of staff who enters the information on the class provision map should be the class teacher. As Massey (2014: 16) comments:

A fundamentally important feature of this system is that class teachers should analyse attainment data in order to track the progress of the children in their class. For teachers to be fully focused on the progress made by the pupils in their class or group across a year they will need to be fully aware of how much progress is being made, and by whom, at each assessment point in the year. The attainment data need to be analysed by those who have taught the children.

- Carry out the first PPMs at the beginning of the summer term.
- Review provision maps and work with the next teacher to prepare transition provision maps for September.
- Carry out the second PPMs before the end of the summer term.
- Review the process with staff. Address any confusions, alter the provision map tables in response to suggestions.

The resultant class provision maps contained the following information:

- type of intervention;
- size and ratio of the group;
- staff involved;
- names of the pupils accessing the intervention;
- entry data by pupil;
- intervention target;
- exit data by pupil;
- outcome by pupil, including evaluation of the need for continued intervention, or not
- Mean/average progress.

Appendix B3 is an example of an annotated class provision map that was produced.

From the collation of the class maps, Susan produced a whole school provision map that included the following information:

- year group and class name;
- provision/resource (this refers to the type of intervention);
- staff/pupil ratio;
- staff involved;
- time costs;
- costs in £;
- Value for money.

Example 2

'Jane', not her real name, a new SENCO in a middle school, was tasked with developing a whole-school provision map from scratch following a period of instability during which three SENCOs had left in succession over the preceding two-year period. Following an audit of SEND provision, she highlighted, as her main concerns, that

- there was no system for recording, reviewing and evaluating provisions;
- pupils, once selected for interventions, remained in them all year, without targets being set or progress being evaluated;
- there were many gaps/failures in the interventions provided caused by the divisions of 'SEN' responsibilities within different school departments;
- there were no clear processes in place for the identification of pupils with special educational needs apart from initial screening;
- there was little CPD to inform differentiation in classrooms or the practice and deployment of LSAs;
- many aspects of provision, especially the recording and reviewing processes, did not comply with the requirements outlined in the SEND Code of Practice (DfE, 2014a).

Given the concerns highlighted, she felt that introducing provision mapping to the school would be a useful first step because it would:

- provide an effective tool for recording who was taking part in interventions, which could then be shared with teachers/home;
- provide a means of evaluating the effectiveness of support put in place for pupils, including the success of new interventions that needed to be introduced, helping to ensure interventions that worked where accessible to the children that needed them;
- help ensure the better identification of pupils with special educational needs, through regular meetings and discussion, and its inclusive approach which enables *all* pupils to be helped and supported in their areas of weakness (Massey, 2014);
- re-engage teachers and LSAs in seeking best-practice for SEN pupils by making it very clear what support is available and how they could help pupils with SEN;
- provide evidence for the need for the SENCO to have more say in how the SEN budget is allocated and spent, by enabling the review of departmental costs against gains for the child.

To keep the task manageable, in the first instance she decided to focus on only one area of need within the department. Cognition and learning needs were chosen as the focus because interventions here would have the largest impact, given that the majority of the children on the SEN list were identified as having problems with weak literacy and numeracy and this was also highlighted on the Department Improvement Plan. Having a provision-mapping system for each year rather than by need was selected in consultation with the senior leadership team (SLT) and the SEN Governor. Quality First Teaching (QfT) methods were to be provided on them and relevant differentiation strategies to be signposted, so that busy teachers could use them when planning learning activities. The format of the Year Provision Maps would also provide all the necessary information to act as an effective recording and tracking tool for the interventions: intervention type, names of pupils, group size, frequency/duration and staffing, entry and exit data, intervention target and outcomes. LSAs would be asked to contribute vital information to the outcomes/comments sections through Intervention Evaluation Sheets.

In addition to the Year Provision Maps, the consultation group felt it would be useful to have a whole-school provision map in order to evaluate the success of the interventions offered by collating all the exit data from the Year Provision Maps into a mean gain over the period of the intervention and calculating cost-effectiveness.

She followed a clearly structured process in developing the plans:

- Whole staff training was delivered on provision mapping ensuring that all parties were clear on
  - the provision-mapping process;
  - the new interventions;
  - how they could access support for any/all of their pupils;
  - how the provision maps were going to be used at future review evenings;
  - the selection of suitable candidates among the students for the pilot interventions.
- Pupil progress meetings were organised to discuss data related to students' progress in cognition and learning.
- The provision maps were populated with the same data used in the pupil progress meetings, in order to provide the 'entry' levels and then these unevaluated provision maps were sent to staff so they knew what interventions the pupils were taking part in.
- The provision maps were evaluated after 7 weeks:
  - The LSAs input a summary of their observations so that the interventions could be evaluated in context.
  - Comments were entered on the provision map (by the SENCO) to aid planning for the next steps of each child, and to help form tutors at Pupil Progress Review Evening.
  - Results were circulated to all staff.
  - A final 30-minute staff meeting was held to review the provision-mapping process.

On each Year Provision Map Jane collated a list of differentiation (Quality First Teaching) strategies by area of need also (see Appendix B4). From the year group maps Jane collated an evaluated whole-school provision map for cognition and learning needs (see Appendix B5). She also evaluated factors influencing the effectiveness of individual interventions (see Appendix B6).

Development of action plan

Given the findings of this project and the needs analysis, an action plan (Table 10.8) was developed to update the next DIP, to ensure improvements were supportive of this provision mapping system.

Evaluating developments in SEND provision and practice

When evaluating the success or value of any initiatives in the area of SEND provision, it is really important to be very objective and aware of pitfalls as well as positives. In

Table 10.8 Departmental improvement plan

Goals/Issues to be dealt with:	*Action Needed by SENCO:*
Short term	
• Improve identification of needs through more thorough assessments before the next provision map starts	• Buy in standardised, diagnostic assessments for reading comprehension, maths skills and reading accuracy.
• Ensure vulnerable groups are highlighted on the provision map e.g. SEN. LSA to help with task of pupil tracking.	• Ask the data manager to tag this information onto data used at PPMs so it is apparent when drawing up the next provision map.
• Improve the accuracy of the SEN list so SEN children can be given the time and attention they need from the SENCO, whilst placing responsibility for underachievement back on the class teacher.	• Use LA Guidance documents to check SEN attainment at The Academy is in line with SEN attributes.
• Continue to improve the department using the provision-mapping system.	• Implement provision mapping in full from September 2014. Get PPMs and PPREs booked into the school diary.
Medium term	
• Make sure all stakeholders are aware of the new system of provision mapping	• Re-write the SEN Policy to include these changes and explain the process by which pupils can access help.
• Continue to tackle gaps in provision for cognition and learning using provision maps to evaluate their effectiveness.	• Source interventions/assessments for maths and writing improvements. For maths, training of teachers with LSAs may be a good idea to help QFT and enable interventions to take place within normal lessons. LSAs will have to be trained in these interventions.
• Improve staff and LSA awareness of SEN issues.	• CPD on active listening for communication and language needs/specific learning difficulties and Autism for teachers.
• Establish IEP equivalents (Pupil Progress Records - PPREs) using information from provision maps to reengage parents and ensure review evenings conform to statutory guidance going forward.	• This process has started but needs to 'build up' over forthcoming review evenings. 3 pupil progress review evenings have been timetabled for next year. SIMS has been set up to allow data entry of review evenings that can then be used to populate the PPRs going forward but poor parent turn out to reviews is a problem; speak to SLT to come up with strategy to change this. Maybe review evenings could be integrated into Parent's Evenings?

(continued)

Table 10.8 Departmental action plan *(continued)*

Goals/Issues to be dealt with:	*Action Needed by SENCO:*
Long term	
• Tackle the problems caused by school division of SEN responsibilities and establish effective provisions in all areas of SEN.	• Meet with SLT, the Hub Leader and the Learning Mentors to discuss the use of provision mapping across these departments. • Restructure Learning Support to enable specialisms of LSAs e.g. literacy/numeracy specialists to aid QFT and carry out these interventions, autism specialist (working from Learning Support rather than the Hub).
• Tackle the problems caused by the poor funding of the SEN department so that resourcing can improve.	• Use evidence gathered from provision maps to 'claim back' funds from PP, looked after children (LAC) and the Hub, to show that the SEN department divisions are resulting in the under-resourcing of the SEN department who provides the majority of interventions. Too use this evidence to get more control of the SEN budget and use this to respond to changing school needs.

evaluating the introduction of the provision-mapping system, 'Jane' noted that there is a potential danger posed by 'inclusive' provision maps where teachers merely put forward their concerns about pupils to their head of department and do not discuss QFT, as happened here; class teachers must not get used to using interventions to prop up poor classroom teaching. For example, 78 pupils were put forward to improve their spelling ability because their spelling age was more than 2 years behind their standard age score. Many more children were below their expected age score across the school, although not to this degree. On reflection, this suggests a school-wide problem with the way spelling was being *taught* and the most cost-effective solution in the long term would be to implement strategies through curriculum support of the English department, rather than to cause unnecessary disruption to lessons by pulling children out for separate interventions. This would need to be dealt with through CPD.

She also noted a number of other limitations in her work:

> However, there are some limitations that must be taken into account before assuming these findings are completely accurate. Inaccuracies were introduced into the provision maps by basing measures of effectiveness on extremely small sample sizes in some cases, using inaccurate assessments for the entry and exit criteria and an actual lack of attendance by pupils/LSAs to their interventions which have skewed the results, especially where N* (phonics) is concerned.

Cost-effectiveness can be calculated by dividing the cost per pupil of the intervention by the average gain experienced by that pupil *because* of the intervention. However, it is worth mentioning that there are ideological problems with the concept of cost-effectiveness (and effectiveness) as applied to SEND provision in that cost-effectiveness requires improvement to be made. For the purpose of this assignment, this improvement has been set at a ratio gain of 2 in line with Brooks' (2007: 32) expectations that 'good impact – sufficient to at least double the standard rate of progress – can be achieved and it is reasonable to expect it'. However, it is important to bear in mind that progress and improvement can be viewed in different ways and the SEND Code of Practice (DFS, 2014a: §6.17) itself defines inadequate progress as that which:

- is significantly slower than that of their peers starting from the same baseline;
- fails to match or better the child's previous rate of progress;
- fails to close the attainment gap between the child and their peers;
- widens the attainment gap.

In terms of cost-effectiveness, it seems that P (maths programme) and N* (phonics) (×3 weekly) are clearly not good value for money. However, these poor results have to be put in the context of the limitations of how their effectiveness has been measured in this project. For example, P (maths programme), used National Curriculum levels to measure progress as this was the only assessment accessible at the time; however, progress with the P (maths programme) should have been measured with the results of mental maths tests, or a standardised test score from a bought-in assessment, as NC levels do not reflect the improvement in basic maths skill and confidence observed in the pupils. Likewise, N* (phonics) data has been greatly skewed by a lack of attendance (either by pupils of LSAs who are taken to cover lessons) as well as the inaccuracies introduced by using old scores of spelling age as a baseline. Therefore, both of these interventions should be re-tested and re-evaluated on improved provision maps that correct the limitations, rather than be dismissed at this stage because these results are inconclusive.

The most cost-effective interventions, which also produced ratio gains of more than 2, are paired reading (for increasing reading age) and intensive N* (phonics) (×4 weekly) (for improving spelling age), although again the limitations should be taken into consideration. The success of N* (phonics) (×4 weekly) undoubtedly had to do with having an effective LSA leading the group, a good cohort who attends, and the concept of economies of scale; if LSAs can work effectively with small groups (as opposed to a one-to-one basis), costs are better spread, and this gives weight to the argument going forward that more effective, small-group interventions need to be introduced to provide for needs.

Overall, while measuring cost-effectiveness is certainly a useful tool to have when SEN budgets are under pressure, it is important to remember that the implications of this for pupils will have to be considered on an individual basis. Sometimes, it will be completely justifiable to choose the most effective intervention for a pupil with a SEN (e.g. T (literacy programme) for reading age) rather than the most cost-effective solution (e.g. paired reading with an LSA) and the right to choose on the basis of individual circumstances must be maintained, with the findings being used to guide decision-making along with the uniqueness of an individual pupils needs.

Finally, any discussion of progress for individual SEN students should bear in mind that they may make progress at a different rate than non-SEN pupils and therefore the guidance used to measure the effectiveness of the provision map (e.g. a ratio gain of 2) must be looked at more flexibly for SEN students once an intervention has been established as effective.

The school budget for special educational needs

The issue of the school budget in the realm of special educational needs can be particularly contentious. As in other areas, the school governing body has the ultimate responsibility for oversight of these funds. Managing resources for pupils requires a clear understanding of a number of issues. Among these are accountability to pupils, parents, the school and the local authority; the principle of equal opportunities; the nature, availability and function of resources; human, physical and financial; ways of embedding the use of unfamiliar technology into the curriculum; and strategies for resource allocation. How a balance is achieved between finite resources, people, space, time and money, and the individual needs of pupils who are experiencing difficulties in learning will vary from school to school. It is very likely, however, that the SENCO will play a key management role.

Schools have an amount identified within their overall budget, called the notional SEN budget. This is not a ring-fenced amount, and it is for the school to provide high-quality appropriate support from the whole of its budget. The SENCO, headteacher and governors should establish a clear picture of the resources available to the school and consider their strategic approach to meeting SEN in the context of the total resources available, including any resources targeted at particular groups, such as the pupil premium.

Schools are expected to provide additional support from their core funding up to the nationally prescribed threshold per student per year not more expensive support. Above this, the LA, usually where the student lives, may provide additional top-up funding. For example, the LA must conduct an assessment of education, health and care needs and prepare an EHC plan where the special educational provision required to meet needs cannot reasonably be provided from within the resources normally available to mainstream schools. The LA is responsible for ensuring that the required resources to support the EHC plan are available.

Pupil premium

The pupil premium is additional funding paid to schools and LAs to raise the attainment of 'disadvantaged' pupils in publicly funded schools and close the gap between them and their peers. 'Disadvantaged' is defined as those with free school meals and those who are or have recently been, looked-after. There is also a grant for supporting children and young people with parents in the regular armed forces (DfE, 2015e). The grant may be spent in the following ways:

- for the purposes of the school, i.e. for the educational benefit of pupils registered at that school;

- on community facilities, e.g. services whose provision furthers any charitable purpose for the benefit of pupils at the school or their families, or people who live or work in the locality in which the school is situated.

OFSTED inspectors are required to investigate the use of this resource during their inspections (Ofsted, 2015):

> §158 When evaluating the effectiveness of leaders, managers and governors, inspectors should gather evidence about the use of the pupil premium in relation to the following key issues:

- the level of pupil premium funding received by the school in the current academic year and levels of funding received in previous academic years;
- how the school has spent the pupil premium and why it has decided to spend it in the way it has;
- any differences made to the learning and progress of disadvantaged pupils as shown by performance data and inspection evidence.

In relation to the governance of a school (§165), inspectors are required to consider whether governors:

- use the pupil premium and other resources to overcome barriers to learning, including reading, writing and mathematics.

An example of the use of pupil premium in a school is:

- Employ Teaching Assistants to give intensive support to these identified children in Maths, Writing and Reading.
- Monitor provision of extra 'after school' booster lessons in numeracy, literacy and hand writing.
- Provide support for year group educational trips and school residentials.
- Hold Science and Literacy workshops.
- Build an ECO Pastoral Care Room in the grounds of the School. School are busy fund-raising for this and it is envisaged this will be completed by 2013/14.
- Implement a new reading and writing scheme for KS1 and KS2 called Read, Write Inc. (Cost £6,500).
- Pastoral care for children who need support in their personal development and well-being.

(http://www.st-andrews23.lancsngfl.ac.uk/index.php?category_id=-1, accessed 28 May 2015)

Auditing special educational provision

Before completing this chapter you might choose to carry out an audit of resources to support learning needs, both human and material, in your own institution.

Reflection 10.3: Audit of special provision

You might like to discuss the following with your line manager, SMT and members of your department:

- What is the school's budget for special educational needs?
- What is the process by which the budget for special educational needs is decided?
- How transparent is this process?
- How are decisions made about the allocation of resources to support pupils' learning needs from what is generally available in school?
- Which (if any) of the following criteria exist for allocating resources:
  - identified pupil learning need
  - the level of need in teaching groups
  - the needs of curriculum areas
  - values and principles expressed in the school's SEN policy
  - any other?

On what basis is support divided between the following?:

- individual pupils
- in-class support
- pupil withdrawal
- curriculum support.

Areas of strength:

____

Areas of weakness:

____

Summary

To summarise this chapter, we would like to ask you to reflect on the coherence of your own record-keeping in SEND provision in your school or college in light of what has been discussed above.

Reflection 10.4: Evaluating the quality of a whole-school provision map

Reflecting on how she would know if her school map was effective, Louise, another Primary SENCO, commented that she would measure success of her school provision map by evaluating the following points (Bell, unpublished). How would you rate your own record-keeping system against these points?:

- Does it document all interventions and support that are in place at [name of school]?
- Are there clear entry and exit points for interventions?
- Can the progress made by pupils be seen clearly and evaluated easily?
- Is staffing of interventions clear?
- Is the document available to all staff and being used to communicate information effectively?
- Are staff using the provision map to help guide them with their planning for specific pupils or groups of pupils?
- From analysing progress data, does it clearly show value for money?
- Does it provide valid evidence of use of resources when in discussions with governors, external agencies, families and the local authority?
- Does it ensure that targets set for pupils are inspirational enough?
- Does it audit how well provision matches need, and recognise gaps in provision?
- Is it a useful document for transferring information at times of school transition?
- Does it provide useful evidence when writing the SEND information report and Local Offer?
- You might choose to evaluate your own provision map using this framework.

11

Policy-making in SEND provision in schools and colleges

Introduction

This chapter focuses on the process and practice of policy-making in the context of statutory requirements in the area of SEND provision. The approach taken will be that policy development in institutions can usefully be seen as an opportunity both to review the effectiveness of current provision overall and also for CPD for staff. The chapter will discuss:

- the principles of policy-making at the whole-school level;
- the requirements of SEND policies;
    - examples of clearly written SEND policy documents underpinned by reference to requirements and supporting research evidence
- preparation for inspection of SEND provision in schools and colleges:
    - examples of what schools or colleges might do to prepare themselves for inspection of their SEND provision
    - audit tools for school or college self-evaluation.

National policy development

Broadly, in England, there is one general route taken by the government to create and develop national policies related to SEND that, in turn, are put into operation through policy and practice in schools and colleges. First, a Green Paper of government intentions is issued for consultation. A White Paper usually follows which can become the basis for legislation in the form of an Act of Parliament. The legislation passed by Parliament can also empower the particular Secretary of State to decide on the details in the form of 'Regulations'. Any Regulations made by a Secretary of State become legislation as part of the Act of Parliament. The actual meaning of the law is ultimately interpreted by the courts if and when features of the legislation are challenged in the courts. However, the Secretary of State through his or her department can then also issue guidance on what he or she believes the legislation might mean for practice. For example, the *Special Educational Needs and Disability Code of Practice: 0 to 25 Years* (DfE, 2014a) is a document with the status of 'statutory guidance' that quotes from the law, that is Acts of Parliament or any associated Regulations made by the Secretary of State, to support the advice it gives. Such a document is intended to be used as a framework against which policy and practice in schools can be evaluated.

In the area of SEND, schools or colleges are expected to develop a number of policy documents in order to ensure that, as far as possible, what is intended in law is reflected in practice. Below we discuss a number of these documents:

- SEND policy and the SEN Information Report;
- policy related to child protection – what is called safeguarding;
- policy related to children and young people with medical conditions;
- accessibility plans;
- behaviour (and discipline) policy, including issues of bullying;
- policy related to literacy difficulties.

Schools' or colleges' SEND policies

According to the SEND Code of Practice (DFEa, 2014a), schools must publish a report called a Special Educational Needs Information Report, or local offer, showing how they implement the school policy. The implication of this is that schools should therefore publish both a SEN Information Report and also a special educational needs and disability policy.

There is an important difference between a 'report' and a 'policy'. Technically, a report is a written account of something that is completed. 'The governing bodies of maintained schools & proprietors of academies must publish information [a SEN Information Report] on their websites about the implementation of the governing body's or the proprietor's policy for pupils with SEN' (DfE, 2014a: §6.79).

A policy, on the other hand, broadly speaking, is a set of principles and expected actions adopted by an institution in relation to a particular area. School policy frameworks need to be cast within an understanding of external requirements, such as the law related to special educational needs and the disability equality legislation referred to above. They should also flow from a coherent set of beliefs and values which are shared across an organisation (Palmer et al., 1994). Policy should therefore be based on a shared understanding of:

- why the school exists: its mission;
- what it believes to be right: its values;
- what it is trying to achieve: its vision;
- what it is going to do to put this into operation: its objectives;
- over-riding principles for action;
- practicalities of implementation: its procedures.

In a school's SEND policy, therefore, the objectives and procedures of the policy for SEND provision should be cast within an understanding of the school's own mission and values. The National Association for Special Educational Needs (NASEN) has issued a very useful *NASEN Help Sheet: Updating SEN Policy for Schools* that advises that a school should reflect its individuality in its statement of policy by including the actual staffing, approaches and practices. Advice on policy development makes it clear that families and young people, as well as school staff, should be involved. There appears to be a general sense that, as Radford (2000: 88) suggests, such development should take place

- within 'an environment in which there are non-judgmental opportunities to reflect on one's beliefs, values, attitudes and feelings about behaviour';
- where families, students and staff are drawn 'into active involvement, using their ideas as part of the process' and are invited 'to take responsibility for decisions taken' and provided with 'opportunities to formulate ideas that will influence future planning, including changes to practical arrangements';
- where staff are confident enough 'to reflect on their own practice'.

The SEN Information Report, i.e. the school's 'Local Offer': what should be included?

The Code of Practice (DfE, 2014a, §6.79,6.83) states the information (i.e., the SEN Information Report) published should be updated annually and any changes to the information occurring during the year should be updated as soon as possible. The information required is set out in the Special Educational Needs and Disability Regulations 2014 and must include:

1. information on the kinds of special educational needs for which provision is made at the school;
2. information, in relation to mainstream schools and maintained nursery schools, on the school's policies for the identification and assessment of pupils with special educational needs;
3. information on the school's policies for making provision for pupils with special educational needs whether or not pupils have EHC Plans, including:
   (a) how the school evaluates the effectiveness of its provision for such pupils;
   (b) the school's arrangements for assessing and reviewing the progress of pupils with special educational needs;
   (c) the school's approach to teaching pupils with special educational needs;
   (d) how the school adapts the curriculum and learning environment for pupils with special educational needs;
   (e) additional support for learning that is available to pupils with special educational needs;
   (f) how the school enables pupils with special educational needs to engage in the activities of the school (including physical activities) together with children who do not have special educational needs; and
   (g) support that is available for improving the emotional, mental and social development of pupils with special educational needs.

4 in relation to mainstream schools and maintained nursery schools, the name and contact details of the SEN co-ordinator;
5 information on the expertise and training of staff in relation to children and young people with special educational needs and about how specialist expertise will be secured;
6 information on how equipment and facilities to support children and young people with special educational needs will be secured;
7 the arrangements for consulting parents of children with special educational needs about, and involving such parents in, the education of their child;
8 the arrangements for consulting young people with special educational needs about, and involving them in, their education;
9 any arrangements made by the governing body or the proprietor relating to the treatment of complaints from parents of pupils with special educational needs concerning the provision made at the school;
10 how the governing body involves other bodies, including health and social services bodies, local authority support services and voluntary organisations, in meeting the needs of pupils with special educational needs and in supporting the families of such pupils;
11 the contact details of support services for the parents of pupils with special educational needs, including those for arrangements made in accordance with Section 32;
12 the school's arrangements for supporting pupils with special educational needs in a transfer between phases of education or in preparation for adulthood and independent living;
13 information on where the local authority's local offer is published.

The above should include arrangements for supporting children and young people who are looked after by the local authority and have SEN.

There is a considerable overlap between information required for the SEND policy and for the SEN Information Report. There is advice in the *Schools' Guide to the 0–25 SEND Code of Practice* (DfE, 2014b: 18) that the two documents can be combined: 'This [i.e. the SEN Information Report] information can be included as part of the school's overall SEN policy and does not need to be a separate document.'

Reflection 11.1: Ensuring clarity in SEND information for families

The Lamb Enquiry (Lamb, 2009: 3) advises that schools should ensure that the information about SEND provision is easily accessible to young people and parents and is set out in clear, straightforward language, so that they understand the provision that is available, how they may support their child and how they and their child can contribute to decision-making, as also advised. The information given in the SEND Policy/SEN Information Report should enable answers to the following questions, frequently asked by parents, as outlined in the schools' *Guide*.

- How does the school know if children/young people need help?
- What should I do if I think my child has special educational needs?

- How will the school know how well my child is doing?
- How will I know how well my child is doing?
- How will the school know that what they are providing is helping my child make progress?
- How will the school staff support my child and how will the curriculum be matched to their needs?
- How will the school support me to support my child's learning?
- How is the decision made about the type and level of support provided to my child?
- What extra-curricular activities are available for my child? How will my child be included in activities outside the classroom, including school trips?
- What support will be available for my child's overall well-being?
- What specialist services and expertise are available in school or can be accessed by the school?
- What training have the staff working with pupils with SEND received? What further training is planned?
- How accessible is the school – indoors and out?
- Whom should I contact if I have any questions or concerns?

Appendix B7 comprises an example of a completed template that you might like to consider when drawing up or revising your own SEND policy and SEN Information Report.

The issue of child protection and safeguarding in schools and colleges

Increasingly since the 1980s with the death of 5-year-old Jasmine Beckford and the ensuing Beckford Report (Panel of Enquiry, 1985), issues of child protection have been the focus across various agencies, including education. Recently, in 2011, Ofsted published a guide on safeguarding in schools that evaluates the features of best practice in safeguarding, based on inspection evidence from a sample of outstanding schools visited by Inspectors. Key features of an outstanding school were identified as:

- high quality leadership and management where safeguarding was seen as a priority;
- stringent vetting procedures;
- rigorous safeguarding procedures and policies;
- easily accessible child protection arrangements;
- a high priority given to training that goes beyond the basic;
- robust arrangements for site security;
- a flexible, relevant and engaging curriculum that is used to promote safeguarding.

Since 2011, a number of other documents have been published by the government on guidance on child protection for schools and other agencies. Currently every school or college must have a Child Protection Policy, often referred to as the Safeguarding

Policy. The aim of the policy is to ensure that the school or college has effective measures in place to safeguard children from the potential risk of harm and that the safety and well-being of the children and young people are of the highest priority.

On 26 March 2015, the government published revised versions of the documents entitled *Working Together to Safeguard Children* (DfE, 2015a) and *Keeping Children Safe in Education* (DfE, 2015b) which set out the responsibilities of all local authorities, schools and further education colleges in England to safeguard and promote the welfare of children and young people. These documents became statutory with immediate effect, and this is guidance to which *all* schools and further education colleges must have regard when carrying out their duties to safeguard and promote the welfare of children. Advice for practitioners has also been updated by the DfE in the following areas: *What to Do If You're Worried a Child Is Being Abused* (DfE, 2015c) and *Information Sharing: Advice for Practitioners* (DfE, 2015d).

Currently, the governing bodies, management committees or proprietors of maintained and independent schools, including academies and free schools, FE and sixth form colleges, pupil referral units and non-maintained special schools have duties in relation to safeguarding and promoting the welfare of students. These organisations are required to have arrangements in place that promote the welfare of their students and ensure they are safeguarded. These arrangements include (DfE, 2015a: Chapter 2, §4):

- a clear line of accountability for the commissioning and provision of services designed to safeguard and promote the welfare of children;
- a senior board level lead to take leadership responsibility for the organisation's safeguarding arrangements;
- a culture of listening to children and taking account of their wishes and feelings, both in individual decisions and the development of services;
- clear whistleblowing procedures, which reflect the principles in Sir Robert Francis's Freedom to Speak Up review and are suitably referenced in staff training and codes of conduct, and a culture that enables issues about safeguarding and promoting the welfare of children to be addressed;
- arrangements which set out clearly the processes for sharing information, with other professionals and with the Local Safeguarding Children Board (LSCB);
- a designated professional lead (or, for health provider organisations, named professionals) for safeguarding. Their role is to support other professionals in their agencies to recognise the needs of children, including rescue from possible abuse or neglect. Designated professional roles should always be explicitly defined in job descriptions. Professionals should be given sufficient time, funding, supervision and support to fulfil their child welfare and safeguarding responsibilities effectively;
- safe recruitment practices for individuals whom the organisation will permit to work regularly with children, including policies on when to obtain a criminal record check; appropriate supervision and support for staff, including undertaking safeguarding training:
  - employers are responsible for ensuring that their staff are competent to carry out their responsibilities for safeguarding and promoting the welfare of

children and creating an environment where staff feel able to raise concerns and feel supported in their safeguarding role;
  - staff should be given a mandatory induction, which includes familiarisation with child protection responsibilities and procedures to be followed if anyone has any concerns about a child's safety or welfare; and
  - all professionals should have regular reviews of their own practice to ensure they improve over time.
- clear policies in line with those from the LSCB for dealing with allegations against people who work with children. Such policies should make a clear distinction between an allegation, a concern about the quality of care or practice or a complaint. An allegation may relate to a person who works with children who has:
  - behaved in a way that has harmed a child, or may have harmed a child;
  - possibly committed a criminal offence against or related to a child; or
  - behaved towards a child or children in a way that indicates they may pose a risk of harm to children.

Policy on supporting students with medical conditions

Section 100 of the Children and Families Act 2014 places a duty on governing bodies of maintained schools, proprietors of academies and management committees of pupil referral units (PRUs) to make arrangements to support pupils at their school with medical conditions to ensure that they are given the same opportunities at school as any other child or young person. Schools and colleges should work with local authorities, health professionals and other support services

> to ensure that children with medical conditions receive a full education. In some cases this will require flexibility and involve, for example, programmes of study that rely on part-time attendance at school in combination with alternative provision arranged by the local authority.
>
> (DfE, 2014c: §6)

Children and young people with medical conditions have the same rights of admission to school or college as others. However:

> in line with their safeguarding duties, governing bodies should ensure that pupils' health is not put at unnecessary risk from, for example, infectious diseases. They therefore do not have to accept a child in school at times where it would be detrimental to the health of that child or others to do so.
>
> (DfE, 2014c: §9)

Governing bodies have the responsibility for ensuring effective implementation of the school's policy, including provision of a named person with overall responsibility for policy implementation. Statutory guidance (*Supporting Pupils at School with Medical Conditions: Statutory Guidance for Governing Bodies of Maintained Schools and Proprietors of Academies in England*, DfE, 2014c: §19) on the contents of individual healthcare plans reads:

When deciding what information should be recorded on individual healthcare plans, the governing body should consider the following:

- the medical condition, its triggers, signs, symptoms and treatments;
- the pupil's resulting needs, including medication (dose, side effects and storage) and other treatments, time, facilities, equipment, testing, access to food and drink where this is used to manage their condition, dietary requirements and environmental issues e.g. crowded corridors, travel time between lessons;
- specific support for the pupil's educational, social and emotional needs – for example, how absences will be managed, requirements for extra time to complete exams, use of rest periods or additional support in catching up with lessons, counselling sessions;
- the level of support needed (some children will be able to take responsibility for their own health needs) including in emergencies. If a child is self-managing their medication, this should be clearly stated with appropriate arrangements for monitoring;
- who will provide this support, their training needs, expectations of their role and confirmation of proficiency to provide support for the child's medical condition from a healthcare professional; and cover arrangements for when they are unavailable;
- who in the school needs to be aware of the child's condition and the support required;
- arrangements for written permission from parents and the head teacher for medication to be administered by a member of staff, or self-administered by the pupil during school hours;
- separate arrangements or procedures required for school trips or other school activities outside of the normal school timetable that will ensure the child can participate, e.g. risk assessments;
- where confidentiality issues are raised by the parent/child, the designated individuals to be entrusted with information about the child's condition; and
- what to do in an emergency, including whom to contact, and contingency arrangements. Some children may have an emergency healthcare plan prepared by their lead clinician that could be used to inform development of their individual healthcare plan.

Any member of school staff may be asked to support pupils with medical conditions and they should take into account the needs of pupils with medical conditions whom they teach. This includes administering medicines, but they cannot be required to do this. 'School staff should receive sufficient and suitable training and achieve the necessary level of competency before they take on responsibility to support children with medical conditions' (DfE, 2014c: 12).

The governors should ensure that the school policy clearly sets out ways in which staff will be supported in assisting pupils with medical conditions, and how to review this. This should specify how training needs are assessed, and how training will be commissioned and provided.

Accessibility plans

In relation to accessibility for disabled pupils, the Equality Act 2010 (Schedule 10) requires the 'responsible body' of a school or college to prepare an 'accessibility plan' and make sure such a plan is put into operation as needed. The intention behind the plan is described as (§2):

- increasing the extent to which disabled pupils can participate in the school's curriculum;
- improving the physical environment of the school for the purpose of increasing the extent to which disabled pupils are able to take advantage of education and benefits, facilities or services provided or offered by the school; and
- improving the delivery to disabled pupils of information which is readily accessible to pupils who are not disabled.

An accessibility plan must be in writing, implemented 'within a reasonable time' in ways that take account of the students' disabilities and 'any preferences expressed by them or their parents' (§3), be kept 'under review during the period to which it relates', and revised if necessary.

Behaviour and the law

In the past few years a number of guidance documents have been published by central government in relation to student behaviour in schools and colleges. One of these is *Behaviour and Discipline in Schools: Advice for Head Teachers and School Staff* (DfE, 2014d). This guide explains the powers members of staff have to discipline pupils. Key points include (DfE, 2014d: 3–4):

- Teachers have statutory authority to discipline pupils for misbehaviour which occurs in school and, in some circumstances, outside of school.
- The power to discipline also applies to all paid staff (unless the head teacher says otherwise) with responsibility for pupils, such as teaching assistants.
- Heads and governing bodies must ensure they have a strong behaviour policy to support staff in managing behaviour, including the use of rewards and sanctions.
- Governing bodies have a duty under Section 175 of the Education Act 2002 requiring them to make arrangements to ensure that their functions are carried out with a view to safeguarding and promoting the welfare of children.

The way in which schools deal with pupils varies widely and behaviour which one school considers to be unacceptable may not be defined as unacceptable by another. If a pupil misbehaves, breaks a school rule or fails to follow a reasonable instruction, legally the teacher can impose a punishment. However, that punishment (including detentions) must satisfy three conditions (DfE, 2014d: §14):

1 The decision to punish a pupil must be made by a paid member of school staff or a member of staff authorised by the head teacher.

2 The decision to punish the pupil and the punishment itself must be made on the school premises or while the pupil is under the charge of the member of staff.
3 It must not breach any other legislation (for example, in respect of disability, Special Educational Needs, race and other equalities and human rights) and it must be reasonable in all the circumstances.

One guiding principle is that of 'reasonableness'. Schools must, for example, consider the personal circumstances of pupils before they decide what action to take. The head teacher and teachers can use reasonable non-physical means to punish a pupil for unacceptable conduct or behaviour. Any punishment must be fair, reasonable and within the school's policy. In determining whether a punishment is reasonable, Section 91 of the Education and Inspections Act 2006 says the penalty must be proportionate in the circumstances and that account must be taken of the pupil's age, any special educational needs or disability they may have, and any religious requirements affecting them. Confiscation of pupils' property is a case in point. Disciplinary penalties may include confiscation and disposal of items. However, the confiscation has to be reasonable in the circumstances. For example, playing loud music on a personal music player might result in confiscation but it would be hard to justify that destroying the player was reasonable. Corporal punishment is against the law in all schools (including nurseries and independent schools). However, a member of staff can use reasonable physical force to break up a fight between pupils or to stop pupils endangering themselves, other pupils or school property or to prevent a pupil from committing a criminal offence.

In deciding what strategies to use, the head teacher must take account of the governors' statement of behaviour principles and any guidance provided by them. We might take three specific examples of issues with which the school might have to deal: (1) screening and searching pupils; (2) protection of vulnerable pupils; and (3) exclusions.

Reflection 11.2: The power to screen and search

It is a criminal offence to carry offensive weapons on school property, and these days schools have a legal right to search without consent for weapons, knives, alcohol, illegal drugs and stolen items.

Every maintained school should have a drugs education programme, suitable for the age and ability of the pupils, and a drugs policy setting out the ways in which the school will deal with drugs on school property.

You might choose to access government guidance on the use of reasonable force (DfE, 2013b) at https://www.gov.uk/government/publications/use-of-reasonable-force-in-schools and consider its relevance to your own institution.

This document indicates that teachers have a legal power to use reasonable force. They can use force to remove a pupil who is disrupting a lesson or to prevent a child leaving a classroom.

Heads can search without consent for an extended list of items including alcohol, illegal drugs and stolen property.

Protection for 'vulnerable' pupils

Behaviour policies themselves should show an awareness of the special needs that many vulnerable children might have. The policy should make sure that vulnerable pupils get the support they need. Vulnerable pupils include:

- pupils with special educational needs;
- pupils with physical or mental health problems;
- migrant and refugee pupils;
- pupils who are being looked after by the local authority.

Pupils in all of these groups may show difficult behaviour and their specific needs should be covered by the discipline and punishment policy of the school.

Exclusions

The procedures which can be used to exclude a pupil from school vary according to the sort of school a child attends. However, it is against the law for the school to discriminate, for example because of disability, when deciding whether to exclude a child. Statutory guidance for schools on exclusions can be found at: https://www.gov.uk/government/uploads/system/uploads/attachment_data/file/269681/Exclusion_from_maintained_schools__academies_and_pupil_referral_units.pdf, accessed 1 June 2015, and can be read alongside the School Discipline (Pupil Exclusions and Reviews) (England) Regulations 2012 that are available at: http://www.legislation.gov.uk/uksi/2012/1033/made, accessed 1 June 2015.

A pupil cannot be excluded temporarily for more than 45 days in any one school year. If a pupil is excluded for more than one or two days, the head teacher should arrange for the pupil to receive school work to do at home and to have it marked when they return to school. If, however, a child has been permanently excluded, the local authority must make sure that other suitable education is provided from the sixth day of their exclusion.

Reflection 11.3: Inspection framework related to behaviour

One of the ways in which the government ensures that schools carry out their statutory obligations is through the use of inspections by its inspection agency, the Office for Standards in Education (Ofsted). The Ofsted document (2014: 4) *Unannounced Behaviour Inspections: Guidance for Inspectors*, outlines the focus of inspections that take place with no prior warning to schools. You might wish to take careful account of this list of bullet points if you are considering what Ofsted inspectors might be looking for in your own school.

The document states:

The inspection will focus sharply on evaluating:

- pupils' attitudes to learning and their conduct around the school and in lessons, both during the inspection and over time;

- how well, and how consistently, pupils' behaviour is managed on a day-to-day basis;
- the extent to which the school's culture promotes and supports good behaviour.

In this guidance document, inspectors are told (2014: 5) that they must take account of:

- pupils' attitudes to learning and their conduct in lessons;
- pupils' conduct around the school, including the way in which they speak to each other and to staff;
- how well leaders and staff model good behaviour to pupils;
- how well leaders and managers model good behaviour management techniques to staff;
- the effectiveness of the management of pupils' behaviour, including how well leaders and managers analyse and use documentary evidence to improve the way behaviour is managed;
- if the school uses exclusion, the impact of this on improving behaviour;
- if fixed term exclusion overall or for any group is above the national average, the extent to which its use is reducing over time, and how well the school is developing the use of alternative strategies to exclusion;
- pupils' views about behaviour and bullying (these views must be gathered from a range of pupils at informal times, not just from a formal discussion);
- any specific issues raised in the previous inspection report about pupils' behaviour and whether these have been tackled effectively and are showing clear signs of improvement.

Requirements of schools' behaviour policies

The school behaviour policy must be publicised in writing to staff, parents and pupils. The guide on behaviour and discipline in schools (DfE, 2014d: §10) exhorts head teachers to have regard to ten particular aspects of school practice that are considered to contribute to positive pupil behaviour when they develop their school behaviour policies:

1. a consistent approach to behaviour management
2. strong school leadership
3. classroom management
4. rewards and sanctions
5. behaviour strategies and the teaching of good behaviour
6. staff development and support
7. pupil support systems
8. liaison with parents and other agencies
9. managing pupil transition
10. organisation and facilities.

These ten aspects of school practice reflect a report on behaviour in schools that was commissioned by central government (the Steer Report) (DfES, 2006) *Section 2: Principles and Practice. What Works in Schools*. The group was asked to identify practical examples of good practice that promote good behaviour and that can be adopted by all schools. The outcomes can be summarised in terms of the link between the quality of teaching and pupil behaviour, the importance of consistently applied policy and practice, and understanding that good behaviour will not necessarily just happen. It needs to be taught by staff who model what they want through their own behaviour and who have access to training and support in behaviour and classroom management.

Reflection 11.4: Auditing behaviour in schools

In the Steer Report (Steer, 2006), key to articulating a school's values is the school's behaviour policy that should be clear, coherent and shared by all the stakeholders in the school. Schools are exhorted to review their behaviour, teaching and learning policies and carry out an audit of student behaviour. In carrying out this audit, ten aspects of effective school practice, reflecting the ten points made above, are identified as supporting positive student behaviour (Steer, 2006, Section 2, §6, §9). You might choose to use these ten points as the basis for an audit of the degree to which behaviour policy is effective at your school:

1 a consistent approach to behaviour management, teaching and learning. Being 'consistent' means that when there is persistent offending or low level disruption, all schools should:
   - ensure staff follow through issues with pupils indicating what must be done to improve;
   - ensure that staff discuss with parents the school's concerns and agree a common way of working to help pupils make improvements to their behaviour; and
   - establish the best way of communicating with parents and provide regular feedback on the progress being made (Steer, 2006: §9).

Good teaching means that all schools should (Steer, 2006: 4):

- identify those pupils who have learning and behavioural difficulties, or come from communities or homes that are in crisis, and agree with staff common ways of managing and meeting their particular needs
- ensure that senior colleagues are highly visible at particular times of the day, to support staff and maintain a sense of calm and order. Critical times in a school day are at the beginning, break and lunch times, changes of lessons (in secondary schools), and the end of the school day; and
- ensure that senior managers regularly walk their building, going into classrooms and assessing how well staff are consistently applying the school's policies on behaviour improvement.

2 Effective school leadership by head teachers and governors that is seen as crucial in developing shared expectations and values and creating a sense of security and good order that supports positive pupil behaviour. Schools are advised to work in partnership with parents to 'set high expectations for pupils and staff in all aspects of the school's life and show how they are to be met. For example:

- by clear codes of conduct;
- by guidance on how to improve their work; and
- a dress code.'

Senior leaders are advised to 'use opportunities such as assemblies to articulate their expectations and reinforce them by their visibility around the building during the day' and also to 'model the behaviour and social skills they want pupils and staff to use' (Steer, 2006: 5). The responsibilities and roles of senior staff for behaviour improvement should be clearly identified.

3 Classroom management, learning and teaching. The school curriculum should be 'accessible to pupils of all abilities and aptitudes' (§15). There should be an agreed teaching and learning policy, negotiated with all stakeholders in the school, that identifies the teaching and classroom management strategies to be followed by all staff. All schools should (§17):
   - ensure all staff follow the learning and teaching policy and behaviour code and apply agreed procedures;
   - plan lessons well, using strategies appropriate to the ability of the pupils;
   - use commonly agreed classroom management and behaviour strategies such as a formal way to start lessons. In secondary schools this could include: All pupils being greeted by the door, brought into the classroom, stood behind their chairs, formally welcomed, asked to sit and the teacher explaining the purpose of the lesson.
   - offer pupils the opportunity to take responsibility for aspects of their learning, working together in pairs, groups and as a whole class;
   - use Assessment for Learning techniques, such as peer and self-assessment, to increase pupils' involvement in their learning and promote good behaviour;
   - collect data on pupils' behaviour and learning and use it, for example, to plan future groupings and to target support on areas where pupils have the greatest difficulty;
   - ensure that all teachers operate a classroom seating plan. This practice needs to be continued after transfer to secondary school. Educational research shows that where pupils are allowed to determine where they sit, their social interactions can inhibit teaching and create behaviour problems.
   - ensure teachers build into their lessons opportunities to receive feedback from pupils on their progress and their future learning needs;
   - recognise that pupils are knowledgeable about their school experience, and have views about what helps them learn and how others' poor behaviour stops them from learning; and
   - give opportunities for class, year and school councils to discuss and make recommendations about behaviour, including bullying, and the effectiveness of rewards and sanctions.

Homework is seen as providing, potentially, a major source of friction and confrontation. 'Planning homework carefully and setting it early in a lesson can significantly increase the number of pupils who subsequently have a clear understanding of what is expected of them. This is particularly helpful to pupils with special educational needs who can be disadvantaged by the volume of work presented (§18).

4 Rewards and sanctions: all schools are expected to have a range of rewards and sanctions that are appropriate and applied fairly and consistently by staff. Planning to improve pupil behaviour should be informed by statistical information about the use and effectiveness of rewards and sanctions. There should also be an agreed system to identify when poor behaviour should be dealt with by classroom teachers and when it should be referred to more senior staff.

5 Behaviour strategies and the teaching of good behaviour: all staff should understand and use consistently, the behaviour management strategies agreed by the school community, and use pupil tracking systems to identify patterns of positive and negative behaviour. This includes having an agreed policy about how to teach pupils 'to manage strong feelings, resolve conflict, work and play cooperatively and be respectful and considerate; and arranging additional small group support for pupils who need it' (§22). Staff should be acquainted with, and use where appropriate the SEAL and SEBS4 materials from the National Strategy to develop pupils' emotional development. New staff should be made aware of the school's behaviour policy and practices.

6 Staff development and support: staff should be trained and supported to implement the school's behaviour policy. All leaders should have access to training to mentor less experienced staff.

7 Pupil support systems: schools should recognise that good pastoral support is focused on academic attainment and supporting pupils to become good citizens, not just on individual badly behaved children. Pastoral staff should ensure that all pupils feel a sense of belonging to the school community by sharing a common dress code that is agreed with parents and families.

8 Liaison with parents and other agencies: there should be a comfortable area where parents can be received. Reception and other staff should know how to welcome parents and be able to deal with distressed and angry parents. Parents and carers should be informed when their children are doing well as well as when there is a problem. Communication between school and home should include new technology such as email and mobile phones. However, 'this should not replace personal contact' (§30).

9 Managing pupil transition: teachers should be given appropriate information about new classes at the beginning of the school year to help the plan work and manage behaviour. Schools should consider a managed entrance at the beginning of the week where there is a high level of pupil mobility to avoid day by day arrivals. They should also draw on the expertise of outside agencies such as Traveller support teams. Buddying from other pupils with named staff as mentors can help new arrivals to a school.

10 Organisation and facilities: attractive, clean environments are conducive to good behaviour and learning, so any graffiti and rubbish should be cleaned up immediately. The fabric of the building is important in making pupils feel they are respected. Toilets should always be clean and supplied with soap, paper towels or hand dryers. There should be discrete areas in the school with seating for pupils to socialise. Play areas should be zoned to separate louder activities from quiet areas. In addition, timetabling should be organised very carefully to ensure:

- 'that teachers are not timetabled for a second year with classes that they had a poor relationships with the previous year;
- 'that pupils with reading difficulties are not timetabled for a whole day without some lesson where they have a practical activity;
- 'that teachers are timetabled so that they can get to their teaching areas quickly; and
- 'that at key points of movement, staff are on duty to supervise.'

Bullying

Bullying can take many forms, and this includes cyber-bullying. Bullying is often associated with an imbalance of power between victim and perpetrator. Bullies trade in secrecy, not from their peers, but from adults. Breaking through this secrecy is crucial in addressing bullying of any kind. There need to be clear, school-wide consequences for bullying, otherwise the bully will continue in the belief that he or she can continue with impunity (Olweus, 1993). Such consequences need to be set out in a formal process for dealing with bullying behaviour in an educational context that emphasises rights-respecting behaviour.

Government guidance *Preventing and Tackling Bullying: Advice for Head Teachers, Staff and Governing Bodies*, (DfE, 2014h: 7–8) comments that schools which deal successfully with the issue of bullying are those that apply sanctions consistently and fairly and look to see if there are underlying motives behind the bullying behaviour that can be addressed. Such 'successful' schools also:

- involve parents to ensure that they are clear that the school does not tolerate bullying and are aware of the procedures to follow if they believe that their child is being bullied;
- involve pupils. All pupils understand the school's approach and are clear about the part they can play to prevent bullying, including when they find themselves as bystanders;
- regularly evaluate and update their approach to take account of developments in technology, for instance, updating 'acceptable use' policies for computers;
- implement disciplinary sanctions;
- openly discuss differences between people that could motivate bullying, such as religion, ethnicity, disability, gender or sexuality. Also children with different family situations, such as looked after children or those with caring responsibilities. Schools can also teach children that using any prejudice-based language is unacceptable;
- use specific organisations or resources for help with particular problems;
- provide effective staff training. Anti-bullying policies are most effective when all school staff understand the principles and purpose of the school's policy, its legal responsibilities regarding bullying, how to resolve problems, and where to seek support;
- work with the wider community such as the police and children's services where bullying is particularly serious or persistent and where a criminal offence may have been committed;

- make it easy for pupils to report bullying so that they are assured that they will be listened to and incidents acted on. Pupils should feel that they can report bullying which may have occurred outside school including cyber-bullying;
- create an inclusive environment. Schools should create a safe environment where pupils can openly discuss the cause of their bullying, without fear of further bullying or discrimination;
- celebrate success. Celebrating success is an important way of creating a positive school ethos around the issue.

Anti-bullying policies

State schools should have an anti-bullying policy which sets out the way that bullying should be dealt with in the school. This includes:

- bullying related to race, religion and culture;
- bullying pupils with disabilities or special educational needs;
- sexist bullying and harassment;
- bullying pupils because of their sexuality or perceived sexuality;
- cyber-bullying (the use of mobile phones and the internet to bully pupils).

Under the Children Act 1989, bullying should be seen as a child protection concern when there is 'reasonable cause to suspect that a child is suffering, or is likely to suffer, significant harm'. If this is the case, staff should report their concerns to their local authority children's social care. Schools may need to draw on a range of external services to support pupils who are being bullied, or to address any underlying issue which has contributed to a child's bullying behaviour (DfE, 2014h).

In England, government guidance advises that schools should discipline pupils who bully, whether inside or outside the school premises. At the same time, the school should look at the reasons for the bullying and whether the bully also needs help. If the bullying is extremely serious and the bully is over the age of 10, the bully could be prosecuted for a criminal offence, for example, assault or harassment. If the bully is under the age of 10, it may be possible to take legal action for negligence against the school and the local education authority for failure in their duty of care to the bullied pupil.

Advice about cyber-bullying

Childnet International and the Department for Children, Schools and Families together issued guidance to schools about how to address cyber-bullying in schools: *Let's Fight It Together. What We Can All Do to Prevent Cyberbullying* (Childnet International and DCSF, 2007–8). Section 4 explains the rationale underpinning this guidance document:

> It is important to equip young people with strategies for getting out of situations involving inappropriate, unwanted or difficult contact online, and to leave them feeling empowered after the session. It is imperative that children and young

people are aware of the school policies and strategies for dealing with cyber-bullying. For example, it is recommended that all children are made aware of what cyberbullying is, what the sanctions are for cyberbullying, and to whom or where they can report cyberbullying behaviour.

Strategies that should be discussed with students include:

- Respect for others: be careful what is said online and what images are sent. Ask permission before photographing someone.
- Forethought: think carefully before posting information on a website. Information could stay online for ever. Do not give your mobile phone numbers to others in a public domain.
- Maintain the confidentiality of passwords: do not disclose these to anyone, and change them regularly.
- Block bullies: websites and services often allow individuals you to block or report someone who is bullying.
- Do not retaliate or reply to bullies.
- Save the evidence of offending messages, pictures or online conversations.
- Report online bullying. Such bullying may be reported to a trusted adult, the provider of the service, the school or the police, if the cyber-bullying is serious.

If pupil safety is compromised, it is important not to promise confidentiality to the child. The child will need to know what will happen to the information, and why. The first point of contact following disclosure should be the designated child protection officer within the institution. An accurate account of what the child has disclosed should be recorded as soon as possible. If possible, the child should be present when the incident is reported to the designated officer.

Practices and procedures to report and respond to incidents of bullying should already be in place in the school. Most cyber-bullying cases can be effectively dealt with in existing systems.

In all cases of bullying, incidents should be properly documented, recorded and investigated, support should be provided for the person being bullied, other staff members and parents and carers should be informed as appropriate, and those found to be bullying should be interviewed and receive appropriate sanctions.

Full cyber-bullying guidance is available at: www.digizen.org/cyberbullying/full-guidance, accessed 1 June 2015.

Reflection 11.5: Checking on the procedures and policies relating to cyber-bullying in schools

At this point you might like to check your own school policy documents on bullying, including cyber-bullying. How far do these documents include what is advised or required?

Policy related to literacy difficulties

Families and carers of children and young people who experience difficulties in literacy acquisition may feel alarmed at the focus on the testing of their children's achievement in literacy against national norms. Currently, in England, a high-stakes assessment regime regulates the teaching of literacy in schools. (High-stakes assessments are those used to make significant educational decisions about students, teachers and schools (Heubert, 2000).) The authors of a research review comparing curriculum and assessment policies for primary education in England with those in other countries (Hall and Øzerk, 2008: 3), for example, note: 'The scale of assessment for the purpose of monitoring and accountability is of quite a different order in England compared to the other countries included in this survey.' Effectively, now, literacy policy in schools is driven by the requirements of the particular Key Stage in English with the whole system held in place by schools' accountability for publicising their pupils' progress and assessment outcomes, and also for their rating by Ofsted during school inspections. There is also a requirement that children aged 6 should take a systematic synthetic phonics test.

While parents and carers of children with literacy difficulties may, as noted above, feel alarmed at the effect on their offspring of such a high-stakes testing environment, there is also a formal recognition that severe dyslexic difficulties are likely to create a barrier to learning. This area of need is acknowledged in the terms of Part 3 of the 2014 Children and Families Act and special provision should be made to address it. In addition, severe dyslexia might also constitute a disability and be covered by the Equality Act (2010) under which schools and local authorities have a duty to be proactive in providing 'reasonable adjustments'. Advice about 'reasonable adjustments' given to schools by the Equality and Human Rights Commission reads:

> You cannot justify a failure to make a reasonable adjustment; where the duty arises, the issue will be whether or not to make the adjustment is 'reasonable' and this is an objective question for the tribunals to ultimately determine.

> The duty is an anticipatory and continuing one that you owe to disabled pupils generally, regardless of whether you know that a particular pupil is disabled or whether you currently have any disabled pupils. You should not wait until an individual disabled pupil approaches you before you consider how to meet the duty. Instead you should plan ahead for the reasonable adjustments you may need to make, regardless of whether you currently have any disabled pupils.
>
> (http://www.equalityhumanrights.com/private-and-public-sector-guidance/education-providers/schools-guidance/key-concepts/reasonable-adjustment, accessed 1 June 2015)

As the Equality and Human Rights Commission comment, this duty runs alongside schools' responsibilities under SEN legislation. For some students, the support that has been made available under the special educational needs framework may mean that the individual does not suffer a substantial disadvantage and there is no need for additional 'reasonable adjustments' to be made. Others may require reasonable adjustments in addition to the SEN provision they are receiving. For some, this may imply special consideration during external examinations, for example, additional time or access to an amanuensis or a word processor. It is clear, therefore, that the level of support a pupil is receiving under SEN legislation is one of the factors for schools to take into account when considering what it would be 'reasonable' to have to do.

Developing an institutional policy on dyslexia

Comparison of a number of principles of policy-making in schools (Wearmouth and Berryman, 2009) would indicate that a school policy related to the inclusion of pupils who are dyslexic:

- should begin with a statement, which indicates the school's general philosophy with regard to addressing dyslexic-type difficulties in schools;
- should also include a definition of what dyslexia is;
- should have a set of aims and objectives in relation to identifying, assessing and addressing dyslexic-type difficulties and including dyslexic pupils in the school curricular activities;
- should also outline a number of proactive and reactive strategies the school aims to take;
- must be regularly reviewed.

Table 11.1 contains a checklist of effective policy and practice related to dyslexic students.

Table 11.1 Checklist of effective policy and practice related to provision for dyslexic students

This might include the following:

- Is there a shared understanding of what dyslexia means across the school community (children, young people, staff, governors and parents)?
- Are dyslexic pupils' views on the difficulties they experience and the extent to which they feel supported and encouraged canvassed regularly?
- Do pupils feel that there will be a consistent response whichever member of staff they talk to about the difficulties they experience?
- Are policy and practice consistent with legislation and guidance on special educational needs and disability equality legislation?
- Is support at transition and for dyslexic pupils clearly identified?
- Do all staff feel they have had adequate training about dyslexia and how to respond to it?
- Are all staff aware of specific techniques they can use to address difficulties in literacy and raise standards of literacy generally?
- Is it clear how the curriculum addresses dyslexic-type difficulties?
- Are there peer support schemes in place?
- Are records kept and analysed for patterns of progress among pupils identified as dyslexic?
- Does this analysis inform changes to practice?
- Do parents know whom to contact if they are worried that their child(ren) might be dyslexic?

Summary

In the past two decades, in particular, a number of documents have emanated from central government that have the status of 'statutory guidance'. It is essential that schools and colleges are thoroughly familiar with these documents, and also with the requirement to have in place particular policies against which their practice can be evaluated, first, by themselves and their own governing bodies, but also externally by the families of their students and by the government's inspection arm, Ofsted.

12

Working with families

Introduction

In a number of countries across the world there is a formal acceptance that parents and carers have the right to know about decisions taken in schools in relation to their children, and that they themselves are, potentially, an important source of additional support in addressing difficulties in learning and behaviour experienced by young people. Crozier and Reay (2005: 155) suggest it is the 'centre piece' in twenty-first-century education policy-making. The right of parents and carers to be consulted at every stage of decision-making about their children is currently enshrined in law in England, for example, in the Children and Families Act 2014. The intention to support families not just to understand, but to access, their legal entitlements also, has been emphasised through the publication of a number of guides to the SEN(D) system for parents and carers, the most recent of which was published by the DfE in 2014. This latest guide both explains the law and also outlines the kinds of questions that parents and carers might ask in schools and colleges to ensure that their children have their needs properly assessed and addressed.

Entitlement in law is not always synonymous with experience in practice, however. Schools have a lot of power to affect the lives of children and their families and carers through the kind of consultation arrangements, assessment and provision that they make. Embedded within the particular discourses, approaches and strategies of schools are a variety of preconceptions about the ability and right of parents, families and communities, from a diversity of backgrounds and cultures, to support the learning and development of their children.

This chapter will begin by outlining, very briefly, the background to current policies on families' rights in decision-making about SEND provision for young people in schools and colleges. This will include research that critiques some of the previously practised models of home–school partnerships as well as the outcomes of the (2009) Lamb Enquiry into ways in which parental confidence in the existing SEN system in education might be enhanced.

It will go on to discuss:

- the legal requirements in relation to partnership work with families and carers and some of the challenges in meeting these, with examples of:
  - what can happen in practice;
  - effective practical initiatives designed to enable more positive working relationships between schools and families and, thus, to meet families' legal entitlements to have account taken of their views.

Definition of terms

A number of different, but related, terms are often used in a rather ill-defined way to describe the relationship between schools or colleges and parents or carers, for example, parental 'involvement', 'engagement' and 'partnership' (Hallgarten, 2000). Involvement can refer to a whole range of activities: good parenting, helping with homework, talking to teachers, attending school functions and other activities, including school PTA and being a school governor. Some researchers have suggested that parental involvement with a school may have little impact on a child's learning (Desforges and Abouchaar, 2003), but can have a significant effect on achievement and well-being when it occurs at home. Nevertheless such involvement within the school can be effective as 'an essential lubricant for at-home involvement' (Desforges and Abouchaar, 2003; 14). 'Parental engagement', on the other hand, implies engagement in the child's learning process (Goodall et al., 2011). It is this engagement that research has shown can have a significantly positive impact on achievement and well-being (Shah, 2001; Deforges and Abouchaar, 2003; Campbell 2011; Wearmouth and Berryman, 2011). Parent partnership involves a 'full sharing of knowledge, skills and experiences' between families and the school and, ideally, 'must be equal' (Jones, 2004: 39). Clearly, such a partnership is seen to have some commonality with aspects of what is defined above as 'involvement', particularly as it relates to the issue of the lubricant for parental involvement at home. It seems logical, therefore, that schools might aim to encourage parental/family involvement in the child's education with engagement and partnership in order that the information families have as experts about their children, combined with the information teachers have about learning and the curriculum, may work together in the interests of all young people particularly, here, of children and young people with SEND, who need additional support to overcome their barriers to learning (DfE, 2014a).

Past experience

Parents and carers have not always had a statutory entitlement over decision-making in their children's education in state schools or colleges. For a long time after education for (almost) all children became compulsory, families had obligations rather than entitlements. In the 1870 Act (p. 471), School Boards were empowered, with the approval of the Education Department, to make byelaws that *required*:

1 [T]he parents of children of such age, not less than five years nor more than thirteen years, as may be fixed by the byelaws, to cause such children (unless there is some reasonable excuse) to attend school.

Much more recently, however, parental engagement in their children's education has been a key issue in education policy in the UK with discussion of this in, for example, the Plowden Report (Central Advisory Council for Education, 1967), the Taylor Report (Committee of Enquiry, 1977), the Warnock Report (DES, 1978) and then the 1981 Education Act.

It is not always straightforward to put parents' and families' rights under the law into operation, however, as a piece of research related to the case of the SEN Register indicates. The original Code of Practice (DfE, 1994) advised schools to maintain a Register of Special Needs without apparently, taking any account of what parents' views about this might be. In the only ever published research study in this area (Wearmouth, 1996), parents of pupils who had been identified as experiencing difficulties in learning in one school were asked whether they would have any reservations about their children's names being included in the school's Register of Special Needs. Of those replying to the letter sent home, a number expressed serious deeply-felt concerns with regard to issues of stigma, confidentiality, segregation and labelling, and withheld their permission to 'register' their children. Given the statutory advice in the Code, the SENCO was left in a very difficult position, asking herself whether there was ever any real intention of involving parents as partners in their children's education – partners with any real say, that is – and what rights parents actually have in practice in this situation. Very little, was her conclusion.

Parents' and families' rights and entitlements: the current situation

In 2009, the Lamb Enquiry into special educational needs and parental confidence in the system concluded that: 'Failure to comply with statutory obligations speaks of an underlying culture where parents and carers of children with SEN can too readily be seen as the problem and as a result parents lose confidence in schools and professionals.' Lamb went on to say: 'As the system stands, it often creates "warrior parents" at odds with the school and feeling they have to fight for what should be their children's by right; conflict in place of trust' (Lamb, 2009: 1.1). The recommendations in this report suggested a new framework for the provision of SEN and disability information that 'puts the relationship between parent and school back at the heart of the process' and 'trades adherence to a "laundry list" of rules for clear principles to guide that relationship' (Lamb, 2009: 1.4). Clearly these recommendations informed the terms of the Children and Families Act (2014) in England.

Section 19 of Part 3 of the Children and Families Act 2014 requires that the views, wishes and feelings of children, young people and their parents, and their participation, must be central to every decision the LA makes in regard to assessing a child or young person's SEN and how to support them. As noted above, to support parents and families to access their legal entitlements the government has published a new guide for parents and carers (DfE, 2014e). It is essential for SENCOs and others working in schools and colleges to be familiar with the contents in order to meet parental or family expectations at the very least. This Guide makes very clear the 'basic principles' that parents and families 'need to keep in mind' when thinking about the special needs of their child: 'All children with special educational needs (SEN) or disabilities should have their needs met, whether they are in early years settings... in school or in college.' It advises parents and families (DfE, 2014e: 11) that '[they] should have a real say in decisions that affect their children, should have access to impartial information, advice and support and know how to challenge decisions they disagree with'.

The Code (§6.17) advises regular assessments of the progress of all students. Information gathering should include discussion early on with both student and parents so that everyone can be clear about the pupil's areas of strength and difficulty, any concerns the parent(s) might have, the outcomes agreed for the child and the next steps. Parents and families are advised in the Guide (DfE, 2014e: 8–9):

> If you think your child has SEN, you should talk to your child's early education setting, school, college or other provider. They will discuss any concerns you have, tell you what they think and explain to you what will happen next.

SENCos would therefore be well advised to be prepared to answer questions such as the following that the Guide suggests (DfE, 2014e: 9):

- Why do you think my child has SEN or a disability?
- How do you know that my child doesn't have SEN or a disability?
- What happens now?

If a student is identified as having SEND, schools are exhorted to put 'SEN provision' in place through a graduated approach in the form of a four-part assess→plan→do→review cycle. SENCOs will need to be prepared for the implications of the family's expectations of their active involvement in the process as the Guide (DfE, 2014e: 9) advises:

> You may be contacted – for example in schools, this will be by your child's teacher or SENCO – if your early years setting, school or college think your child needs SEN support. Or you can approach your child's school or other setting if you think your child might have SEN. You will be involved and your views will be needed throughout the process, and you will be kept up to date with the progress made.

If the child or young person still does not make the progress that is expected, the school or parents should consider requesting an Education, Health and Care needs assessment and provide evidence of the action taken by the school as part of its SEN support. It is expected that both parents and students will be actively involved in requesting, creating and assessing the effectiveness of the individual plan (DfE, 2014a: 22):

> [S]ometimes a child or young person needs a more intensive level of specialist help that cannot be met from the resources available to schools and other settings to provide SEN support. In these circumstances, you or your child's school or other setting could consider asking your local authority for an Education, Health and Care (EHC) needs assessment for your child.

During the preparation of the plan the views of the following should be sought and recorded: the parents, the young person, representatives of relevant agencies and any others who provide support. Guidance is also given (DfE, 2014a: 31) that:

> If your child has an EHC plan, you can make a request for a non-maintained special school, or for an independent school or independent specialist college (where approved for this purpose by the Secretary of State and published in a list available to all parents and young people). The local authority must comply with your preference and name the school or college in the EHC plan unless provision there is considered to not meet their needs, not represent good value for money or would impact negatively on the education of others.

You may also request a place at an independent school or independent specialist college that is not on the published list and the local authority must consider your request. The local authority is not under the same duty to name the provider and should be satisfied that the institution would admit the child or young person before naming it in a plan since these providers are not subject to the duty to admit a child or young person even if named in their plan.

Where an independent school is named on the EHC plan the local authority is obliged to provide the funding to meet the provision set out in the plan.

Families are advised, specifically, that they can challenge the outcome of decision-making at this stage (DfE, 2014a: 24):

> If you disagree with your local authority's decisions on:

- not proceeding with an EHC needs assessment;
- not producing an EHC plan;

or

> The special educational support that is included in the EHC plan,
> then you have the right to challenge it.

The local authority has the duty to make arrangements for independent services to resolve disagreements and provide mediation (DfE, 2014a: 42). The SEND Tribunal is a legal body, to which families can appeal 'if your local authority decides:

- not to carry out an EHC needs assessment or re-assessment for your child;
- not to draw up an EHC plan for your child, once they have done an assessment;
- not to amend your child's EHC plan after the annual review or re-assessment;
- to cease to maintain your child's EHC plan.'

You can also appeal 'if you disagree with what your local authority includes in your child's EHC plan'.

However, before resorting to an appeal to the SEND Tribunal, families have to demonstrate that they have contacted a mediation adviser.

Two other important areas with which SENCOs should be familiar in relation to families' entitlements are those of personal budgets, and the 'local offer'. The Code of Practice (DfE, 2014a: §48) outlines how the LA is obliged to consider identifying a personal budget for educational provision for a child or young person if the parent requests it when they are carrying out an EHC needs assessment or when they are reviewing an EHC plan. The personal budget is the notional amount of money that would be needed to cover the cost of making the special educational provision specified in the EHC plan. A head teacher or principal has a veto if he or she does not agree to a direct payment being made for special educational provision which would need to be delivered in the school or college.

In relation to the 'local offer', the parents' Guide (DfE, 2014e: 16) describes how each LA is required '[to] identify education, health and social care services in their local area provided for children, young people and families who have SEN or disabilities and include them in an information directory called the Local Offer'.

It is expected that local services reflect what local people need:

> Your local authority must ask children, parents and young people what they think the Local Offer should include, and how they think people should be able to access it…They must publish what children, young people and parents tell them about their Local Offer and say clearly what they will do about the comments they receive.

Issue of power in the home–school relationship

A positive reaction of schools to the involvement of parents is a strong foundation stone on which to build. However, there should be no doubt about some of the gaps, misunderstandings and lack of knowledge that exist, even in schools as effective generally as the ones studied in Wragg et al.'s (1998) summary of the manner of parental involvement in the reading development of their children in the schools surveyed during the Leverhulme Primary Improvement Project. Unwittingly perhaps, some schools may patronise their children's parents by glossing over their concerns, assuming that they are capable of very little beyond the most rudimentary, or, sometimes in the case of some minority ethnic families, assuming too readily that they may not be equipped to help (Wragg et al., 1998. 269–70).

Reflection 12.1: Power relationships in schools' relationships with parents and carers

Similar issues to those raised by Wragg et al. were highlighted by Dale (1996). Five common partnership arrangements between schools and parents or carers that Dale identified clearly reflect different kinds of power relationships in some common home–school literacy programmes. Among them are:

1 the traditional 'Expert Model' in which the professional is assumed to have the expertise to decide what needs to be done, and parental involvement is not of prime importance except to provide information;

2 the 'Transplant Model', where the role of professionals is to control decision-making and transplant skills and expertise to the parents to help them become teachers;
3 the 'Consumer Model' where, as consumers, parents have the power to draw upon their own expertise and knowledge about their children in deciding what services they need for their child. In some schools this model might be experienced as uncomfortable for a number of reasons. Parents might be felt to usurp some of the power and control more usually owned by education professionals. Also, there may be a very real concern about the way in which education is viewed as a commodity in the UK (Gewirtz et al., 1995) and an inherent inequality in a marketised system which ensures that children whose parents are the most literate, persistent and articulate are advantaged (Audit Commission, 1992; Gross, 1996);
4 the 'Empowerment Model', where the professional's role is to recognise the family's own support network and to empower and support family members to meet their own needs;
5 the 'Negotiating Model', where negotiations between parents and professionals over the differences and commonalities between their perspectives are assumed to lead to the best decisions for the children.

In some settings, parents may welcome and initially require strong directives from teachers in supporting the learning and behaviour of their children, especially for children who experience difficulties. The expert model implied here is reflected in the UK by initiatives such as Topping's (1995) 'Paired Reading' programme, for example, in which teachers give strong direction to parents about how the technique should operate. Topping describes the rules of his method as clearly behaviourist in orientation: 'Much verbal praise and non-verbal approval for specific reading behaviours is incorporated. Undesirable behaviours are *engineered out* of the system by *engineering in* incompatible positive behaviours' (Topping, 1995: 46).

While some parents may welcome such clear directives from teachers, others may be very concerned about involving themselves in initiatives where the intention is to 'engineer out/in' behaviour seen as 'desirable' by those outside the child's family and home community.

It is clearly the case that some parents or carers are unable, or unwilling, to support the progress of their child through school as a result, for example, of stress within the family. Factors, for example, bereavement, can cause intolerable stress with a huge impact on the children in the family. In an interview (Wearmouth, unpublished), an inmate of one of Her Majesty's prisons related the following experience from his childhood:

> [Wh]en I was seven years old, my Mum was killed in a car crash and this seemed to devastate our family, you know. My Dad turned to drink and I had a sister, a year-old sister and up until then it was kind of a normal happy life, really, you know. I remember before then I was just a normal child, you know.... Fairly soon my Dad met another woman and we moved in with her. She had two kids, and we kind of moved in with the kids and everything but he wasn't very happy at all – always drank pints...She didn't like me very much this lady and I was relegated

really... She would compare us, me and the oldest son who was going to grow up to be a lady killer, but I was an ugly bastard. It was quite cruel stuff... We... lived in her house but occasionally they would argue and fight and he would, you know... real physical violence, and she would throw my Dad out! So, he would take me and my sister down to the local Police Station.

Reflection 12.2: Power issues in the home – school partnership

Russell (1997: 79) makes a plea to schools to take their power very seriously. Have a look at the points she makes below, and reflect on the extent to which you feel your school matches up to what she asks for:

- Please accept and value our children (and ourselves as families) as we are.
- Please celebrate difference.
- Please try and accept our children as children first. Don't attach labels to them unless you mean to do something.
- Please recognise your power over our lives. We live with the consequences of your opinions and decisions.
- Please understand the stress many families are under. The cancelled appointment, the waiting list no one gets to the top of, all the discussions about resources – it's our lives you're talking about.
- Don't put fashionable fads and treatments on to us unless you are going to be around to see them through. And don't forget families have many members, many responsibilities. Sometimes, we can't please everyone.
- Do recognise that sometimes we are right! Please believe us and listen to what we know that we and our children need.
- Sometimes we are sad, tired and depressed. Please value us as caring and committed families and try to go on working with us.

Facilitating family engagement

Rix and Simmons (2004) report how Bangabandu School in East London, for example, had a high commitment to parental participation and had consequently opened up their school to parents, extended families and the wider community in diverse ways. The school managed to do this when, in the following ways:

- Classes had 'authors' breakfasts' where family members were invited to have refreshments and see their child's written work for the term.
- Parents were regularly invited into assembly.
- A toddlers group met once a week with a toy library which was popular with extended family members.
- A summertime Mela, or fete, offered opportunities for families to mix and experience the diverse food and cultures that exist there (Phillips and Jenner, 2004).
- The school had a commitment to the use of home languages and bilingual staff were employed to work closely with both students and families.

Strategies such as those listed above promoted a community-style environment, creating a lot of continuous and open communication between the school and the parents of all children, and it consequently strived to provide a supportive learning culture for all. Additional resources were made available to this inner-city flagship school by the government and are no longer available. Nevertheless, an initiative to create a more constant and welcoming atmosphere for a school's or college's families may still be a viable, although a long-term, method of encouraging parent–school partnerships.

Byatt (2014) outlined several barriers to parental engagement, including lack of transport and lack of communication skills, and suggested that, as well as informal and non-learning-related activities being provided in school, meetings off-site, home visits and flexible meeting times would further encourage parents to participate. She even suggested that meetings held in public houses are an effective way of increasing attendance among fathers, although this clearly would not be an entirely inclusive strategy in a school with a large minority ethnic population opposed to the drinking of alcohol.

Reflection 12.3: Parents in classrooms

In many schools, parents come in to assist teachers in classrooms. From your own experience, how far do you go along with the points below?

Parental involvement should be a part of accepted practice within agreed policies. Schools should have clear policies for parental involvement and may have a teacher with responsibility for partnership with parents.

There is always room for conflict and misunderstanding to arise between the adults in a classroom, and this can be very detrimental to children's learning and behaviour. Lorenz (1998) notes a number of fears among teachers about involving parents in classroom activities that may, or may not, be well-founded:

- Where parents are not paid for their help in class, they may not be reliable.
- Parents may be over-enthusiastic in offering assistance to children.
- There may be breaches of confidentiality.
- Children may show off in front of parents.
- There may be complaints from other parents.
- Parents may favour their own children.
- Parents may criticise teachers inside, or outside, the classroom.

Lorenz's solution is to be proactive in negotiating clear roles and boundaries from the start. She advises:

- discussing and agreeing which skills the parents are offering;
- thinking about parents' degree of confidence in assisting with classroom activities and organising their support in a way that plays to their strengths;
- ensuring parents are fully aware that the teacher is responsible for the group and that the teacher remains in control;
- clarifying what is needed and expected and that the teacher is responsible for the conceptual content of the lesson;
- overtly valuing the help parents offer and not taking parental help for granted;
- limiting the size of the student group working with parents.

Two SENCOs' experiences: Anna and Nickie

Anna, a SENCO in an infant school, identified the relationship between home and school as problematic from an initial audit of the school's SEND provision. Discussions with teachers showed that while in theory they agreed with improving parent partnership, they were unsure how to go about it and some were concerned that it could weaken their position as experts. Using the scale devised by Jones (2004) and based on Dale (1996) (see above), Anna assessed the school as being at level 1 (expert model). Professionals took control and made the decisions regarding children with SEND and the parents appeared to be passive recipients of services. She wrote:

> Teachers often use educational jargon and can sometimes be (unintentionally) insensitive to parents, showing little empathy. Our school is typical of many schools in that it has a range of strategies for making contact with parents, e.g. open evening, school productions, assemblies, prospectus, newsletters, reports and parent–teacher reviews. However, these are all on the teachers' terms and can benefit the teachers rather than the parents. Whilst it was obviously better to discuss children's IEPs with parents rather than give them a couple of minutes to sign them at the end of parent consultations, it was clear that this was not going to be sufficient to develop parental partnerships as needed, or required by the Lamb Inquiry or Code of Practice. [Our system] still involved the teachers imparting knowledge to the parent much more than an equal sharing of ideas.

In order to elicit information from the parents and to develop more effective parental partnerships, Anna decided to hold a less formal coffee morning. All parents of children on the special needs register were invited by an informal flyer, followed up by asking (and gently reminding) each parent two days before if they could attend.

> The coffee morning took place after drop off in the morning, in the staff room. Younger siblings were welcome, (so as to make it easier for some parents to attend), the set-up was informal. Parents chatted and had refreshments until all the parents were there. I then explained how SEN works in our village school, describing the different methods of identifying children with SEN, how we address this initially through Quality First Teaching, then school-based interventions , then assessment and advice from external agencies. I showed resources and evidence from some of the interventions we use (Fischer Family Trust Wave 3 Intervention (FFT), SpLD base programmes, Stile resources, 100 high frequency words etc.).

The parents had a chance to chat between themselves very informally to enable them to say what they really thought and raise issues which mattered to them rather than respond to an agenda set by Anna. There were two key areas from the discussion: (1) ways to support children at home; and (2) communication issues.

Anna reflected on this:

> Overall, the SENCO Coffee morning worked well on three levels – it allowed the participants to get to know each other better, to get to know me better and vice versa and it also allowed me to discover issues which concerned the parents and to try to rectify any problems and inform any gaps in knowledge and therefore develop more effective parent partnerships.

She concluded that:

> In order to achieve better communication and therefore more effective parental partnerships I have organised more SENCO coffee mornings and drop in sessions on a half termly basis (as preferred by the majority of the parents at my initial coffee morning) and am in the process of setting up a SENCO email address which is available to parents to email me directly. Canter and Canter (2001), Ekins (2011), and Goodall et al. (2011) explain that we need to find different ways of communicating with parents as they will have different needs; some will be working and cannot attend school time meetings, some have child care issues etc., therefore by introducing different methods of communication I hope to make it easier for parent–SENCO and SENCO–parent contact.
>
> (Fenelon, unpublished)

A second SENCO, Nickie, noticed that the SEN register showed clearly that Year 3 had the highest number of children identified as requiring extra provision to support their mathematical thinking, with 10 children having a Group Education Plan in place. From conversations with the Year 3 class teacher, it became clear that although provision had been put in place to help the children identified make more progress in mathematics, she had concerns in regard to the negative attitudes that some children in her class were showing towards Numeracy. In particular these were issues regarding anxiety in relation to mathematics homework and lack of motivation to join in classroom activities and discussions focussed on mathematics. In addition, homework tasks, especially those that were Numeracy focused, were not being completed, and, as a result, children were not acquiring basic skills such as facility with times tables that would enable them to further develop their problem-solving skills. Initial conversations between Nickie and parents of children in this year group also highlighted that the anxiety that their children were showing in regards to Numeracy and the tension that homework activities often created, were a worry to them also and an area that needed addressing.

Nickie therefore decided to set up a trial (Chamberlain, unpublished) with what she called 'Go-home maths bags', both to improve lines of communication with parents and also to investigate how these numeracy games played at home might help to build up 'a network of cognitive connections between the four experiences of mathematics: concrete experiences, symbols, language and pictures' (Haylock and Cockburn, 2009: 9). The playing of maths games can help to ensure that these links are reinforced and so build mathematical understanding. The Field Report (2010: 5) outlines very clearly how the links between poverty, parent education, good parenting and the opportunities for learning and development can influence a child's life chances. It also recommends (2010: 93) that parents undertake activities with their child(ren) 'which have a positive effect on their development, such as… playing with letters and numbers'.

Nickie hoped that this trial would result in more frequent dialogue (by phone, face-to-face, and written comments) between class teacher and parents regarding difficulties or successes experienced by pupils, especially if this dialogue was instigated by the home. She also anticipated that it would help alleviate some of the associated stress and anxiety that are often associated with homework activities, and the accompanying lack of self-esteem that can come with it by providing an enjoyable way of consolidating mathematic concepts at home, the use of maths games.

Nickie describes how she set up the trial:

> A resource was purchased by school at a cost of £160 that contained 30 games per level, each in its own zip lock bag, and that came complete with game, instructions on how to play it, and any resources that were needed (dice, game card, dominoes, spinners). As the children I intended to target were academically below the level of an average yr3 child, I chose to use the level that was designed to use with year 2. My rationale for this was that I very much wanted pupils to have an immediate sense of success when playing the games, to avoid coming across mathematical concepts that they were unsure of, and to be able to 'lead' the play somewhat when using it with either their parents or siblings. In addition to the resources that were included, I supplemented it with mathematical apparatus from school that the children were familiar using (Numicon, number lines).
>
> I held an informal meeting with three of the children's parents to discuss the advantages of using maths games to engage children's learning, to lead them through the maths games on offer, and to highlight the kind of mathematic language to use when playing the games with their child (the other parent was spoken to over the phone).
>
> The children were encouraged to play the games at home as many times as they wanted to, and to exchange the games with myself when they required a different one. A booklet was designed to record the game that was used, the amount of times played, and space for the children to record 'what I found easy' and 'what I found hard'. Space was also provided for parents to add comments on the success of the game.
>
> The views of the class teacher were sought at the beginning and end of the trial as were those of the parent and pupil.

When questioned as to their views in regards to mathematics before the intervention, the majority of the children expressed some negative perceptions. One child commented 'When there are really hard sums I feel angry and frustrated.' This negativity was most pronounced in relation to their views on the current homework set. Again the majority expressed dislike at completing homework especially the retention and learning of times tables. They were perceptive in their evaluation of their own academic achievement, with many of them aware of their own strengths and weaknesses.

At the end of the five-week intervention, the most marked difference in perceptions were those surrounding the subject of homework. All were very enthusiastic in regards to playing the mathematics games, commenting on how much they enjoyed playing them with their family. One child commented though that 'the games were good, but it would have been nice to have more people to play with'. They also expressed fewer negative perceptions in regards to maths lessons and themselves as learners, one in particular, stating 'especially addition Lotto, I'm really good at that'.

When questioned before the intervention on the attitudes of their child in relation to the current mathematic homework set, the parents were unanimous in the negative perceptions their child displayed and the high level of tension and stress that completing it created. This was most evident in the responses from one parent, 'a lot of the time it is a real struggle... He will stop listening and get upset.' And in response to the question on the time spent on mathematic homework, 'as little time as possible'.

When questioned again at the end of the intervention, the feedback given echoed and reinforced the views expressed by both the teacher and pupils themselves. The parents commented on how significantly the levels of tension had been reduced, and how enjoyable playing the games had been. Additionally, the parents noticed in their children an increased confidence and willingness to use mathematic language, 'he was able to explain the games to me... he even corrected me when I got a couple of answers wrong' which again was most obvious in the perceptions in relation to Child C.

The time period over which the trial operated was too short to facilitate a reliable level of measured improvement in mathematics learning. However, Nickie noted that the child who played the games most frequently with his parents appeared to gain the greatest benefit in terms of increased confidence and increased classroom participation.

Although some parents were not engaged, the benefits felt by other parents, the enjoyment felt by children playing the games and the positive impact on their self-esteem make this a trial worth expanding and investing in further as a school.

The SENCO and senior leadership team made the decision to purchase an additional mathematics games resources to cover the age range Years 1–4 at a further investment of £380 in order to widen the scope of the trial, with an aim to enhance the provision already in place to nurture effective home-school links.

Summary

The *Review of Best Practice in Parental Engagement* (DfE, 2011: 21) recommends that if 'school-home links are to be sustainable and supportive of children's attainment, they will form part of a whole school approach to parental engagement and be informed by an on-going needs assessment'. To draw this chapter to a conclusion, therefore, you might like to complete the template in Table 12.1 to audit the working relationship between school or college and the families of children and young people with SEND.

Table 12.1 Whole-school needs analysis related to parental/family involvement

How does the school involve parents/carers in the progress and development of their children?

How are parents/carers involved when the school is concerned about a child's progress?

Areas of strength

Areas for improvement

What opportunities are there for parents/carers to express a concern about a child's progress?

Areas of strength

Areas for improvement

How effectively does the school respond?

Areas of strength

Areas for improvement

How does the school attempt to involve parent/carers in planning provision to meet the special learning needs of a child?

How does the school work with parents/carers to plan short-term targets and to review progress?

Areas of strength

Areas for improvement

What information is made available to parents/carers about the special educational provision at the school, and in the local authority?

How are parents/carers informed of appropriate sources of support that may be available?

Areas of strength

Areas for improvement

What is the procedure for parental/carers' complaints about the effectiveness of the special provision made to meet pupils' special learning needs?

How is this complaints procedure evaluated?

Areas of strength

Areas for improvement

13

Collaborating with other professionals

Introduction

Multi-agency collaborative working practices have been encouraged by the government in England as paramount for the safety of children since the 1980s, with subsequent recommendations about training in joint working practices for health professionals, social workers, teachers and others (Dunhill, 2009). For teachers, parents and families, knowing when and how to interact with the vast array of professionals, inside and outside the school, who may become involved with a particular child is very important to the student's welfare and progress, albeit confusing and time-consuming on occasions.

This chapter will outline the range of people with whom the SENCO might be expected to work and their likely role: teaching assistants (TAs), outside agencies (Health and Social Care in particular), and so on. It will go on to discuss:

- research associated with the usefulness and cost-effectiveness of TAs in addressing the needs of young people with SEND in classrooms:
    - the challenges raised by some recent research studies;
    - ways that some experienced SENCOs have addressed these challenges;
    - real-life examples of useful TA role descriptors;
- the role of specialist external agencies in supporting provision for SEND in schools and colleges: when and how to seek advice. This will also include consideration of the issue of the 'Local Offer', that is the local authorities' published list of specialist support available in the local area that is required in recent (2014) legislation, with examples of good practice;
- the legal requirements in relation to collaboration with Health and Social Care agencies over Education, Health and Care plans. This discussion will include:
    - long-standing challenges in achieving effective inter-agency working;
    - examples of good practice.

Effective use of support staff in classrooms

Teaching assistants (TAs) and other support staff – 'paraprofessionals' - are part of a large workforce in schools. The rapid expansion in numbers of TAs has shifted the focus of TAs' work from simply preparing resources, general assistance, clearing up, student welfare, and so on, to duties much more clearly focused on student learning and achievement (Wearmouth, 2009). Most schools employ assistants in classrooms but their roles vary. They may, or may not, have some formal training.

Ideally partnerships between teachers and support staff should be built on a foundation of mutual respect and trust and a common understanding of how to address the difficulties in learning that some students might face. Having said this, positive relationships are not created automatically. They often develop out of accommodations made by all parties as they negotiate their ways of working and establish their working relationships. The potential for clashes inherent in a situation where, traditionally and conventionally, one professional has been seen to be in control alone is clear (Wearmouth, 2009). If the adults are not in close agreement, or do not get on, students will play one off against another. Students often have a strong sense of where power and control lies in the classroom and of fairness.

Cremin et al. (2003) comment that having teaching assistants in a classroom does not necessarily lead to improved learning and behaviour for students. Balshaw's (1991) description of LSAs, for example, as potentially being 'overgrown students', 'piggy in the middle', 'spies in the classroom' or 'dogsbodies' illustrates how things can go seriously wrong with the implied lack of respect that is unhealthy for everyone.

In the past twenty years there has been a huge investment in increasing levels of support staff, and providing training. Between 1997 and 2003, there was a 99 per cent increase in TAs in English schools but limited research evidence about their impact and effectiveness. The evidence that existed was mostly based on teachers' reports. Teachers had been largely positive and reported that in classrooms supported by TAs there was more one to one attention and support for children with SEN, more productive group work, creative/practical lessons, more effective classroom management and a positive effect on children's learning outcomes (Blatchford et al., 2004). However, relatively few studies provided evidence on which to base conclusions about impact beyond such teacher reports. A systematic literature review (Alborz et al., 2009) concluded that, if TAs are to make an impact on pupil progress, certain prerequisites need to be taken into consideration:

- TAs can help pupils with literature and language problems to make significant learning gains but they need to be trained and supported to do so.
- 'Sensitive' TA support can facilitate pupil engagement in learning and social activities with teacher and peers, but these TAs need to be skilled at encouraging interaction and aware when pupils need to undertake self-directed actions.
- TAs can also promote social and emotional adjustment but they are less successful in therapeutic tasks for children with emotional and behavioural problems.
- For teachers, use of TAs can allow them to engage pupils in more creative and practical activities, class-related workload can be reduced, but management workload can be increased.

Findings from a study that used a number of indicators to evaluate the effectiveness of TAs in schools, the Deployment and Impact of Support Staff (DISS) project (Blatchford et al., 2009), indicated that:

- TAs impacted positively on teachers' workloads, job satisfaction and levels of stress. They were able to focus their attention on individual pupils and minimise disruptive behaviour.
- TAs spent the majority of their time working with small groups or 1:1, usually those pupils with SEN or lower attaining, much more rarely with high and middle attaining pupils.
- Teachers tended to spend the majority of their time leading or supervising the whole class. Comparatively little of their time was spent working with groups or individual pupils, and when they did, it was rarely with pupils with SEN.
- TAs were often expected to lead interventions which tended to be separate from the whole class teaching and learning environment.
- In general, pupils receiving the greatest support from TAs made less progress than similar pupils who had less TA support. This remained the case even after allowance had been made for influencing factors such as SEN, English as an additional language (EAL), free school meals (FSM) and prior attainment.
- TAs tended to be focused on finishing a set task, rather than encouraging independent learning through open questioning and focused discussion, whereas teachers tended to extend learning through specific feedback and more detailed explanations of new concepts to ensure understanding.
- There was a consistently expressed view that teachers and TAs had little or no designated planning and feedback time. This often leads to TAs feeling insufficiently prepared and dependent on teacher input to gain subject knowledge and task requirements.
- Teachers had very often not received training on deploying and managing TAs.

One conclusion of the project was that the lack of impact on pupil achievement related to the way in which TAs were poorly prepared for the pedagogical role they were usually deployed to do, with a tendency to be reactive rather than proactive when addressing pupil needs, thus creating pupil dependency on them rather than fostering independent learning. Some of the recommendations from this report relate to preparedness, deployment and the practice of support staff:

- *Preparedness*: more needs to be done to prepare teachers with the necessary skills and preparation to manage support staff and to prepare classroom based, support staff for their role in schools, especially for the pedagogical role with pupils. More time should be available for joint planning and feedback, and for considering how TAs might be deployed effectively.
- *Deployment:* support staff should not routinely support lower attaining pupils. Instead, pupils in most need should get more teacher time. Teachers should take responsibility for curriculum and pedagogical planning for all pupils in the class.
- *Practice:* conceptualising the pedagogical role of TAs needs to be built into professional development, school deployment decisions and the management, support and monitoring of support staff.

A further study, the Effective Deployment of Teaching Assistants (EDTA) project (Blatchford et al., 2012), put the recommendations from DISS into effect in ten primary schools over the course of one year. The evaluation showed that the trials conducted by each school improved the way school leaders and teachers thought about and deployed TAs:

- Preparedness: TAs' pre-lesson preparation was improved over the year, as were the quality and clarity of teachers' lesson plans. Teachers made more effort to meet with TAs before lessons, and some schools adjusted TAs' hours of work to create meeting time. The tasks and expectations of TA roles were made explicit in planning.
- Deployment: TAs worked more often with middle- and high attaining pupils, spent less time in a passive role and withdrew pupils as little as possible from the classroom to help maintain contact with the mainstream curriculum, and teachers spent more time with low-attaining pupils and those with SEN. There was a greater emphasis on peer support, collaborative group work and self-help strategies in the classroom.
- In terms of practice, there was a growing focus on changing the nature TA/pupil talk and giving pupils longer to respond, on open, rather than closed, questioning, on enhancing pupil understanding rather than task completion, and on encouraging autonomy in learning rather than adult dependency.
- Teachers also became more aware of the significance of the role of the TA, and TAs felt more valued and appreciated, enabling them to carry out their tasks with greater confidence.

A recent survey of 210 school leaders by UNISON (2013) generated overwhelming support for the role and impact of TAs, with the above findings being considered too generalised. Recruitment, deployment, management and training are often inconsistent, but, when systematic, TA impact on raising attainment is deemed to be effective. Interestingly, nearly all respondents stated that they employed TAs to work with individual pupils, small groups and those with SEN, adding weight to the possibility that teachers are delegating their teaching responsibility for lower-attaining pupils to, predominantly, less well-qualified TAs.

Enhancing TAs' (cost) effectiveness: one SENCO's experience

Karen, a SENCO in a primary school, decided to investigate ways to enhance the effectiveness of TAs in her school after discussion following a senior leadership team (SLT) learning walk had suggested that TAs were inconsistently deployed. Some were actively engaged in meaningful small group discussion or 1:1 intervention, while others were carrying out administrative tasks and many simply sat passively listening to the teacher. Subsequent SLT discussion identified this as an area of concern. With no school policy in place to offer guidance in recognised good practice, and the expectations of the TA role, differences in interpretation and efficiency of deployment were inevitable. It was therefore necessary to establish to what extent teachers were directing their TAs effectively, and how TAs were actually supporting and promoting learning within the classroom. With such a potentially valuable, and expensive, resource available to support pupil learning, it was imperative that TAs be utilised effectively to maximise pupil learning.

With an annual spend of over £100,000 just on classroom-based TAs, inconsistent progress of pupils with SEN across the school and the School Development Plan (SDP) focus on 'Closing the Gap' to improve outcomes for pupils with SEN, it was crucial that the school made the best possible use of this asset to ensure that all pupils were receiving high-quality learning support.

All TAs needed to be managed and deployed for maximum impact on pupil progress. However, it was also recognised that pupil and class needs differed, dependent on many factors including age, so one generic format or expectation of TA deployment was not necessarily appropriate either. It was anticipated that this analysis of how TAs are deployed in classrooms across the school, the perceptions and expectations of their role held by both teachers and TAs and any potential data evidence, would enable the SLT to make their expectations of TA deployment more clearly defined, thereby promoting optimum pupil progress.

The methods of data collection included:

- A learning walk to gain an initial, overall, impression of TA deployment.
- Identification of current teacher and TA perceptions of their deployment (through questionnaires) and triangulation of evidence through observations to confirm what was actually happening.
- Data analysis of progress of pupils with SEN in each class, excluding those with statements, overall and by core subject as an indicator of TA impact on progress, followed by comparison of data with the type and level of TA support to which these children had access.
- Interviews with TAs to establish their perceptions of their role in the classroom (see Table 13.1).
- Analysis of TA role descriptors to ensure relevance of expectations.
- Investigation of pupil/small group intervention support: whether targets and outcomes were specified and the accuracy of record-keeping.
- Scrutiny of teachers' planning documents to establish level of differentiation and clarity of teacher direction of TA deployment.
- Audit of availability of dedicated shared planning/talk time between teachers and TAs.

Findings from the analysis of the data and their implications indicated:

- TAs estimated that they spent 54 per cent of their time working with lower-attaining pupils, with teachers only dedicating 9 per cent of theirs. This was in line with the findings of both the DISS and UNISON reports which highlight how TAs spent a disproportionate amount of their time with these pupils. The figure of 9 per cent of teacher-directed input towards these pupils was totally inadequate and likely to impact negatively on these children's progress, as the majority of the teaching they received was being delivered by their 1:1 TA, who was not necessarily sufficiently skilled to do so.

Table 13.1 Teaching assistant questionnaire

How would you describe your role within the classroom?
Do you have a current job description – are you familiar with it and is it sufficiently detailed? Has it ever been reviewed?
Does your actual role reflect your job description?
What TA training have you had? Qualifications? What would you like?
Do you have designated planning/talking time to discuss pupil progress and next steps for learning?
Is communication adequate? If not, how would you like things to change?
How are plans shared with you? Do you have a plan for every lesson?
Do you always know what your role is in a lesson and what you are expected to achieve? Are you fully prepared?
Do you work equally amongst all groups?
What percentage of your time is spent doing interventions with targeted pupils as opposed to general group support?
Do you collect any formal evidence of pupil progress?
Do you know which children are on the SEN register and what their learning needs are? Are IEPs/Statements shared with you?
What is the most enjoyable aspect of your job?
What is the least enjoyable aspect?

- Lack of dedicated time for communication between teachers and TAs was highlighted by both, again in line with the DISS report findings, with the vast majority of pre- and post-lesson discussion being brief and ad hoc.
- Another cause for concern was the extent to which 84 per cent of TAs felt that they were left to plan and prepare interventions with no teacher input. Greater clarification on roles and expectations in this area was required. Time needed to be set aside for teacher/TA communication, both in order to promote pupil outcomes, but also to conform with the job descriptor, 'In conjunction with the classroom teacher, adapt lessons to meet the needs of individual children and small groups', as specified in the principal accountabilities of their job description.
- Some 32 per cent of TAs stated that they gained their subject knowledge by listening to the teacher's lesson delivery as part of the class audience, so, in effect, had no additional information to share with pupils to broaden their knowledge and understanding. Some 42 per cent of TAs felt that they only learnt the task expectations, and their role in achieving this, when the teacher informed the whole class, rather than having any time to prepare themselves in ways to enhance pupil learning. Additional training was required to enable TAs to optimally perform the role, particularly in terms of how to best support children

with significant development needs, behaviour management and monitoring and tracking progress and providing feedback.

- Observations of pupil–TA interactions indicated a lack of open questioning, with pupils making some suggestions, but then often copying TA-generated work from a whiteboard into their books, signifying a definite lack of independent learning. While there was task differentiation in lessons, this did not generally extend to those pupils with SEN, for whom there was little or no evidence of additional differentiation, particularly in Key Stage 1, an observation that was supported by the subsequent planning scrutiny. The observation pro-forma is included in Appendix B8.
- A detailed literacy and numeracy planning scrutiny of all teachers' plans indicated an overall inconsistency in identifying which groups should be teacher or TA led, no clear rotation among groups, and neither the role of the TA within the group, nor pupil outcomes, were made sufficiently clear. The variability of planning in regards to TA deployment and differentiation of tasks and activities for pupils who experienced difficulties in learning led Karen to compile a planning checklist in order to raise standards, particularly in ensuring that the class teacher directs equal, or more, of their high quality teaching input towards lower-achieving pupils in order to maximise their progress, while ensuring that TA support is more clearly specified and rotated across all groups, rather than primarily towards the lower-attaining pupils.

Reflection 13.1: Checklist for planning to include children with SEND in classrooms

Here is the checklist compiled to guide teachers' lesson planning to incorporate the work of TAs in their classrooms. You might like to consider how far this list might be appropriate for teachers in your own context:

- Ensure all gifted and talented (G&T) and pupils with SEN are clearly identified on plans, along with current levels.
- Incorporate IEP/G&T targets into plans – perhaps in a box at the top of unit plans – to ensure that they are being worked towards and enable on-going evaluation.
- When appropriate, link IEP targets to learning objectives/success criteria.
- Always include an achievable success criterion that reflects the task you have set your pupils with SEN.
- If pupils identified as having SEN are being supported by an adult within the lower attainers' group, even if on a differentiated task, make this clear.
- Make clear which adult is working with each group, on a rotational basis, to ensure class teacher spends *at least* as much time working with G&T and SEN pupils as others to ensure they receive sufficient high quality teaching input in order to optimise progress.
- If possible, direct any 1:1 TAs to work with another group to enable you to work with their named child for at least one literacy and numeracy lesson every week.

- Differentiate effectively, and differently, for pupils with SEN, otherwise why have you identified them as having SEN? Need to identify SEN task and support very specifically, linked to success criteria.
- Specify what, and with whom, teaching assistants are doing at all times of the lesson, including whole class input and plenary, rather than just stating 'TA to work with LAPs', or TA to 'work with SEN as necessary to build and develop skills'. Make clear what the task is and ensure that your TA is prepared in advance with sufficient subject knowledge to be able to open up discussion with their group.
- If you do not have a large number of children with SEN, you could write their maths/literacy targets next to their name in the box at the top of the plan which identifies pupils with SEN. This would make it easier to monitor when a target has been met and respond more quickly to setting a new one.
- Ensure next steps for learning are clearly specified and appropriate to all pupils.
- Consider when it may be beneficial for pupils with SEND to be pre-taught new concepts, so that they can participate more fully during carpet time, either by CT or TA, and include on plans. This is a good use of TA support as it enables pupils with SEND to access whole class teaching more effectively. A 1:1 TA could work with all the SEND children in the class, or even year group, the previous afternoon to deliver this. However, you do need to have effective communication with your TA so they know what the next teaching steps are.

- There was insufficient evidence to make a judgement on the impact of the interventions in years 1, 2 and 6 as the data related to broad National Curriculum levels rather than more specific entry and exit criteria. This further highlights the need for more detailed provision mapping in order to evaluate the effectiveness of interventions.
- Pupils with SEN in Key Stage 1 made less progress than pupils overall. However, in Key Stage 2, these pupils made better than average progress in both reading and maths. Interestingly, pupils with statements of SEN made accelerated progress in all areas of the curriculum, suggesting that their 1:1 TA support was highly effective in maximising their progress.
- This research generally supported the findings of the DISS report in relation to TA deployment, with TAs spending the vast majority of their time supporting LAPs and those with SEN, during which time there was a demonstrable lack of child-initiated talk and independent learning, with pupils heavily reliant on TA guidance in completing tasks. Lack of talking, planning and feedback time was also highlighted as an area of concern, concurring with Blatchford et al.'s findings that TAs often felt poorly prepared and consequently lacked confidence within the classroom.

Taking into account all of these factors, and referring to the EDTA project's findings regarding the importance of taking account of the characteristics of TAs, their preparedness, management and deployment, it seemed likely that a policy governing all these areas would ensure greater consistency and effectiveness in their practice. The SENCO, in discussion with the senior management team, decided the following:

- A TA policy was to be implemented, to clarify their role and level of expected support for pupils and teachers, the curriculum and school wide responsibilities.
- When recruiting in future, there would be a minimum qualification requirement, and an expectation that TAs would be observed working with a group of children before being offered employment.
- An effective performance management process would be introduced, aimed at raising standards and encouraging the TAs' own continual professional development.
- Regular training would be offered to TAs to improve their performance through enhanced knowledge of the curriculum, effective questioning to enhance independent learning, behaviour management strategies or any other identified areas of need.
- All teachers and TAs would have timetabled planning and discussion time to improve communication and enable TAs to be more prepared and proactive within the classroom.
- Teachers' plans would be scrutinised, focusing on TAs being clearly directed and prepared for their role within every lesson and explicit task differentiation, particularly for those pupils with SEN. Plans would need to be shared in advance and clearly specify the rotation of both TA and teacher across all groups to ensure quality teaching is received by all pupils.
- A number of issues would be addressed through a radical change in TA deployment: TAs being left to plan and deliver interventions in isolation from the teacher with very little support; lack of clear focus and purpose in the TAs' work; slow response to identified need; inconsistent provision mapping. While all classes would still receive some, albeit reduced, classroom TA support, a new, more holistic, learning mentor role would be developed. Key Stage 1, lower and upper Key Stage 2 would each have 20 hours access weekly to a learning mentor TA who would support specifically targeted children identified with needs ranging through academic, behavioural, social and home support-based. All these TAs are highly experienced and would work under the direction of the SENCO, addressing a range of components contributing to poor academic success, with early identification leading to effective intervention to promote enhanced pupil achievement. The school provision map would be adapted to monitor the impact and cost effectiveness of this initiative.
- Learning mentors would maintain detailed records and map provision carefully in order to justify their role.
- An on-going and focused planning scrutiny with regular class drop-ins and learning walks is essential to ensure teachers are continually directing their TAs effectively to facilitate the independent learning of pupils. Simply writing a policy would not, in itself, achieve this. Teachers would need to be trained and encouraged to adopt a more progressive approach to TA deployment.

One of the exemplar job descriptions that was subsequently developed for TAs is included in Reflection 13.2.

Reflection 13.2: Level 2 exemplar job description for TAs

You might like to consider how far this job description would be useful in your own context.

Job Title: Teaching Assistant – Level 2
School/Service: [name]
Reports to: [name]
Grade: Level 2
Location: [name]
Hours: [number] (subject to maximum 32.5 hours per week)

Role:
Support the classroom teacher to facilitate the active participation of children in the academic and social activities of the school. Contribute to raising standards of achievement for all pupils.

Principal Accountabilities

1. **Support for children**
   - In conjunction with the classroom teacher, adapt lessons to meet the needs of individual children and small groups.
   - Take responsibility for delivering learning activities with small groups who would benefit from a different learning approach as agreed.
   - Establish and maintain supportive relationships with individual pupils, small groups and parents/carers to ensure they understand and can achieve the tasks.
   - Provide learning support to children with significant care needs, or where English is not their first language.
   - Support children with significant development needs, e.g. cognitive ability, EBD, learning skills, etc. as directed.
   - Encourage and promote inclusion in the classroom, ensuring all pupils feel involved with tasks and activities.
2. **Support for the curriculum**
   - Support the school curriculum, including literacy and numeracy activities.
   - Suggest areas where ICT might be used to enrich pupil learning.
   - Provide targeted support to enhance learning and improve attainment.
3. **Support for the teacher**
   - Assist in maintaining class records and contribute to reports on pupil progress and development as directed.
   - Monitor and track progress and provide feedback to assist in developing individual plans for children with special needs.
   - Contribute to the planning and evaluation of work programmes for individual pupils and groups.
   - Organise the learning environment and develop classroom resources as required.
   - Undertake support activities for the teacher as required, e.g. photocopying, preparation of materials, mounting displays.
   - Contribute to the management of pupil behaviour, including anticipating and taking action to prevent potential problems arising.

4. Support for the school

- Develop and maintain effective working relationships with other staff and parents or carers.
- Contribute to the maintenance of a safe and healthy environment.
- Attend and actively participate in staff meetings.
- Participate in and support the professional development of other teaching assistants as required.
- Assist in facilitating school events, e.g. school plays, events.

(Brindley, unpublished)

Collaboration between professionals

There are two particular areas in schools where work with other professionals is important: classroom learning and child protection. Crucial to the success of implementing the terms of the 2014 Children and Families Act Part 3 is the effectiveness of multi-agency working across children's services, health and education. Assessment of children and young people's special educational needs and disabilities and additional support needs, whether statutory or not, may require effective inter-agency collaboration in order to ensure that they are supported with the special/additional provision that they need to engage with the school or college curriculum and make good progress.

The new statutory assessment of SEND and production of Education, Health and Care plans introduced by the Children and Families Act 2014, by definition, require collaboration. In England also there is the issue of the continuation of the Common Assessment Framework (CAF) process described below, which, in some ways, appears to duplicate the EHC assessment process. The relationship between the CAF process and that of EHCs does not seem to be entirely clear at the time of writing (May, 2015). Some LAs have published documents that differentiate between the two, for example, in Hertfordshire:

> CAF is a separate early intervention. The EHC plan and arrangements are for those children and young people with complex needs. With the new EHC plan arrangements, the CAF will continue to be used where appropriate.
>
> (Hertfordshire Special Educational Needs and Disability Pathfinder, n/d)

In Devon LA however, the parent partnership service advises that assessment carried out through the CAF might be incorporated into plans for children whose needs are not so severe that they require statutory assessment:

> For children who do not meet the level of need required for a statutory assessment, parents and carers may be offered a plan that is non-statutory, but that still identifies their child's needs and the support that will be put in place. This might incorporate other assessments that are carried out through education, health and social care, such as the current Common Assessment Framework.
>
> (Devon Parent Partnership Service, n/d, www.parentpartnershipdevon.org.uk)

Inter-agency collaboration in child protection issues and the CAF

The concept of 'special educational needs' covers a wide area that may go well beyond school and the conventional realm of 'education' into, sometimes, health and welfare. In the past it has often been quite difficult for schools to work closely with outside agencies to protect the welfare of individual students seen by teachers as at risk of injury or abuse. In terms of child welfare, there is a long history of problems in inter-agency work in, for example, the exchange of information between agencies and of disputes over responsibility for offering particular services, sometimes with duplication of interventions by different agencies working on the same case (Roaf and Lloyd, 1995). The three primary care agencies, Education, Health and Social Services, have tended to operate to different legislative frameworks with different priorities and definitions of what constitutes a need. Lack of clear structure to determine responsibilities in inter-agency working could also generate considerable tension, especially when resources were under pressure. The loser has been the client and his or her parents or carer. Roaf and Lloyd (1995) quote the frustration of one young person's parents who commented that their son had been offending while truanting from school. They went on to say that they felt like tennis balls because education professionals said it was a problem for social services, and social services said it was a problem for education, and they were just going backwards and forwards from one to the other.

System failure is illustrated, most notably, in recent years, in the case of the tragic death of Victoria Climbié, a child known to be at risk by both educational and social services. In 2003, alongside the formal response to the report into her death, the government published a Green Paper, *Every Child Matters*, followed by the Children Act (2004) that gave legal force to five interdependent outcomes (DfES, 2004). The clear failure in the system re-stated the need for closer co-operation between agencies which exist to support children in difficulties and their families or carers. The 'Every Child Matters' (ECM) agenda sought to resolve these difficulties by unifying the range of children's services. All local education authorities combined with other services to become local authorities (LAs). One important implication for all teachers, particularly classroom teachers, is to listen carefully to what students say and how they behave, and work closely with, and under the guidance of, the teacher(s) designated to oversee the safety and well-being of the students in the school.

As part of this agenda, a CAF for use across the children's workforce has been developed to provide a shared framework for enabling decisions 'about how best to meet [children's] needs, in terms of both what the family can do and also what services could be provided' (CWDC, 2009: para 1.11). As a result of the common assessment discussion, concerns about the child might be resolved, or particular actions for the professional undertaking the CAF and his or her service might be agreed with a date for review and monitoring progress. Alternatively, actions might be identified for other agencies. This involves sharing the assessment with these agencies, subject to the appropriate consent of the child or young person/family; and forming a team around the child (TAC) to support the child or young person. The actions needed would be agreed with the other agencies, and a plan and responsibilities for delivering the actions recorded on the CAF form (CWDC, 2009).

Clearly, in the attempt to ensure the 'joined-up thinking' that is required by the 2004 Children Act and the ECM agenda, in schools there is a potential overlap between assessment associated with provision for special educational needs and that carried out for the CAF. However, the CAF is not intended to replace other statutory assessments, but to complement or be integrated with them. The CAF is also not intended for assessment of a child where there is any suggestion of harm. Guidance given by the CWDC (2009: para 1.4) states: 'The CAF is not for a child or young person about whom you have concerns that they might be suffering, or may be at risk of suffering, harm. In such instances, you should follow your Local Safeguarding Children Board (LSCB) safeguarding procedures without delay.'

So far there have been mixed reports of the effectiveness of integrated children's services in addressing children's needs. In a study of 14 local authorities (Kinder et al., 2008), children, young people and parents reported a range of improvements in outcomes: getting on well with school work, feeling safer and feeling happier. Practitioners, however, raised a number of concerns, including workload implications, a reported lack of sign-up from some agencies, for example schools and health, issues around communication and leadership, loss of professional identity and distinctiveness and resource issues and different service priorities that could inhibit the embedding of integrated children's services in some instances.

In 2009, Laming confirmed that significant problems remained in the 'day-to-day reality of working across organisational boundaries and cultures, sharing information to protect children' (Laming, 2009: para 1.6). There were training issues still to be resolved and data systems to be improved (para 1.5). Ultimately children's safety depends on individual staff having the time and the skill 'to understand the child or young person and their family circumstances'. Laming also felt that 'Staff across frontline services... need to be able to notice signs of distress in children of all ages, but particularly amongst very young children who are not able to voice concerns and for whom bedwetting, head-banging and other signs may well be a cry for help' (para 3.1).

It is obvious that where cultures and core professional beliefs conflict, multiagency working is likely to be inhibited (Nethercott, 2015). Key to effective multiagency working (Atkinson et al., 2007) is the establishment of clear and realistic aims and objectives that are understood by everyone, with a shared vision and culture and strategic management commitment and drive.

Co-location and the improved lines of communication that can result from this (Atkinson et al., 2007) can enhance common values and the development of a shared vision. Having said this, however, there is some evidence (Collins and McCray, 2012) that professionally qualified workers from education, health and social care backgrounds may be less willing to include practitioners from voluntary organisations with a lower, vocational, level of qualifications, possibly as a result of concerns about issues of confidentiality. Collins and McCray concluded that the inclusive, co-operative process that has been envisaged in policy is not yet reflected in practice, hence casting doubt on whether professionals yet have the capability to deliver services within a multi-agency environment.

As Nethercott (2015) notes, reports from many child protection reviews within the UK over the past twenty years (Laming, 2003; Reder and Duncan 2003; Brandon et al., 2008; Brandon et al., 2009; RBSCB 2012) have concluded that a lack of communication between agencies has contributed to the death or serious abuse of a child. Communication difficulties may include the problems created by the use of differing terminologies (Taylor and Daniel 1999) as well as the unwillingness at times to become involved in difficult situations, including those relating (Corby, 2006) to child protection.

The issue of professional identity is of crucial importance in considering how to establish effective collaboration among the various agencies. Working together may lead to greater understanding of the roles of other professions (Whiting et al., 2008). However, it may also often result in a sense of threat to the individual's sense of his or her own professional identity with a consequent decrease in collaboration within the multi-agency team (Hudson, 2002). Particularly in teams with no clearly defined responsibilities communication may be at a surface level, but with underlying tensions resulting in avoidant behaviours and little action by the group (Stuart, 2012).

Challenges in developing Education, Health and Care plans

A number of 'Key challenges and enabling factors' were identified during the piloting of EHC plans (DfE, 2014f: 14). In some cases, these issues were interpreted as 'fundamental to the new process' (DfE, 2014f). The first identified challenge was 'ensuring sufficiency and consistency of multi-agency working' that might be addressed by:

- increased levels of strategic and operational commitment to contribute to the new process;
- provision of clear guidance to all professionals detailing expectations of how, when and why they should be involved;
- creation of 'champions' or 'spearheads' for individual agencies (and services within these) to act as the point of contact for the EHC planning process;
- introduction of proportionate approaches to multi-agency working, e.g. use of multi-media to enable capacity-constrained professionals to input to meetings.

The second was 'resourcing the delivery of a more family-centred process' to be addressed by:

- creation of dedicated EHC co-ordinators who have sufficient time to undertake the required family-facing elements of the process, which in turn will mean limiting their caseload;
- adoption of proportionate approaches to key working and family engagement based on the complexity of the child or young person's needs.

Next was 'meeting the reduced 20 week statutory timeframe', potentially to be addressed by:

- alignment of early years and school paperwork to enable efficient translation of pre-referral information into the EHC planning process;
- creating efficiencies between agencies through sharing of assessments and reports;

- introduction of proportionate approaches to multi-agency working, e.g. use of multi-media to enable capacity-constrained professionals to make an input to meetings;
- development of integrated resourcing and funding mechanisms.

Fourth was the 'sharing of information between agencies and with families' that might be achieved by:

- having the family as the holder of all information and paperwork and relying on them to give permission and transfer it from place to place;
- development of an integrated IT system that enables all relevant professionals and families to access the 'live' EHC plan and grants differing levels of permissions for distinct parties to edit the plan.

Fifth was 'increased paperwork' that might need the following:

- providing the EHC plan co-ordinators with sufficient time to draft the summary assessment;
- training for EHC plan co-ordinators in interpreting assessments and drafting in plain English.

Next was 'ensuring all families have the capacity to engage' (p. 17), that might mean:

- time needs to be allocated to EHC plan co-ordinators to allow them to be flexible to family needs;
- EHC plan co-ordinators also need training in communicating expectations and flexibilities to families, and in negotiating time with them;
- providing independent advice and support for families.

Finally (p. 17), there was 'negotiating between family members when conflicts arise' that could involve the following:

- clarity in the Code of Practice about whose views take precedence when there is a difference of opinion between young people and their parents;
- key workers, independent supporters and EHC plan co-ordinators need to be sure to identify any differences at an early stage, perhaps through taking separate soundings from each member of the family;
- they also need to have good negotiation and mediation skills to enable them to conclude an agreed plan.

Summary

In a systematic literature review, *Multi-Agency Working and Its Implications for Practice* (Atkinson et al., 2007), a number of factors were identified as essential to effective multi-agency practice. To summarise and draw this chapter to a conclusion we would like to invite you to have a look at the list in Reflection 13.3 and reflect on the degree to which these factors are evident in any multi-agency working arrangements in which you are involved.

Reflection 13 3: Auditing essential factors in multi-agency partnerships

These are all answers given by practitioners as to what the essential factors in multi-agency partnerships were:

- 'clarifying roles and responsibilities';
- 'securing commitment at all levels . . . engendering trust and mutual respect';
- 'fostering understanding between agencies (e.g. through joint training and recognition of individual expertise)';
- 'developing effective multi-agency processes: ensuring effective communication and information sharing';
- securing the 'necessary resources for multi-agency work and . . . securing adequate and sustained funding (e.g. through pooled budgets';
- 'ensuring continuity of staffing . . . and an adequate time allocation';
- 'ensuring effective leadership . . . although also dependent on effective governance and management arrangements . . . and an effective performance management system';
- 'providing sufficient time for the development of multi-agency working';
- 'the provision of joint training';
- 'agreement of joint aims and objectives'.

14

Developing effective SEND provision

Introduction

This chapter will focus explicitly on clear, high quality examples of initiatives undertaken by SENCOs to develop SEND provision across their schools. It will indicate ways in which practising SENCOs have:

- identified areas of provision requiring improvement;
- identified specific weaknesses within these areas;
- designed interventions to address these weaknesses;
- set out the aims and objectives against which they might later evaluate their interventions;
- implemented and evaluated their work;
- set out the implications for future developments in their school or college SEND provision and ways in which these might be included in the subsequent School or College Development Plan.

Identifying areas for improvement in SEND provision in schools

There are a number of ways in which SENCOs might evaluate the quality of provision for SEND in their school or college. One might be to scrutinise the school provision map for evidence of gaps, and of areas of provision that appear to be less effective in supporting young people to make progress in achievement and behaviour, and so on. Another might be to carry out a formal audit of provision, in discussion with SMT and other staff. Appendix B8 is a suggested template for such an audit that has been used very successfully by many SENCOs working towards the National Award for SEN(D) Co-ordination at the University of Bedfordshire. You might choose to adapt the template for your own purposes, either as a basis for a programme of development in SEND provision, or in preparation for an OFSTED inspection (or both, if appropriate).

Example of an initiative to raise reading levels in a secondary school

The example below of a small-scale intervention to raise the confidence level and reading comprehension of a small cohort of secondary school-aged students was carried out by one SENCO, Claire, on a recent National Award for SEN co-ordination course. It is reported in her own words.

Introduction

Mine is a secondary school in an urban, economically-deprived area of the country. I carried out the whole-school needs analysis and it became obvious that the school's student intake had a significant proportion of each cohort with low literacy levels and that these students did not appear to make satisfactory progress in literacy development after they arrived. I also realised that many of these students attracted money to the school through the pupil premium initiative, so it would be possible to justify pupil premium resources to support an initiative to raise these students' reading levels.

I wanted to know if working intensively to practise reading using peer leaders could improve confidence levels and comprehension of texts for readers. I had hoped an outcome would be that both the readers and the leaders would gain in confidence and motivation from their experience, and that it would raise awareness in the school of the 'need to read'. I also wanted to know if the readers and leaders gained anything else from working together, for example, socially.

A low level of literacy across many students in the school has been an issue repeatedly raised by Ofsted and HMI inspectors. Increasingly, some students with low literacy levels are becoming disaffected and disengaged, and presenting with poor behaviour, believing that they are not capable of achieving. Children become aware of failure very quickly and they lose confidence when they see their classmates making progress whilst they struggle (Wray et al., 2000). I intended to use questionnaires to evaluate the programme and 'Motivation to Learn' (MTL) data (the school's internal measure for motivation/effort) as well as current and predicted National Curriculum Working levels to give a clear indication of student progress.

In my opinion, much of the poor behaviour displayed in lessons is a result of a lack of access to the curriculum due to poor literacy, particularly reading, and particularly amongst boys (commented on in our recent Ofsted inspection, March 2013), as well as poor differentiation and low teacher expectation in some challenging groups. [...] I have little experience of working in the area of literacy, therefore, working with student readers, although new, was something which I needed to develop skills in, as it is such a significant problem in my school. I hoped this would give me more confidence and understanding of this area of special needs provision.

I anticipated that a successful outcome to this intervention could lead to a wider-scale reading intervention programme becoming properly embedded in the school day for more students. I negotiated with the Head the Paired Reading programme, and he agreed to fund the buying of refreshments and the reward for attendance at the end.

Topping (1995) recommends starting with a small target group for the first 'venture'. The advantage of working with a small cohort of students was it allowed me to control the programme logistics, such as chasing students to attend, getting to hear them all read whilst circulating during the sessions, and covering any leader absence with teaching assistants.

It was also important to get parents involved, which I intended to do by setting up parental workshops to explain exactly how I would be working with their children.

I took advice from colleagues in selecting readers. I did not select those with challenging behavioural needs or those with poor attendance records. This was because I was mindful of the Year 10 leaders, and giving them a positive experience of working with others.

After student selection, I checked chronological reading ages of readers to ascertain their level of need (to inform my book selection) and asked the Head of Year 10 for student leader recommendations.

A plan of my intentions

I set out my plan as follows:

- Select readers, from the special needs register with a chronological reading age of 8/9 years or below.
- Select leaders from Year 10 with a chronological reading age at least 2–3 years above their reader. (Using leaders from the same year group: less logistically demanding.)
- Complete a training session to train leaders how to undertake paired reading. (When training leaders, I repeatedly stressed the importance of praise and reassurance, as I did in the parental workshop.) Topping (1995, cited in Wearmouth, 2009: 127) discusses the need for much verbal praise and non-verbal approval from helpers.
- Run a workshop to inform parents of how I and the year 10 students intended to work with their children. Hornby (2000 p.60) notes 'In all paired reading approaches the key factors in ensuring effectiveness are how well parents are trained... to ensure parents correctly implement the procedures at home.'
- Record confidence levels on a scale of 1–10 about how readers felt about their ability to read/read aloud in class at the beginning, middle and end of the programme. 10 = very uncomfortable, 1 = very confident.
- Run the sessions three times per week, either before or after school for approximately 15–20 minutes.
- Readers choose a book of interest and read simultaneously with the leader: 'the tutor modulating speed... giving a good model of competent reading" (Topping, 1995:46) prompting unknown words, after 4–5 seconds.
- Encourage readers to choose to read independently, leaders to speak only if the reader got stuck on a word to model the correct pronunciation. (Described by Glynn and McNaughton, 1985 as 'Pause prompt praise', cited in Wearmouth, 2009: 127.)
- Ask leaders to stop the reader after two paragraphs to review the text to develop the reader's comprehension skills. Gamble and Yates (2008) describe the pausing in narrative as 'an opportunity to predict what may happen next in the story'; an important part of reading comprehension.

- Ask leaders to complete a log book each session to track and record how confidently the reader read each session.
- Assess the reading ages of the students at the end of the school year (just after completion of the paired reading).
- Questionnaires to be completed by readers and leaders at the end of the programme, and teachers to be asked for feedback.

Out of the thirteen chosen readers, four were girls and the remaining nine, boys.

I also collected data on leaders, to determine whether there was enough of a difference between the reader and the leader's chronological reading age (enabling the leader to be supportive).

I was therefore able to collect evidence of progress from the leaders' perspectives from two sources:

- in the form of peer assessment in the log books used each day to record the readers' progress;
- questionnaires to teachers and support staff at the end of the intervention where they were asked to comment on any noticeable changes in student participation or attitude in lessons since the start of the intervention.

I also measured the students' progress using a tick box attitude line/box to describe where they felt they were on the 1–10 scale.

Findings

The results show that all but one student showed an increase in their confidence and self-belief in their perceived reading level/ability.

Fluidity of reading was interrupted by stopping readers every two paragraphs.

Although Topping (1995, cited in Wearmouth 2009: 126) describes the process of paired reading as 'the child choosing high interest reading material irrespective of its readability level from any source', I found that, when readers chose high interest books that were too challenging, their confidence level dipped initially. However, throughout the programme, readers and leaders worked together to record progress in a Reader's Log book. As Goodlad (1998: 238) suggests: 'Initial bonding occurs fairly quickly . . . usually after the first few meetings . . . the relationship must be comfortable and grounded in connectedness.'

Seven students exceeded the end of year (EOY) grades they were set at the beginning of the year, three fell below their EOY target and two met their target grade.

Eight out of thirteen students achieved the 'benchmark' 95 per cent or above attendance level, two fell just short, and 3 fell at 90 per cent or below which would be considered a concern. There appears to be a possible correlation for students 5 and 13 between their underachievement in their EOY target and their attendance percentage. The students who have better attendance largely appear to be those who have achieved greater success in terms of exceeding EOY target grades.

Ten members of staff noted improvements in reading confidence for six students, and five students now volunteering to read which has not happened previously in their lessons. Other comments talk about a definite improvement in reading delivery and about improvements in attempting work before asking for help, being able to access work more easily, and the reading/attempting of more challenging texts aloud. Most importantly, teachers talked about a number of the students appearing to have a better understanding of the texts being read, or the recipes in food technology lessons. The Head of Year 10 also commented on Year 10 leaders having gained in confidence in their own ability to help others.

At the end of the programme all twelve students indicated that they enjoyed paired reading, wanted to continue with it in the following year, and they felt their reading had improved, and eleven out of the twelve that their understanding of text had improved. Five had already identified family members who would read with them at home. Comments they made about their experience of paired reading included:

> I feel more confident about reading in lessons. The best part was meeting my leader.

> My reading has improved, I am happier about reading and I have made a new friend. My understanding has improved, I understand the sentences more.

Leaders also completed an evaluation questionnaire. Students were overwhelmingly positive about their experience and involvement in the programme. The majority commented that the best thing about taking part had been that they were able to help other students, and that they had made new friends. Others commented that the best part was 'seeing the improvement in their partner's reading'. Some said the most rewarding part had been seeing readers' progress, especially those who really struggled to read initially and were now growing in confidence as they could read more books in the sessions, or could read more challenging texts.

Personal reflections

The findings indicate the intervention has been successful in developing confidence levels in readers. The evaluations show that each student's perception was of improvement in their reading level. However, I am unable to verify whether this is so. I would have needed to test their reading age before and after the intervention. However, test instructions say to only test twice per year, at least 6 months apart. They were due to be tested for a second time at the end of term.

Lack of reading age data does not detract from the anecdotal evidence which shows clear impact on the understanding, confidence and fluidity of reading of some of the individuals. Students and teachers alike give examples of improved understanding of texts and work, with some readers now voluntarily reading aloud in lessons, having declared a strong dislike for reading aloud on their initial feelings scale. This is not conclusive evidence of improving reading confidence and comprehension, but strongly indicates the possibility of both having occurred.

In week 6, the leaders went on work experience, forcing me to think about working differently and economically with the readers to avoid paying twelve teaching assistants (TA) to partner each reader. I grouped readers together to read short plays aloud with the aid of three TAs. Readers rose to the challenge well; friendships had developed within the group after six weeks. Readers appeared keen to try rather than being stressed. Ames and Archer (1988) (cited in Wearmouth, 2009), discuss the possible 'damaging nature of public comparison with higher-achieving' peers, similarly, Elkin (2010: 87) warns against 'exposing weaker readers too often to the experience of hearing another child read effortlessly'. I believe from their reaction, my readers had reached a level of trust between them not to be concerned in this situation.

Whilst reading with them, I was struck by how their lack of literacy impacted on the accessibility and understanding of the humour and irony in the plays, something which a more confident reader with good comprehension would have accessed without difficulty. 'To comprehend a text fully means understanding the genre, the purpose it serves, the context it fits and so on' (Glynn et al., 2006: 75–6).

I set up the pairings, based on my first impressions when meeting the Year 7 and 8 students without the leaders, and the training I conducted with leaders alone. In some cases, I tried to match personality, and thought about the gender and confidence level of readers when pairing. I paired a reader with low self-esteem with a very 'cool' male leader who he would probably never have come into contact with during his time in school. He commented positively on this in his evaluation. I believe the successful outcome of the programme can be partly attributed to this selective pairing.

This research project has already contributed academically and socially to the lives of the readers, and has impacted on their lessons positively by enhancing their understanding of their work (verified by their teachers) and of texts they read. There are small indications that some readers who were less engaged previously have started to behave more positively. I have also identified a correlation between good attendance, motivation/effort and achievement by analysing predicted and end-of-year target grades. However, I have only examined English data as it was most closely linked to this intervention.

Recommendations

- To continue the paired reading programme (on a smaller scale than envisaged by colleagues on SLT), in order to make it a more manageable and useful experience to readers.
- Select 20 readers, 10 from each year group (Year 7 and those who have taken part this year from Year 8), and 20 leaders, 10 each from Years 10 and 11.
- Complete the paired reading programme three times per week, for one full term, after school, three times per week.
- Change the reading group after one full term to bring in 20 more weak readers, and continue the paired reading with the first group once a week in registration time rather than after school so they are still monitored, but they are working more independently and with continued family support.
- Leaders need only check understanding at the end of a page or a section rather than every two paragraphs.
- Try to engage more parents in their child's reading at home through paired reading.

- Run workshops open to those beyond the programme, and track what is read at home to compare data for those reading additionally and those not.
- Develop a reading group of students from the pilot paired readers in the second term when they would have developed their skills and confidence further with a view to developing a love of reading and books into later life.
- Develop spelling and grammar interventions for the lowest attaining students to complete in addition to paired reading practice.

Conclusion

There is a clear case for further development of reading interventions such as this one, evidenced by the data collected.

Readers developed newly found confidence levels and showed improvements in achievement and engagement in lessons by the end of the seven-week period. If this intervention was to continue, I believe that it would begin to show an impact on the overall literacy of these students, and consequently their exam data at Key Stage 4. Importantly, whether the chronological reading age of these readers remained the same or improved, the readers *think* that they are better readers, and therefore are not scared to try to read aloud in lessons, or to attempt work without help. This is the truly remarkable outcome of this intervention; that such a simple process can do so much to lift the confidence and change the attitude of a struggling reader, most of whom declared at the beginning that they hated reading, especially aloud.

(Mythen, unpublished)

Example of an initiative to improve the educational provision and learning outcomes of pupils with an autistic spectrum condition

To determine which aspect of SEN was a priority for school development in a large, LA mainstream primary school, the SENCO, Vanessa, held a discussion with the senior leadership team based on the school needs analysis. This led to focusing on the school's provision for pupils with an autistic spectrum condition. The evidence they used during this discussion included:

- Evaluations of learning walks and lesson observations that indicated some pupils with the condition had behavioural difficulties which were seen as a barrier to their learning and the team was concerned that staff did not have the necessary knowledge and skills to meet pupils' individual needs effectively.
- A continual trend of increasing numbers of autistic pupils being admitted to the school.
- Staff comments that showed a lack of confidence and understanding of how to support pupils with autistic tendencies.

Close observation of one pupil had indicated limited engagement with little response to teaching and organised classroom activities. In this case, staff admitted a sense of failure as they did not feel they were able to adequately support this pupil.

Jordan (2001: 18) discusses how autism has consequences for how it is seen in an individual:

> It is normal for us to 'see' the world according to the meaning we expect to see; it is very hard to see it in any other way. The main implication is that apparently bizarre or puzzling behaviour does have meaning and function for the child with autism, but that meaning is not necessary the one normally attributed to it.

This initiative is reported here in Vanessa's own words.

A significant aspect I sought to research was language and communication. Jordan explained that it is communication that is the main problem in autism, not necessarily speech and language; this changed the direction of my work.

> Children with autism will need to be taught communicative functions and what communication is about. The dimensions of communication should be tackled one step at a time. There are specific problems in language and communication in autism but these are best dealt with, not by trying to suppress them, but by understanding their function for the child and helping him or her develop towards meaningful communication.
>
> (Jordan, 2001: 72)

I was aware that pupils with an autistic spectrum condition may share the same diagnosis and have similar difficulties but each pupil is unique with different strengths, and difficulties can vary. This inevitably means pupil response to interventions will differ, so to avoid generalising I took a case study approach as a method for beginning to understand aspects of autism, firmly ground my findings, enable me to learn from my experience and start to develop a model for improving the provision for all pupils at our school who have autistic tendencies.

Ethical considerations

Before I started, I invited the parents into school to discuss the purpose of the project and seek their permission for their child to participate. I explained how I would keep real names unrecognisable to maintain confidentiality and made it clear that all video material would only be viewed by the staff involved with their child for educational purposes and would be deleted at the end of the project. I discussed how I would keep them informed of my findings and interventions I wanted to introduce. I told them that at any time they were free to withdraw from the project. I then explained the project to all staff involved and sought their permission.

I intentionally chose a pupil from the Reception classes since it is commonly recognised that early intervention positively influences achieving successful pupil outcomes.

I took a problem-solving approach as suggested by Wearmouth (2009: 17):

> Find out about the learner and the expectations of the particular curriculum area.

Find out about the difficulties s/he experiences.

Think about the barriers to learning in the classroom environment.

Reflect on what will best address those barriers to help the learner to achieve in the classroom.

Initial assessment

My initial observations confirmed why staff working with 'Ray' were anxious about how much of the curriculum he was able to access. Staff adapted the class activities they considered appropriate to his level, however, he rarely responded and frequently resisted adult attempts to engage in tasks using a 'hand over hand' approach and often behaved in a distressed state. This tended to mean staff allowed him a greater amount of freedom to act on his own agenda, normally engaging in his special interest of spinning objects repetitively or wandering around without any purposeful attention towards the activities on offer.

My initial assessment of Ray identified a number of barriers:

- The adult-initiated activities were not matched to his current level of functioning and he had no motivation or reason to follow adult direction.
- Ray hadn't yet learnt the prerequisite skills for a readiness to learn, e.g. he hadn't yet learnt to sit at a table, hold joint attention with an adult or comply with adult direction.
- Ray didn't know what was expected of him which could explain his troubled behaviour was due to anxiety.

Actions

Although barriers to Ray's learning had been identified, I wasn't entirely sure how to address them. I drew on the recommendations from the specialist advisor who had previously observed Ray and had suggested the TEACCH pre-school curriculum which included 'Shoebox tasks', designed specifically for children with an autistic spectrum condition.

> They are based on the TEACCH principle, which is devised on the theory that people with ASC need to know 'What do I have to do?', 'How much do I have to do?' and 'How will I know when I am finished?'
>
> A symbol or photo of the activity is placed in the 'Now' area and a motivating activity or choice is put in the 'Then' area.
>
> (Specialist advisor report)

We introduced the 'Shoebox tasks' and as suggested, used the 'Now' and 'Then' approach. Since Ray responded to sensory experiences, we collected a range of sensory objects and toys to use as motivators for 'Then' tasks.

Outcomes

Staff liked the tasks because they did not require language, only Ray's visual skills. Ray quickly responded positively to the tasks and after two months using a variety of shoebox tasks he has learnt 'early learning readiness skills', demonstrated by the fact he can now sit at a workstation in a distraction-free area, maintain joint attention with an adult for several minutes and using a 'hand over hand' approach or, on good days, independently complete a number of tasks. Ray is still given opportunities to act on his own agenda but these are short and planned into his timetable.

Action: monitoring pupil progress

Through staff discussion we agreed the activities needed to meet pupil's individual needs and the activities and subjects the pupil could potentially access with his class. As the number of new activities increased, the pupil's differentiated curriculum started to develop and I was keen to monitor pupil responses and progress but realised I wasn't able to sustain my current number of observations. I needed to develop methods for gaining this information that were manageable.

The teaching assistants working with Ray and another autistic pupil started to work more closely as they shared the same shoebox tasks and resources. They agreed to take it in turns to video themselves working with the pupil on adult-assisted tasks and when the pupil was working on independent tasks. We decided to video the same tasks intermittently in hope of gaining evidence of progress. I viewed the videos regularly to monitor pupil progress and gave staff advice accordingly, usually on how to develop or adjust the task. As this process of monitoring got underway, I discovered how it had a positive impact on staff professional development (discussed further in the next section).

I asked staff to keep a record of pupil activities with a brief written description on pupil progress.

Outcomes

The pupil progress logs were useful at determining which tasks were unsuccessful and to consider why. Through a discussion with one of Ray's teaching assistants we established that one task just needed to be presented in a different way. Ray was required to remove a coloured chip from a matching chip and post it in a pot. I explained that if he took the chip from the pot and placed it on the matching chip, this would be cognitively more demanding (video date/task). The pupil now responds positively to the task and we have been able to progress him on to matching more than one object with the same colour (video).

This example demonstrates that as a result of being actively involved in the process of monitoring pupil progress, I was able to provide specific support and guidance to staff which in turn they implemented. This had an influence on the quality of provision.

Action: professional development opportunities

The staff working directly with Ray had no previous experience of working with pupils who have an autistic spectrum condition and admitted their lack of confidence, although they had attended the INSET I had given to raise general awareness and understanding about autistic spectrum conditions. I needed to provide staff with support to help them apply their new learning so I decided to organise regular, professional discussion group sessions for them.

These meetings included:

- opportunities for staff to report on pupil progress, reflect on pupil responses and discuss what was going well and what hadn't been successful and possible reasons;
- discussing and agreeing future actions such as adapting activities or trying a different approach;
- decisions about activities that would contribute to improving staff confidence and practice, such as planning visits to an autistic spectrum conditions provision and a special school, and organising a speech and language therapist to demonstrate how to work with the pupils.

Outcomes

On reflection I found the regular supervision meetings with staff had perhaps the greatest impact on improving pupils' provision. These supervision sessions had many positive outcomes:

- They enabled me to better understand the individual circumstances for pupil and staff, hence I was able to provide explicit advice.
- Staff contributed to the process of evaluating current practice and encouraging staff to become reflective practitioners.
- Staff motivation increased as they could see their own professional practice improve.
- Professional relationships improved mutual respect and collaboration between staff.

Case study outcomes

One of the teaching assistants had been reluctant to trial the 'Intensive Interaction' approach that had been recommended. She admitted feeling self-conscious and although the purpose of the intervention had been explained, she didn't appear convinced. In one of our supervision meetings we watched a video of her and Ray during an early 'Intensive Interaction' session. During the viewing I drew her attention to examples where Ray communicated to her non-verbally. At the end, she commented that she hadn't realised how responsive and communicative he had been and that it was difficult to perceive his response while she concentrated on her role. She later told me this supervision session helped her realise how the approach helped her enter 'his world', something she wanted to achieve but didn't know how. She later acknowledged that since viewing the video her confidence has improved and she has noticed Ray's eye contact had increased. I learnt how this approach can positively develop adult–pupil relationship, something which can be challenging when a pupil doesn't speak.

Attitudes and expectations

A number of staff openly expressed they believed Ray would do better attending a special school that would have the resources and skills to 'cope' with pupils like Ray. I found these comments suggested an attitude of failure towards the pupils and our team which if I didn't attempt to address, could potentially be a barrier to staff's commitment to trial new approaches and interventions and recognise pupils' small steps of progress. I was also concerned that this attitude could potentially reduce appropriate high expectations of pupils' learning and behaviour.

Developing pupil language and communication

> In school Ray primarily babbles and makes noises. He speaks the occasional single word, normally echoed from a familiar song. He gets adults' attention by taking them by the hand and leading them to what he would like. When he is happy he smiles and bounces up and down. He shows distress by screaming and throwing himself to the floor.
>
> (Educational Psychologist report)

Parents discussed how Ray's limited communication was the one area they found the most difficult to manage and staff expressed that his communication difficulties were a barrier to access learning. Ray's speech and language report provided a summary of his communication and language delay and offered advice to support his development. Although these recommendations appeared straightforward, in practice, we found them difficult to implement especially taking account of Ray's difficulties as a whole. I found myself asking questions such as: what does a language programme look like? What methods could be used for alternative communication?

We started looking at visual supports. Staff took photographs of places and everyday objects Ray would use, e.g. toilet, playground. The plan was to show Ray the photograph, e.g. his lunch box and say 'lunchtime' and take Ray to the hall to collect his lunch box.

The specialist advisor thought the photographs were too distracting and he would benefit from simple pictures. Ray's speech and language therapist thought he would be better shown the photograph and the object. None of us had any previous experience working with a pupil with such limited communication and the professionals were offering different advice; this caused some confusion and at the same time staff were frustrated since it took a great deal of effort just to gain Ray's attention to the photograph and hear the spoken word because he would avoid most adult attempts to communicate unless he had initiated it.

Conversations with staff frequently centred on Ray's lack of speech. Ideas on how to encourage it were discussed, e.g. nursery rhymes, action songs, picture books and providing opportunities for adults to model spoken language during activities and experiences. However, observations and discussions showed staff were unsure how to use their own speech and language to support his development. One video entitled 'What colour?' showed the TA asking Ray a question, e.g. TA holds up a coloured shape and asks 'What colour?' Ray looked at her and rocked from side to side. After a few seconds he took the shape and posted it in the box. The TA said 'The colour?' No verbal response. This continued for another four shapes. My evaluation of this activity led me to wonder how it supported Ray's speech and language. Yes, he heard spoken language and the intention was to encourage him to respond verbally but we could assume from his response one or all possible reasons:

- he did not know what was expected of him;
- he did not understand the language;
- he was not motivated to speak;
- the subject (colours) had little meaning and was too abstract for him.

Ray's speech and language therapist thought we could start teaching him to communicate a request. She showed us putting a desirable object (bubbles) out of his reach so he would be motivated to make a request for them. The adult then modelled the spoken language, 'Ray wants bubbles' followed by blowing a bubble. Staff tried this approach with the bubbles but he was not always motivated by them so we tried other 'desirable objects' but he only seemed interested in spinners and a sensory water toy but even then his interest was fleeting. In any case these objects were already given as motivators for finishing a task. Ray's limited interests were seen as a barrier to using this approach.

Action

After reading the work of Jordan (2001) and speaking to different professionals, I realised that perhaps we had all been placing too much emphasis on developing Ray's speech and language and the mode of communication (photographs, pictures or objects) and not addressing the fundamental issue of learning what communication was before he could learn to use a system of communication. Jordan discusses the problem of prioritising speech:

> Language and communication are so closely bound together in normal development that it does not often occur to the parent that speech alone is not the answer. Parents of children with autism who do develop speech soon realise, however, the speaking child with autism may still not be able to communicate, to express needs, or to explain what the matter is when s/he is upset. Speech in fact may become a barrier to communication in some cases, with the child talking incessantly, leaving no space for communication.
>
> (Jordan, 2001: 52)

Staff needed a great deal of support understanding and accepting Ray may never use speech and it was agreed developing his communication and using alternative methods would be a priority. To give staff an example, I used the video clip titled, 'What colour?' to illustrate. As an alternative to speech Ray could have been given a choice of coloured shapes to match the adults either by pointing or posting the matching colour or else pressing the matching colour on a speaking device to 'speak' the word to him.

I drew attention to the non-verbal communication the task did promote' joint attention and interaction, helping staff become more aware of the features of non-verbal communication.

Attention

I came to understand that the early stage of communication is attention. The approach the speech and language therapist promotes is the principle that children will only give attention if the experience is highly motivating, fun and therefore a memorable experience. I decided to set up a small 'Attention Autism' group for Ray and three other pupils with limited attention.

Communicating a request

To help Ray begin to understand the purpose of communication by making requests, we needed something highly motivating. This proved a challenge owing to his limited interests, so we finally opted for food, something his parents suggested. With guidance from his speech and language therapist we discussed which visual support to use. We decided against an object representing a cake since he was likely to put it in his mouth or throw it on the floor. We considered a photograph but decided a simple drawing was the best option. The cake was cut up into small pieces and placed in sight but out of reach. Ray was then taught that when he tapped the drawing he was given some cake.

Outcomes

All staff and parents report that Ray's attention has improved. He is now able to sit and, together with another pupil, gain adult attention for several minutes to complete a task.

Since Ray's attention skills have improved, he is now able to benefit from visual supports. For example, the 'finished' card is placed on the table; he looks at it for a few seconds and places the task in the finished tray.

Staff are more confident about which visual supports to use and have no problem in using a combination to suit the purpose and situation, e.g. photographs for familiar objects, simple pictures/symbols for instructions, e.g. 'work time' and 'choose' and drawings to support spontaneous communication. The therapist suggests drawings since they are a convenient method for communicating unexpected requests and supporting spontaneous communication because it is not always possible to have the appropriate picture for every situation.

At our family support group, one of the TAs demonstrated the technique of communicating a request by tapping a drawing. Ray still initially needs 'hand over hand' to tap the drawing but after a few examples he taps the drawing himself. Parents expressed their pleasure at witnessing Ray communicate 'more cake'. We gave parents an opportunity to try the method themselves and encouraged them to use the approach at home. It is too early to evaluate the impact except research agrees that when home and school use a consistent approach, it helps the child generalise their learning to different situations and contexts (Autism Education Trust/CRAE, 2011).

Summary

Although Ray's educational statement identifies developing a language programme, we recognise these are long-term targets. Following the advice from professionals we have prioritised the fundamental skills we need to develop, first, Ray's understanding of communication and increasing attention skills.

Evaluating the impact of each intervention on improving the pupil's speech, language and communication is difficult to say, since the process to identify appropriate actions has taken a considerable amount of time and we have only just started implementing appropriate interventions. However, early indications show the pupils responding.

Discussion and analysis of my findings

In doing this action research I learnt there is a 'gap' between knowing what good practice is based on professional recommendations and staff having the skills to deliver effective practice and how it was vital for me, the SENCO, to 'bridge that gap'. Therefore it is fundamental for SENCOs to have adept knowledge and skills within this area of SEN, however, this in itself does not make the difference to pupil outcomes, they must have the skills to lead those working with the pupils to implement good practice.

I discovered each theme fed into each other, e.g. recommendations from professionals supported professional development and monitoring progress which then led to improving practice and pupil outcomes. Professional development and monitoring pupil progress were at the heart of improving practice and on reflection it was these two processes that were the most challenging but had the greatest impact on improving practice. They were closely linked since I centred the evaluation of pupil progress within staff's professional development opportunities. Although a lengthy course of action, it means there is sustainability in what I did since four teaching assistants now have experience and skills which they can transfer to support other pupils with an autistic spectrum condition.

In the context of supporting pupils with an autistic spectrum condition, we all learnt normal instincts can mislead due to the many factors affecting pupil response, therefore careful consideration and a willingness to recognise that intuition could be inaccurate when trying to understand pupils' behaviour are needed. It was this understanding that improved the staff–pupil relationship and how challenging behaviour was perceived and managed more effectively than at the start of the project (conversations with staff).

Involving professionals was essential for improving pupil outcomes, it guided our actions, although I found they can have different opinions, but as my confidence grew it was useful to consider different views, and in consultation with parents and staff, decide on the approach most suited to the pupil, within the school and classroom context.

A model for professional development

Since regular staff supervision had a positive impact on pupil outcomes, I am planning to develop this further next year for a group of TAs working with pupils who have similar

SEN difficulties. I am considering pairing TAs, using a critical friend approach, and promoting the development of reflective practice, perhaps using video as a tool to reflect on practice and pupil learning outcomes.

Ethical issues

A common approach adopted has been 'hand over hand'. This was something I hadn't previously encountered and has been a matter of personal debate. I understand how it teaches skills more explicitly than modelling for pupils with severe learning difficulties; however, it raised the issue of whether it is an invasive approach since Ray was often resistant and would frequently become distressed.

(Leaves, unpublished)

Appendix B10 contains an individual behaviour support plan for this young man.

Summary

This chapter has focused on ways in which two practising SENCOs designed, implemented and evaluated interventions to address weaknesses in SEND provision in their schools which they had identified from an initial institutional audit (Appendix B9) designed to support a programme of development or preparation for an Ofsted inspection (or both). (At the time of writing, the most recent document guiding Ofsted inspectors during the inspection process is Ofsted, (2015) *School Inspection Handbook*, Manchester: Ofsted).

To conclude this chapter, we summarise the reflections of one of these SENCOs on what she concluded is important for all SENCOs to know, understand and do:

- It is essential for SENCOs to find out about a range of needs, the impact they can have on individual pupils and barriers to learning. They should have the skills to deliver good practice themselves and have the leadership skills to lead others effectively.
- Professional development opportunities and monitoring pupil progress can have a profound influence on improving pupil outcomes.
- Managing challenging behaviour can usefully involve the process of functional analysis and proactive strategies.
- Involving well-informed, experienced external professionals to guide practice can be crucial in SENCOs' professional development and that of other staff working with pupils.
- It is necessary to promote positive, and challenge negative, attitudes since they affect pupil–staff relationships and expectations of achievement and progress.
- Many of the approaches and strategies which are used for pupils with specific conditions are also effective for pupils who experience other kinds of needs.

Appendix A1

National Award for Special Education Needs Co-ordination learning outcomes mapped against chapters

NASENCo learning outcomes	*Chapter in this book*
Part A: Professional Knowledge and Understanding	
1 *The statutory and regulatory context for SEN and disability equality and the implications for practice in their school or work setting:* • Guidance within the SEN Code of Practice and how it is interpreted locally • Mediation and the SEND Tribunal • The Local Offer • New funding models, including the right to personal budgets.	Chapter 3 *Current statutory and regulatory frameworks for SEND*
• Ofsted Frameworks relevant to their school or work setting	Chapter 10 *Achieving coherence and cost-effectiveness in provision* Chapter 11 *Policy-making in SEND provision in schools and colleges* Chapter 14 *Developing effective SEND provision*
• The policy and legislative context for health and social care, including safeguarding and the health and well-being agenda • Relevant guidance on data protection and confidentiality, health and safety, including governor accountabilities	Chapter 11 *Policy-making in SEND provision in schools and colleges*

(continued)

(Continued)

NASENCo learning outcomes	*Chapter in this book*
2 *The principles and practice of leadership in different contexts*: • The characteristics of highly effective leadership • Leadership and management processes and tools that support change in schools • The role of leadership and professional challenge in supporting and promoting a culture of continuous professional development linked to improvement • Their own leadership, including strengths and areas for development • The professional qualities of effective team leadership	Chapter 10 *Achieving coherence and cost-effectiveness in provision* Chapter 11 *Policy-making in SEND provision in schools and colleges* Chapter 14 *Developing effective SEND provision*
3 *How SEN and disabilities affect pupils' participation and learning:* • The breadth and complexity of the causes of under-achievement • How children's development is affected by SEN and disabilities, including mental health needs, and the quality of teaching they receive • High incidence SEN and their implications for teaching and learning and inclusive practice	Chapter 4 *Understanding communication and interaction needs* Chapter 5 *Understanding cognition and learning needs* Chapter 6 *Understanding social, emotional and mental health needs* Chapter 7 *Understanding sensory and physical difficulties and needs*
• Planning provision for children and young people with more severe and complex SEN	Chapter 9 *Planning provision for individual needs*
4 *Strategies for improving outcomes for pupils with SEN or disabilities:* • Theories of learning as the basis upon which to design effective interventions • Removing barriers to participation and learning for children and young people with SEN or disabilities • Addressing discrimination, stereotyping and bullying related to SEN and disability • The potential of new technologies to support communication, teaching and learning for children and young people with SEN or disabilities • Relevant theory, research and inspection evidence about effective practice in including pupils with SEN or disabilities	Chapter 2 *Models of learning and behaviour in the SEND field* Chapter 4 *Understanding communication and interaction needs* Chapter 5 *Understanding cognition and learning needs* Chapter 6 *Understanding social, emotional and mental health needs* Chapter 7 *Understanding sensory and physical difficulties and needs* Chapter 8 *Assessment of learning, behaviour, physical and sensory needs* Chapter 9 *Planning provision for individual needs*
• Theories of learning as the basis upon which to design effective interventions	Chapter 2 *Models of learning and behaviour in the SEND field*

NASENCo learning outcomes	Chapter in this book
Part B: Leading and Co-ordinating Provision	
5 *Work strategically with senior colleagues and governors to:* • Advise on and influence the strategic development of a person-centred and inclusive ethos, policies, priorities and practices • Promote a whole school culture of high expectations and best practice in teaching and learning to improve outcomes for children and young people with SEN and/ or disabilities • Ensure that the school's SEN policy is embedded within the school's performance management, self-evaluation and improvement planning • Establish systems to collect, analyse and interpret data, including Raise On-line, to inform policy and practice, raise expectations and set challenging targets for children and young people with SEN or disabilities	Chapter 10 *Achieving coherence and cost-effectiveness in provision* Chapter 11 *Policy-making in SEND provision in schools and colleges*
• Commission, secure and deploy appropriate resources to reinforce the teaching of children and young people with SEN or disabilities, and evaluate and report upon their impact on progress, outcomes and cost- effectiveness	Chapter 13 *Collaborating with other professionals*
6 *Lead, develop and, where necessary, challenge senior leaders, colleagues and governors to:* • Understand and meet their statutory responsibilities towards children and young people with SEN or disabilities • Promote improvement in teaching and learning to identify, assess and meet the needs of children and young people with SEN or disabilities, within a person-centred approach • Model effective practice, coach and mentor colleagues • Lead the professional development of staff so that all staff improve their practice and take responsibility for removing barriers to participation and learning • Deploy and manage staff effectively to ensure the most efficient use of resources to improve progress of children and young people with SEN and/or disabilities	Chapter 3 *Current statutory and regulatory frameworks for SEND* Chapter 11 *Policy-making in SEND provision in schools and colleges*

(continued)

(Continued)

NASENCo learning outcomes	*Chapter in this book*
7 *Critically evaluate evidence about learning, teaching and assessment in relation to pupils with SEN to inform practice and enable senior leaders and teachers to:* • Select, use and adapt approaches, strategies and resources for assessment to personalise provision for children and young people with SEN and/or disabilities • Draw upon relevant research and inspection evidence about teaching and learning in relation to pupils with SEN and/or disabilities to improve practice	Chapter 8 *Assessment of learning, behaviour, physical and sensory needs* Chapter 9 *Planning provision for individual needs*
• Undertake small-scale practitioner enquiry to identify, develop and rigorously evaluate effective practice in teaching pupils with SEN or disabilities	Chapter 14 *Developing effective SEND provision*
8 *Draw on external sources of support and expertise to:* • Engage with the Local Offer to develop effective working partnerships with professionals in other services and agencies, including voluntary organisations, to support a coherent, co-ordinated and effective approach to supporting children and young people with SEN or disabilities • Promote, facilitate and support effective multi-agency working for all children and young people with SEN, through, e.g. person-centred planning, 'team around a child or family', the Common Assessment Framework and the Education, Health and Care Plan • Interpret specialist information from other professionals and agencies and demonstrate how it has been used to improve teaching and learning and outcomes for children and young people with SEN and/or disabilities • Ensure continuity of support and progression at key transition points for children and young people with SEN and/or disabilities	Chapter 12 *Working with families* Chapter 13 *Collaborating with other professionals*

NASENCo learning outcomes	*Chapter in this book*
9 *Develop, implement, monitor and evaluate systems to:* • Identify pupils who may have SEN or disabilities • Inform all staff about the learning needs, emotional, social and mental health needs and achievement of children and young people with SEN or disabilities • Set challenging targets for children and young people with SEN and/or disabilities • Plan and intervene to meet the needs of children and young people with SEN or disabilities • Record and review the progress of children and young people with SEN or disabilities • Make effective use of data to evaluate and report upon the effectiveness of provision and its impact on progress and outcomes for pupils with SEN or disabilities • Ensure appropriate arrangements are put in place for children and young people sitting national tests and examinations or undertaking other forms of accreditation	Chapter 8 *Assessment of learning, behaviour, physical and sensory needs* Chapter 9 *Planning provision for individual needs* Chapter 10 *Achieving coherence and cost-effectiveness in provision*
Part C: Personal and Professional Qualities	
• There are high expectations for all children and young people with SEN and/or disabilities • Person-centred approaches build upon and extend the experiences, interests, skills and knowledge of children and young people with SEN or disabilities • The voice of children and young people with SEN or disabilities is heard and influences the decisions that are made about their learning and well-being	*Introduction* Chapter 2 *Models of learning and behaviour in the SEND field* Chapter 3 *Current statutory and regulatory frameworks for SEND* Chapter 4 *Planning provision for individual needs*
• Family leadership is encouraged and parents and carers are equal partners in securing their child's achievement, progress and well-being	Chapter 12 *Working with families*

Appendix B1

Access to Learning Plan strategies

Access to Learning Plan	Specifics according to students
Issue: low reading ages *Strategies:* • Careful choice of texts • Paired reading • Pick out appropriate passages for students • Differentiated homework to focus on reading skills • TA support while class reading	Sig below (8) Karl, Jeff, Sam, Dan, Mike, Henry, Peter, Kerry. Sig group: • Scaffold writing frames for Peter, Kerry and Karl • Differentiated reading/texts for Henry • Spelling list A (except Sam and Dan) • Written instructions simple & short (Mike to read back) • Class reading work as group with teacher/TA • Paired reading/tasks with a stronger student NOTE: Do not forget stretch and challenge through text choices for three students (Trevor, Kylie, Max) who have higher reading ages
Issue: weak conceptual ability – students struggle with texts and abstract ideas. *Strategies:* • Try to keep teaching using concrete examples • Link abstract ideas to concrete examples • Use visuals to support texts	Sig below (8) Karl, Jeff, Sam, Dan, Mike, Henry, Peter, Kerry. Sig group: • Scaffold writing frames for Peter, Kerry and Karl • Differentiated reading/texts for Henry • Spelling list A (except Sam and Dan) • Written instructions simple & short (Mike to read back) • Class reading work as group with teacher/TA • Paired reading/tasks with a stronger student NOTE: Do not forget stretch and challenge through text choices three students (Trevor, Kylie, Max) who have higher reading ages

(continued)

Access to Learning Plan	Specifics according to students
Issue: ____________ Strategies: ____________	
Issue: ____________ Strategies: ____________	
Issue: ____________ Strategies: ____________	
Issue: ____________ Strategies: ____________	

Access to Learning: Too talkative

- Change seating plan layout according to task/activity.
- Count up/down to a verbal cue re: talking reminder.
- Combine desirable and less desirable tasks (think about how to order lesson tasks). More desirable = less talking!!
- Set noise level rules/expectations for different tasks, e.g. talking/discussion time, quiet working.
- Use visual/auditory cues to signal that the talking has gone beyond an acceptable level, for example, alarm, arrow moves from green to orange or red zone on talking chart.
- Excessive talking level; names on board/sanction.

Access to Learning: Confidence

- Explicit verbal praise.
- Targeted questioning.
- Paired support tasks.
- Thinking/warning time for questions.
- Differentiated tasks designed around confidence.
- Positive letter/phone call home to encourage them.
- Comments to improve given verbally and in written form.
- Additional scaffolding, e.g. writing frames.

Access to Learning: Low reading level

- Choice of texts.
- Paired reading.
- Pick out appropriate passages for students.

- Differentiated homework to focus on reading skills.
- TA support while class reading.
- Pre-select texts for student to familiarise themselves with before reading aloud in class.
- Visual dictionary in book (word/pictures).
- Give minimum/maximum amounts for written tasks, e.g. 3 lines minimum, 7 maximum.
- Bullet point instructions using simple language.
- Use a range of teaching/learning styles (VAK).
- Differentiated worksheets.

Access to Learning: Dyslexia (SPLD)

- Tend to have a poor auditory short-term memory, so an outline of what will be taught is helpful, as well as frequent plenaries reviewing what has been learnt.
- Break tasks into chunks of easy-to-remember information.
- Can have poor visual memory, so information displayed on board should be given in a handout as copying is likely to be inaccurate.
- Seat near teacher for easy access to help, or alternatively with a well-motivated, supportive peer.
- Ensure writing on board is well spaced and alternates between colours on each line (or every other line is underlined).
- Leave writing up on board long enough for students to read/take in/write down information.
- Check written tasks for accuracy/understanding e.g. recording homework.
- Important information should be given in written form, not verbally.
- Don't ask student to read aloud (1:1 with TA or to you quietly), OR give pre-selected material to practise at home before lesson.
- Select text/write instructions in format appropriate to their reading level to avoid losing meaning/comprehension when stumbling on every word.
- Use key words with visual cues in back of book/on walls to be used for reference/revision.
- Encourage proof reading to improve spelling (unable to spontaneously correct, but can be trained to look for errors particular to them).
- Only ask to re-write display work, poor handwriting is often an issue, so work produced is often very challenging to write and spell correctly.
- Tasks for a dyslexic child require more thought, take longer, and don't come easily. Set tasks appropriate to their needs for homework, and set a time limit for them to work on it, e.g. 45 mins.
- There will be a difference between the information they can get written down and that which they can give verbally, so ask questions to check further understanding. In group discussions, ask their opinions.
- Reduce talking time, give small amounts of key information using simple language.
- Make questions clear and precise, giving prompts of prior knowledge to aid recall.

Access to Learning: Speech, language and communication difficulties

- Think about group selection as group work can be difficult as some students lack social skills. Give specific tasks/responsibilities within group.
- Give homework/written tasks as pre-prepared sheet rather than recording from verbal instructions.
- Use storyboarding in cartoon form to help gain understanding of complex texts.
- Plan questions that can have a yes/no response rather than extensive language, or give multiple choice options.
- Acknowledge students' efforts, avoid sarcasm/indirect language, use simple language to aid understanding.
- Provide opportunities to practise new vocabulary in written and verbal sentences.
- Provide writing frames/headings/narrative plans for written tasks, especially sequencing, or extended writing tasks.
- Regularly re-focus the student's attention, especially before giving instructions.
- When listening/watching information, ask student to listen for a specific fact/answer.
- Provide visual reminders for new vocabulary, e.g. pictures, prompt cards, symbols, etc.
- Always speak/give instructions facing the student, (not the whiteboard, for example), position them where they can see/hear you clearly; away from windows/doors which may distract them.
- Always use student's name before issuing an instruction to 'cue' them in.
- Avoid words that have more than one meaning, sarcasm/irony.

Access to Learning: General learning difficulty

- Break complex topics and procedures into simple components; check understanding frequently.
- Re-visit concepts in different contexts, relate to everyday concepts.
- Direct experiences will help gain understanding, e.g. showing and feeling object being discussed, e.g. artefacts in history/RE.
- Use lots of visual stimuli to reinforce 'do's and don'ts', e.g. safety rules in science/technology, or to cement concepts.
- Use visual timelines to help with abstract concepts, the pictures will help students to visualise.
- In maths and science, measure liquids, objects, use real coins to work out money problems.
- Small group work will aid development better than teacher-directed instructions to the whole group. Use TA to work with individual or small group.
- Over-learn concepts and work at a slower pace for student to consolidate learning.

Access to Learning: Dyscalculia (SPLD)

- Can have issues with working memory, therefore over-learning skills and concepts will be necessary.
- Make the presentation of worksheets clear and uncluttered.
- Use ICT to aid learning.
- Draw diagrams of problems to aid problem solving.
- Encourage partner discussion of problems to explain methods to each other.
- Teach students to use mnemonics to help remember facts/information.
- Link to real-life situations, use real objects, e.g. coins to solve problems.
- Allow extra time to complete task.
- Use practical activities whenever possible to help understanding of concepts.

Access to Learning: ADD/ADHD

- Provide legitimate opportunities for students to be out of their seat; giving out books, etc. Or, set a task where pupils need to give their answer by jumping on laminated answer sheets on the floor, e.g. jump on the noun, adjective, verb, etc, chemical symbol, correct number.
- Throwing objects between peers to practise sequencing, times tables, reactivity lists, keywords/new vocabulary, etc.
- Chunk work into smaller sections, they will often be overwhelmed by lengthy texts/pages of instructions.
- Allow verbal responses when student is particularly 'hyper'/unresponsive. Manage writing tasks by using a TA in short term.
- Give them something to doodle on/occupy them during lengthy explanations (stress ball) so they can focus on listening without distracting others.
- Sit student close to you between calm/well-behaved students, away from distractions such as doors and windows.
- Avoid changes in routine where possible, or pre-warn of changes you know are coming up. Give a time countdown to signal '5 minutes until the end of an activity, 3 minutes, last minute' to make transitions between tasks easier.
- Praise publicly for good behaviour, and reprimand quietly to avoid confrontation.
- Sequencing can be a problem for some, so practising these skills by writing a checklist, or telling you what they will do next to complete a task will help.
- If your teaching style is very animated/upbeat, be aware that although engaging for most, ADD/ADHD students may find it overly stimulating. Adjust your volume/intensity accordingly.
- Re-direct calmly, but firmly if off-track, giving brief instructions to complete task, check work, then give next instruction on completion.
- Reinforce behaviour reminders/refer to visual reminders.
- Write important information where it can be easily referenced and remind where it is.

Access to Learning: Dyspraxia (SPLD)

- Limit amount of writing required.
- Allow use of laptop.
- Keep your lesson format/classroom well ordered to aid their organisation in your lessons.
- Use visual dictionaries/cues/pictures to help with understanding.
- Can react anxiously to unplanned/sudden changes in routine, stressful.
- Visual reminders for different tasks on different days of week, e.g., bring homework on Tuesdays.
- Create social stories about events outside normal routine. Include detailed steps about what will happen and how.
- Countdown to transitions between activities (5 minutes, 3 minutes, 1 minute, to ease transition between tasks).
- Check accuracy and understanding of recorded homework task.

Access to Learning: Attendance

- Liaise with school attendance officer/parents.
- Photocopy other students' work so notes can be copied up/sent home if absent long term.
- Targeted 1:1 help in class by teacher/TA to ensure understanding and continuity in learning.
- Additional work provided to catch up if student is able to cope.

Access to Learning: Oppositional defiance disorder (ODD)

- Address concerns quietly and privately to avoid confrontation and an audience.
- Do not interrupt student until he or she finishes talking.
- Decide which behaviours you will ignore, focus on only a few to tackle.
- Establish a rapport so student views you as reasonable/fair and will therefore work with you, not against you.
- Establish clear classroom rules. What are your 'non-negotiables'? Display them clearly in teaching space to refer back to.
- Notify them of upcoming changes in routine/lessons to prepare them, and so additional support could be provided if necessary.
- Avoid bringing previous arguments/incidents up at a later date.
- Avoid power struggles and 'show downs' don't raise voice, silence is better than engaging in an argument.
- Set appropriately challenging work, too easy = boredom, too hard = frustration.
- Keep student busy with minimal unstructured time/keep transitions brief.
- When decisions need to be made, try to limit options/choices to two things only. ODD students are more likely to complete a chosen task.

- Use praise for positive responses.
- Alternate between their 'preferred' tasks and non-preferred tasks, praise for completion of non-preferred by rewarding with a preferred task.
- They will often struggle with social interaction, so select tasks which encourage these skills, but choose their working group carefully.
- Plan your responses to particular behaviours presented. An emotional response from you will escalate the situation. Follow through with your actions calmly and quietly.

Access to Learning: Social, emotional/behavioural difficulties

- Alternate difficult tasks (introduction of new material) with tasks they are competent in, to increase motivation/reduce stress.
- Provide choice in tasks/control opportunities to increase their intrinsic motivation.
- Use positive language and a calm approach.
- Have a clear set of classroom rules displayed in teaching space to refer to.
- EBD students need immediate consequences for negative behaviour, balance these with rewards.
- Consistently apply your classroom rules and sanctions to avoid conflict/confrontation through inconsistency.
- Give countdown warnings of changes in task/activity to aid transitions between tasks as these times can be stressful (5 mins, 3 mins, 1 min).
- Provide cues for transitions between transitions. Music? Timers? Visual cues?
- Seat next to a positive role model towards front of classroom in an aisle seat so there is easy teacher/TA access.
- Have minimal free/unstructured time.
- Break down/chunk assignment/class work.
- Use positive reinforcement to motivate EBD students and break cycle of negative behaviours.
- Try to avoid excessive reprimanding/prompting (singling out of student in front of class).
- Familiarise yourself with student's SEN profile which will indicate possible trigger points that prompt inappropriate behaviours.
- Note those behaviours that are characteristic of the student, plan for your response where possible.

Access to Learning: Autism/Asperger's Syndrome

- Tend to be very set in their ways, and find ALL changes in routine difficult to manage. Therefore, pre-warn of changes directly or via SSC/NP. Most have an exit card, remind them quietly that they can use it if they are anxious.
- May have difficulty in controlling temper and get easily frustrated. Often misread visual cues/facial expressions, etc. Try to ignore as much of this behaviour as possible as drawing attention to it will increase their anxiety further.

- Giving instructions with a raised voice may lead them to think they are being shouted at. Talk quietly and calmly.
- Often take information/instructions literally. Give clear, concise instructions: don't overload with information, use literal language, using their name before instructions are given to 'cue them in'.
- Break tasks into smaller chunks when possible, by putting less information on worksheet, or by covering the remainder of the sheet, only showing task they are working on.
- Can often exhibit very attention-seeking behaviour, frequently interrupting. Continuously reinforce classroom rules/expectations. Use visual cues to help remind students of rules.
- Some may have sensory needs, strong smells, humming noises from heaters, etc., and certain lighting can all trigger feelings of anxiety/inability to cope. Also general classroom noise can be difficult. Sit them away from noisy students/objects. Ask advice from NP/read profile about specific triggers.
- Find it incredibly difficult to discuss emotions as they don't understand them. Therefore some subject-based discussions may be difficult. Encourage them to use their exit card if not coping with subject content. Or pre-warn NP so a social story can be written.
- Pair/group work can be difficult as they often struggle with social interaction. Select working partners carefully. Try to pair with a trusted peer, or make sure there is at least one in the group.

Access to Learning: EAL students

- Familiarise yourself with student's profile as they will all be working at different levels.
- Use drama activities such as role plays to practise speaking and listening skills.
- Use barrier games where students are separated by a barrier and have to speak and listen to complete tasks. E.g. find partner by asking and answering questions of the rest of the group to find correct partner.
- Use language prompts to aid written work, e.g. 'I think… because…' or 'You could…'
- Use talk frames on cards to support students' language development and focus their thinking.
- Use paired talking activities to 'safely' practise/rehearse what they will say to the rest of the group.
- Be a good role model for the English language/correct other students. E.g. 'We were' instead of 'we was', 'I did' instead of 'I done'. EAL students benefit from hearing good pronunciation and good modelling of the English language.
- Assign specific roles in group work so their opinion is heard/shared and they take their turn properly.
- Change your methods of differentiation regularly so students practise a range of skills.
- EAL students can benefit from classroom wall displays when used as 'working walls'. Working walls support learning of concepts, skills, and keywords from current or recent lessons. They may include brainstorms, mind maps and new vocabulary (keywords).

Access to Learning: Able, gifted and talented

- Give opportunities for stretch and challenge in all activities/tasks.
- Give opportunities to apply and combine learning objectives in less familiar contexts.
- Give opportunities to accelerate learning through content/tasks.
- Encourage independent/reflective working.
- Use targeted, and follow-up questioning, e.g. 'What makes you think that?'
- Set tasks that require higher order thinking skills.
- Differentiate by:
    - outcome
    - task
    - process
    - pupil grouping
    - personalising content/learning to individuals
    - provision (access to experts/outside speakers)
    - learning style
    - self-direction/choice.

Access to Learning: Medical/Young Carer/CLA Student

- Supportive seating plan (partner who will support and encourage after absence).
- Liaison with SENCO if asked to provide work.
- Work provided/sent home if student is absent for a significant period/if requested by parents.
- Rest breaks given if necessary.
- Allow student to leave a few minutes early to avoid busy corridors.
- Additional help with practical tasks from TA or teacher.

Access to Learning: Concentration

- Consider seating plan, place away from distractions whenever possible.
- Short-timed tasks; check progress regularly.
- Bullet point instructions, simple language.
- Short-term targets for completion of work/assignments.

(Mythen, unpublished)

Appendix B2

Example of an individual provision map for an autistic young man

This is an example of an IPM negotiated for a young man who experienced autistic-type difficulties.

Student: [name] Year: 10	Tutor Group: [name]	Area of Need Autistic spectrum disorder	IPM updated: [date]
Area of need	Additional and different provision/resource	Expected outcome	
Wave 1: Quality First Teaching for all			
Literacy (including current levels)	N/A		
Numeracy (including current levels)	Projected GCSE D/E Support [name of student] by: • providing him with prepared worksheets/graphs • allowing extra time when using mathematical equipment • ensuring tasks and instructions are clear and visual • seating with/near good role models • avoiding changing routine/seating plan	[. . .] will: • be able to work more independently • continue to attend Maths lesson in mainstream • achieve a GCSE in maths	

(continued)

(Continued)

Wave 2: Additional support programme(s) to reach potential		
Literacy		
Numeracy		
Wave 3: Individual		
Literacy	Individual literacy 1: 1 in the specialist unit.	Student will: • be able to explore a range of non-fiction reading materials • absorb information on a wide range of topics related to the curriculum on offer • develop a greater understanding of language • increase his vocabulary • retrieve some information from simple texts independently, complete short written tasks with minimal support
Numeracy		
Emotional and Social	Has an assigned adult to support lunch breaks in the dining hall. Life skill/social skills lessons. Variety of trips and visits to aid this.	

Chronology of intervention

Student: [name]			On roll:			Off roll:		
Date	Yr	Intervention	Timescale	Ratio	Staff	Data	Review impact/ outcome	Next action
	11	Individual and reduced timetable.	Ongoing	1:1 and 1:2	ASC			
	11	ASC Provision placement	Ongoing					

Advice to teachers

Owing to [name]'s autism he is inflexible a very rigid thinker and resistant to following instructions. He can be upset/stressed/anxious about change. It will help him if you do the following:

- Do everything you can to communicate with him with him very clearly, in short, clear sentences/phrases.
- Listen carefully to what he is trying to communicate to you.
- Don't expect him to know what you would like him to do unless you tell him very clearly.
- Prepare him in advance for any change in routines.
- Remember he needs praise and reassurance.
- Avoid group work, give him a previously prepared task.
- Provide a schedule of tasks and activities.
- Provide a structured work sheet.
- Monitor your own language for ambiguity.
- Be firm regarding behaviour/shouting out inappropriate comments.
- When [name] becomes particularly stressed, reduce demands/social interaction.
- Be prepared to remove either [name] or others to a quiet, safe place if necessary.

Current targets

[Name] will be able to do the following:

- Focus on a task for 5 minutes independently.
- Follow instructions and work methodically on structured tasks.
- Practise life and independence skills both at home and school for at least two weeks.

Appendix B3

Annotated class provision map

Year ___________
Yellow Class
Date ___________
Term ___________

Intervention	*Group size*	*Frequency duration/staff*	*Pupil*	*Entry data*	*Target/comments*[1]	*Exit data*	*Outcomes/comments*
Reading	1:1	4 x 20 mins x 6 weeks/TA		6.0 years 4.6 years 4.7 years 4.9 years 5.7 years 5.6 years 4.6 years	To make 2/3 months progress on the Salford reading scheme. *This teacher practises the Salford test before doing the 'real thing'. Massey (2013) states the need for robust data. This will need to be discussed in a staff meeting.*	6:8 5:4 5:1 5:11 7:3 6:4 5:1	*This column should say what the next steps are, rather than describing where the children are. The provision map needs redesigning.* Come off Changing school
Maths	1:1 1:2	4 x 15 mins x 6 weeks/TA		1B 1B 1B	To find one more than a number to 10 *This target has not been met although progress has been made. If the target is changed, the children will forget what they have learnt. This would need to be discussed in the PPMs.*	1B 1B 1B	Able to find one more on numbers to 10. X is able to find one more wthan a number to 10 but is not consistent. Target met. *It also shows that we need fresh ideas for maths intervention and resources that work. The provision map informs the whole school provision map.* *One would not be as effective without the other.*

(continued)

(Continued)

Intervention	*Group size*	*Frequency duration/staff*	*Pupil*	*Entry data*	*Target/comments*	*Exit data*	*Outcomes/comments*
P S E	1:1	Daily			To sit and focus for a complete whole group story time or small group activity time without adult prompts.		Student can sit for a whole class lesson at times, depending on the subject. This is improving daily but still needs reminding
					To respond appropriately to questioning using his own vocabulary and without repeating the adult.		He shows he is working when he asks a question first at carpet time, but he will revert back to repeating others when he is asked back to repeating others when he is asked a question later on.

[1]The comments that Susan annotated to this map have been formatted in italics.

Appendix B4

Year 8 pilot provision map for cognition and learning needs

Differentiation by need

Weak literacy and dyslexia

- Give short, simple instructions.
- Allow extra thinking time to take up instructions and complete tasks.
- Model tasks and show finished examples
- Get pupil to repeat back instructions to you.
- Use strategies such as checklists, reminder notes, use of expanding file to support organisation.
- Print out homework instructions in numbered steps.
- Enlist the support of a peer helper.
- Plan multi-sensory activities.
- Don't make the children read aloud but praise them if they choose to.
- Use tinted overlays, cream paper, pastel-coloured backgrounds on smartboard.
- Look for alternatives to extended writing e.g. presentations, role-play, mind maps, matching labels to pictures/maps/diagrams.
- Scaffold writing with simple writing frames.
- Minimise copying by providing handouts/missing word exercises.
- Highlight information on the smartboard to be copied in a different colour and tell pupils to concentrate on these parts only.
- Encourage use of keyword lists and VCOP pyramids.
- Encourage pupil to use spelling strategy every time they ask for a spelling, e.g. make and break (break word into syllables) or look, cover, write, check.

Weak numeracy and dyscalculia

- Break tasks down into clear steps (process criteria) and model.
- Provide time for recap and consolidation at each stage and revisit basic skills often.
- Allow students thinking time to complete tasks.
- Encourage pupils to use scrap paper to work out complex sums rather than do it all in their heads.

- Use a variety of visual and kinaesthetic resources – objects, images and models.
- Provide number squares and prepared formats for recording calculations.
- Provide help/cue cards for different operations/vocabulary.
- Use small numbers when introducing new concepts.
- Ask lots of questions, rephrasing your sentences and using different vocabulary.
- Establish a routine of estimate-calculate-check.

Working memory

- Give short, simple instructions.
- Allow extra thinking time to take up instructions and complete tasks
- Get pupils to repeat back instructions to you.
- Use strategies such as checklists, stepped instructions and reminder notes.
- Plan multi-sensory activities.
- Use writing frames.
- Provide cue cards for complicated instructions.
- Always provide time for recap and consolidation at each stage and revisit basic skills often.

ASD

- Seat student in an area free from displays and distractions.
- Use very clear classroom routines, e.g. lining up, equipment check, student holding object when it is their turn to talk.
- Display classroom rules with pictures.
- Constantly reinforce and teach social skills, e.g. how to ask for help, what to do when praised – say what to do NOT what not to do.
- Illustrate expectations visually, e.g. use a noise-ometer, examples of finished work.
- Support presentations with charts, diagrams, pictures or objects.
- Set tasks with clear goals, e.g. 'write three sentences about…' rather than 'write about…' 'or you must answer two questions/listen for 5 minutes'.
- Use a visual way of showing the pupil what they will be doing, e.g. a written list supported by pictures, a clock face divided into sections.
- Use short simple instructions, given one at a time.
- Repeat instructions in same words.
- Support writing with writing frames, missing word exercises, Q + A boxes, etc.
- Avoid metaphorical language and idioms.
- Use student's name before asking them anything.
- Redirect conversations back to task.
- Prevent repetitive questions or comments by giving pupils a set number of cards, once the cards are finished, no more questions.
- Allow student to work alone if possible.
- Give clear roles and rules in writing if group work is planned.
- Use incentives based on pupil's interests.
- If pupil becomes anxious, allow them to move to an agreed calm-down area.
- Model that making mistakes is OK and part of the learning process.

Details of interventions

Intervention	Ratio	Frequency/ staff	Pupils	Entry data	Intervention target	Exit Data	Outcomes/comments
Paired Reading & Comprehension	1:1	2 x 15 mins	[illegible]	10yrs 5mths	Reading age should improve by a ratio gain of 2 (e.g. improvement of 3.5 months in a 7-week period)	9yrs 5mth (−12)	Only attended 2 sessions; negative progress.
			[illegible]	12yrs 5mths		12yrs 7m (+2)	*Some progress
			[illegible]	11yrs 8mths		13yrs 3m (+18)	*Excellent progress
			[illegible]	9yrs 11mths		10yrs 11 (+12)	*Excellent progress
			[illegible]	9yrs 6mths		10yrs 11 (+17)	Good attendance; good reader but struggles on longer words; excellent progress
			[illegible]	10yrs 3mths		10yrs 11 (+8)	*Good progress
			[illegible]	10yrs 5mths		10yrs 3m (−2)	Good attendance; negative progress.
			[illegible]	10yrs 7mths		10yrs 11 (+4)	Good attendance; good progress
			[illegible]	12yrs 3mths		12yrs 7m (+4)	Good attendance; good progress
			[illegible]	11yrs 5mths		11yrs 10 (+5)	Good attendance; good progress
			[illegible]	12yrs 0mths		13yrs 3 (+15)	Attends regularly and is learning to read a little slower which improves her accuracy; excellent progress.
			[illegible]	9yrs 7mths		11yrs 5m (+22)	Excellent progress

(continued)

Details of interventions *(Continued)*

Intervention	*Ratio*	*Frequency/ staff*	*Pupils*	*Entry data*	*Intervention target*	*Exit Data*	*Outcomes/comments*
N* (phonics programme)	1:5	2x20 mins LSA		10yrs 0	Improvement in spelling age above *assumed* age-related progress, e.g. all children would have been expected to make 8 months progress from their baseline in September to their spelling re-test in May, and this should show acceleration with the N* (phonics) intervention (more than 8 months indicates success).	11yrs 0 (+12)	Good progress
				8yrs 9		10yrs 0 (+13)	Good attendance; good progress
				10yrs 1		11yrs 6 (+15)	Good attendance; good progress
				11yrs 0		11yrs 0 (0)	Good attendance; no progress
				10yrs 0		14yrs 4 (+52)	Excellent attendance; excellent progress!?
				10yrs 3		11yrs 8 (+17)	Regular attendance; good progress
				10yrs 5		11yrs 8 (+15)	Excellent attendance; good progress
				11yrs 0		12yrs 2 (+14)	Excellent attendance; good progress
				10yrs 0		11yrs 2 (+14)	Good attendance; good progress. Works hard.
				9yrs 4		9yrs 8 (+4)	Regular attendance; slow progress
				10yrs 1		10yrs 5 (+4)	Regular attendance; slow progress
				10yrs 6		11yrs 4 (+10)	Good attendance; good progress
				10yrs 6		11yrs 8 (+14)	Regular attendance; good progress
				10yrs 8		13yrs 2 (+30)	Excellent attendance; excellent progress
				10yrs 3		12yrs 0 (+21)	Good progress
				10yrs 0		10yrs 8 (+8)	Good attendance; good progress
				10yrs 0		11yrs 2 (+14)	Poor attendance; good progress
				10yrs		11yrs 0 (+12)	Good attendance; good progress
				9yrs 3		9yrs 4 (+1)	Regular attendance; poor progress
				10yrs 3		11yrs 6 (+15)	Good attendance; good progress

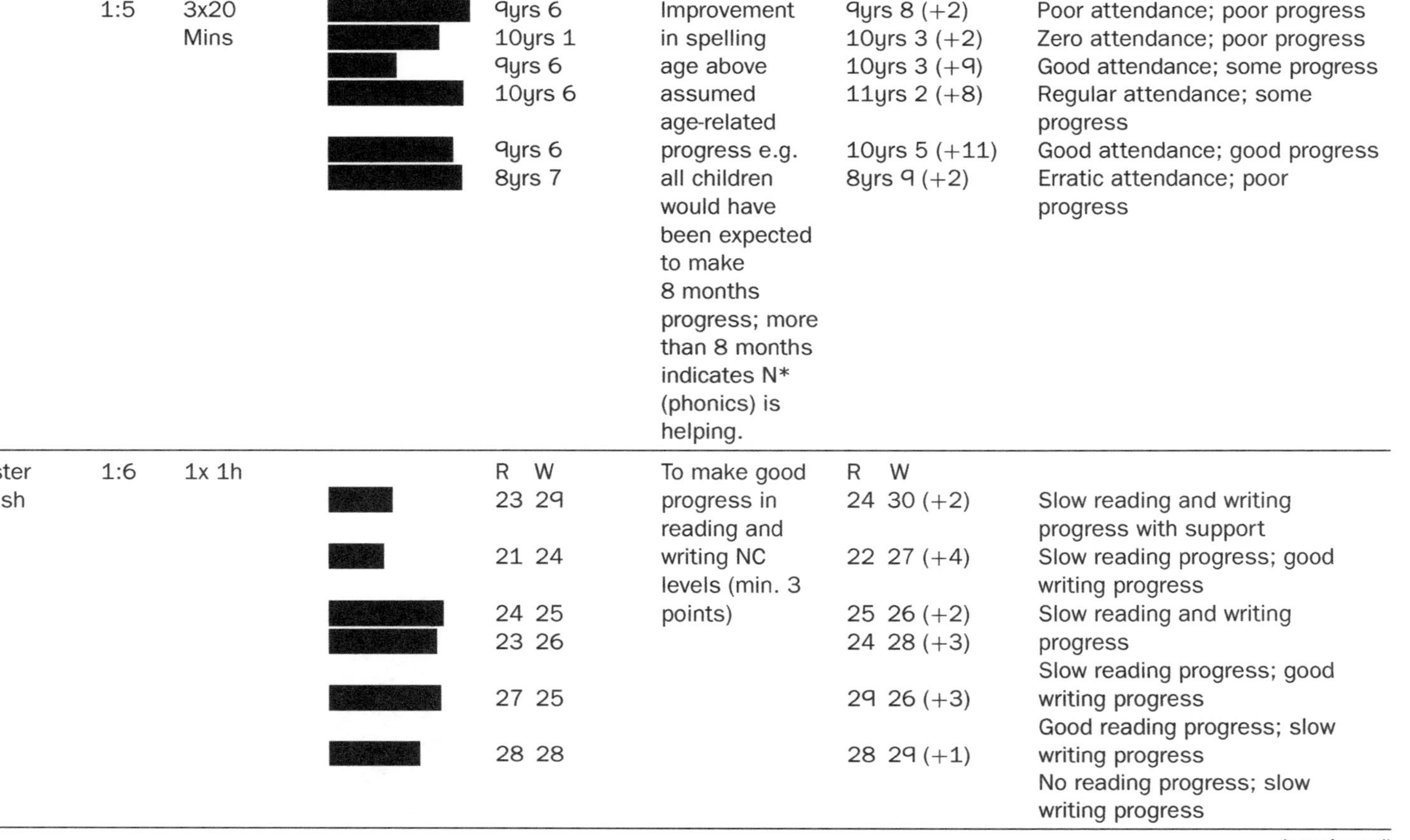

	1:5	3x20 Mins		9yrs 6	Improvement in spelling age above assumed age-related progress e.g. all children would have been expected to make 8 months progress; more than 8 months indicates N* (phonics) is helping.	9yrs 8 (+2)	Poor attendance; poor progress
				10yrs 1		10yrs 3 (+2)	Zero attendance; poor progress
				9yrs 6		10yrs 3 (+9)	Good attendance; some progress
				10yrs 6		11yrs 2 (+8)	Regular attendance; some progress
				9yrs 6		10yrs 5 (+11)	Good attendance; good progress
				8yrs 7		8yrs 9 (+2)	Erratic attendance; poor progress
Booster English	1:6	1x 1h		R W	To make good progress in reading and writing NC levels (min. 3 points)	R W	
				23 29		24 30 (+2)	Slow reading and writing progress with support
				21 24		22 27 (+4)	Slow reading progress; good writing progress
				24 25		25 26 (+2)	Slow reading and writing progress
				23 26		24 28 (+3)	Slow reading progress; good writing progress
				27 25		29 26 (+3)	Good reading progress; slow writing progress
				28 28		28 29 (+1)	No reading progress; slow writing progress

(continued)

Details of interventions *(Continued)*

Booster Maths	1:5	1x 1h		24	To make good progress in maths NC level (minimum 3 points)	27 (+3)	Good progress
				25		26 (+1)	Slow progress
				25		25 (+0)	No progress made
				26		27 (+1)	Slow progress
				22		23 (+1)	Slow progress
				24		27 (+3)	Good progress
				24		25 (+1)	Slow progress
				25		26 (+1)	Slow progress
				26		28 (+2)	Good progress
				24		25 (+1)	Slow progress

Note: Pupils' names have been blacked out to maintain anonymity.

Appendix B5

Evaluated school provision map for cognition and learning needs

Intervention type	*Frequency, duration & staff*	*Group size*	*No. of pupils*	*Total cost of intervention*	*Cost per pupil*	*Mean gain over 7 weeks*	*Ratio Gain (months)*	*Cost per pupil per month gained*
Peer Reading	1 x 15 minutes PEER	1:1	18	£0.00	£0.00	–2.7 months reading age	1: –1.5	£0.00 (but negative gain)
Paired Reading	1 x 15 mins LSA 1 x 15 mins PEER	1:1	11	£155.16	£14.11	4.6 months reading age	1: 2.6	£3.07
Paired Reading	2 x 15 mins LSA	1:1	27	£761.67	£28.21	10.4 months reading age	1: 5.9	£2.71
Intensive Reading Comprehension	4 x 15 mins LSA	1:1	1	£56.42	£56.42	8 months reading age	1: 4.6	£7.05
N* (phonics)	2 x 20 mins LSA	5	58	£451.36	£7.78	1.1 month spelling age	1: 0.6	£7.07
N* (phonics)	3 x 20 mins LSA	5	11	£169.26	£15.39	0.4 months spelling age	1: 0.2	£38.47
N* (phonics)	4 x 20 mins LSA	5	5	£75.23	£15.05	4 months spelling age	1: 2.3	£3.76
W* (PHONICS)	4 X 15 mins LSA	1:1	4	£400.91	£100.23	8.5 months spelling age	1: 4.9	£11.79
T (literacy programme)	4 x 20 mins LSA	1:1	1	£100.23	£100.23	14 months reading age	1: 8	£7.16
P (maths programme)	4 x 20 mins LSA	1:1	25	£2,380.67	£95.23	1.8 NC points	1: 1.03	£52.90
Booster English	1 hour TEACHER	1:6	4	£371.00	£16.86	1.6 NC points	1: 0.9	£10.54
Booster Maths	1 hour TEACHER	1:7	3	£277.20	£14.59	1.3 NC points	1: 0.7	£11.27

Appendix B6

Factors influencing the effectiveness of interventions, and next steps

Intervention	*Evaluation of effectiveness*	*Next steps/action to be taken*
Peer Reading	This intervention has shown a negative gain. There are at least two explanations for this: First, the assessment (based on the Suffolk Reading Scale, 1987) could have introduced error due to the 'snapshot' nature of this kind of summative assessment. Second, as this was a peer scheme, it was organised by the Head of English before I took over as SENCO. On investigation, the children were not trained in how to use their time effectively. They also did not keep any records of attendance or use a levelled reading scheme. It is most likely that children have not attended any reading sessions, given the lack of pupils around school observed reading with a peer during registration time, and the reading may have been inappropriate if sessions had gone ahead, e.g. too easy/hard.	Committed reading buddies need to be selected by the HOD and put forward for training in the Pause, Prompt, Praise reading method (Arnold et al., 1987) and record-keeping. A levelled reading scheme should be used by peer readers, along with a recording book so progress can be monitored and children have access to appropriate materials. A reward system for the reading buddies and attendees needs to be instigated to encourage regular attendance. This is an opportunity that is currently being wasted.
Paired Reading	Paired reading is effective and children with two sessions with an LSA are making the best gains. This is the most cost-effective method for improving reading age found in this study. This may be attributable to the fact that LSAs were trained in Pause, Prompt, Praise before the provision maps commenced, and were also shown how to record pupil mistakes carefully (miscues) so that they could work on these in the sessions as well as read. However, it has to be said that there is a possibility that the gains for this intervention have become 'muddled' with other interventions, e.g. many of those pupils doing Paired Reading were also taking part in N* (phonics) and this could be skewing the results. Also, as the intervention targeted reading age, these results are limited by the drawbacks of the Suffolk Reading test detailed above as well.	Identify children's reading needs more clearly and use these to make a more specific target for the provision map, e.g. assessment needs to show if the child needs help decoding text or comprehending it. This requires a reading assessment to be bought in that could provide clearer entry and exit criteria, e.g. Literacy Diagnostic. Support the Wave 3 Paired reading with Wave 2 guided reading groups to enable more pupils to receive support. This will require guided reading books and materials to be bought in.

1:1 Reading Comprehension	This is an effective intervention but it is expensive. Again, the effectiveness could be skewed by the fact that: (1) only one person received this intervention; and (2) reading age alone does not show an actual improvement in comprehension.	Interventions for comprehension need to be assessed and evaluated against more specific targets, e.g. AFs or a diagnostic test in order to get a more accurate picture of what is going on and distinguish this from reading ability. A Wave 2 equivalent needs to be introduced to ensure more of the children who need support with comprehension can access appropriate help. SENCO to ensure QFT is in place to aid understanding, e.g. through CPD on 'Active listening', provision of keyword lists on schemes of work, etc.
N* (phonics)	N* (phonics) results were very mixed and therefore inconclusive, due to a number of problems with the entry and exit level assessments e.g.: • Pupils were screened for poor spelling using the Vernon Spelling Test (Vernon, 1977) and then put on computers to undertake the N* (phonics) Spelling Challenge/ Assessment. This allowed the computer to design an individualised spelling programme for each child which covered their gaps in spelling knowledge. It was assumed at this stage that this assessment would also provide the entry data for the provision map. However, the assessment could not be pulled off the programme and used in a meaningful way on the provision map, e.g. it only told you that the child was on island 4 of 10, for instance.	Next time the paper-based N* (phonics) assessment should be used to provide the entry and exit criteria for the provision map. This will provide very specific target for different N* (phonics) groups, e.g. improve awareness of split-diagraphs/CVCC spellings, etc. Pupils should be grouped by ability on the outcome of this test; this will allow the LSA to direct learning activities and begin to use the printable worksheets/ games from N* (phonics) to enhance the N* (phonics) sessions further and provide opportunities for overlearning and variety. This may help to increase pupil attendance, althoughN* (phonics) sessions are generally popular except for a minority of disengaged pupils who do not turn up. A positive reward may help with this going forward.

(continued)

(continued)

Intervention	*Evaluation of effectiveness*	*Next steps/action to be taken*
	• To make up for this oversight, the only data on which progress could be measured was the original screening data. The Vernon test had originally been undertaken in October. It was redone during the exam week in May to provide exit data. As the Vernon test was based on providing a standard age score for spelling, and 8 months had elapsed between assessments, 8 months had to be taken away from the progress seen in spelling age from the exit data. The spelling data is therefore based on the assumption that children who took part in N* (phonics) would make more than the 'normal' 8 months progress; this is seriously flawed in that many of the children selected for this intervention had never made 'normal' progress and were in fact at least 2 years behind. Therefore, any improvement in the rate of progress cannot been seen. • Another problem is that the Vernon Test does not necessarily reflect the N* (phonics) programme of spelling as it is an old test, whereas the N* (phonics) learning activities are centred on a newer synthetic phonics approach. Besides these assessment problems, anomalies have been introduced into the results for N* (phonics) interventions by operational problems. Individual results vary enormously. Reasons for this may be: • Poor attendance of pupils and LSAs to run the sessions (because of cover requirements, SATS, etc.) along with inaccurate assessment could explain the negative gains; if pupils were really struggling with spelling and made little progress before the intervention, then did not attend as regularly as they should have, the assessments would assume that they have not made any progress because they had not *done* enough to make over 8 months progress.	LSA to be made responsible for one group; before different LSAs may have been rostered on to provide the N* (phonics) sessions. Next time a new intervention is introduced, make sure that it is evaluated on a cohort that is receiving no other similar intervention and whose entry/exit criteria are very distinct. Better assessment of need to distinguish between cognitive difference and language disorders.

	• Positive gains, that fall outside the limits of standard deviation shown on the graph, can be attributed to the combined effect of other interventions. It is a flaw of the design of this pilot that assessmentsare not specific enough, nor provide separate cohorts, to study the effect of an individual intervention. The four individuals who showed such gains were participating in W* (PHONICS) and extra reading. • Negative gains that fall outside the limits of the standard deviation shown on the graph, are also probably due to a variety of factors rather than failures of N* (phonics) such as inaccuracies introduced by the summative nature of the Vernon test, inconsistencies in the quality of the intervention as it was delivered by different LSAs in order to use LSA time efficiently, poor attitude and attendance of pupil, or even misdiagnosis of the need (e.g. spelling problems could indicate a language processing deficit rather than a spelling problem and cause even more confusion to the child involved).	
W* (PHONICS)	This proved to be an effective intervention; the sample size studied was very small with only four pupils undertaking this intervention. Of the four, one child showed a poor attitude to the intervention and did not attend regularly. As a result, this has skewed the results. The results would have also been skewed by the fact that all of these pupils were undergoing other interventions at the same time, making it impossible to say which intervention is responsible for what gain.	Use a diagnostic literacy assessment to pin-point area for improvement.

(continued)

(continued)

Intervention	*Evaluation of effectiveness*	*Next steps/action to be taken*
T (literacy programme)	This proved to be the most effective intervention for reading improvement but was based on only one pupil. Again, this very positive result may have been skewed by the fact that this pupil was undergoing other interventions at the same time, making it impossible to say which intervention is responsible for what gain.	Use a diagnostic literacy assessment to pin-point area for improvement.
P (maths programme)	The LSAs, pupils and parents reported greatly improved confidence and better performance in mental maths tests as a result of this intervention but the intervention itself was not shown to be effective. The main problem here, was the use of NC levels rather than a more specific diagnostic assessment on which to evaluate the results.	Use a diagnostic maths assessment, or a specific AF, to measure the success of this intervention next time.
Booster English	Shown not to be effective but, as this was assessed by an improvement in NC level, concerns over whether the 7-week time period measured would be enough to allow this.	Allocate groups based on the findings of a specific diagnostic assessment, e.g. it may be better to have different reading and writing groups rather than putting children with different needs in the same set for teaching.
Booster Maths	Shown not to be effective but, as this was assessed by an improvement in NC level, concerns over whether the 7-week time period measured would be enough to allow this.	Allocate groups based on the findings of a specific diagnostic assessment for numeracy. Ensure the use of 'concrete' examples.

Appendix B7

Example of completed template for a school or college SEND policy and Information Report

Special Educational Needs and Disability (SEND) Policy/Special Educational Needs Information Report

Name of school ______________________
Date: [add date of this current version]

This policy is written in line with the requirements of:

- Children and Families Act 2014 and associated regulations;
- *Special Educational Needs and Disability Code of Practice 0–25 years* (DfE, 2014a);
- Equality Act 2010;
- Schools Admissions Code (DfE, 2012).

It is updated annually.

This policy should be read in conjunction with the following school policies: any other linked policies, e.g. Behaviour/Discipline Policy, Equalities Policy, Safeguarding Policy, Homework Policy, Dyslexia Policy.

This policy was developed with [give details of how the policy was developed and in consultation with whom, e.g. by the SENCO in liaison with the school's SEND governor, senior leadership team, all staff, parents of young people with SEND, and so on]. It will be reviewed annually.

Definition of SEN

By law, a child or young person has special educational needs if he or she has a learning difficulty or disability which calls for special educational provision to be made for him or her (Children and Families Act, 2014, Part 3, §20 (1)) and the educational provision that is required to meet the needs is 'special'. According to theChildren and Families Act 2014, Part 3, §20 (2), a young person has such a difficulty if s/he experiences

- significantly greater difficulty in learning than the majority of' same-age peers, or
- s/he has a disability which prevents him (or her) from making use of (educational) facilities 'of a kind generally provided for' same-age peers in mainstream educational institutions.

Definition of disability

Many children and young people who have SEN may also have a disability under the Equality Act 2010. This is defined as 'a physical or mental impairment which has a long-term and substantial adverse effect on their ability to carry out normal day-to-day activities'. According to the SEN Code of Practice (DfE, 2014a: 5): 'long-term' is defined as 'a year or more' and 'substantial' is defined as 'more than minor or trivial'. This may include children and young people with long-term medical conditions for whom adjustments will be made as required by the Equality Act, 2010.

Aims and objectives

Set out the following:

- the statement of the school's mission statement, or otherwise umbrella statement of values;
- the overall aims for the school's approach to SEND practice and provision as compatible with the mission statement;
- the objectives, for example:
  - operate a whole-school approach to identifying and providing for students with SEND;
  - ensure school practices conform to the requirements of the SEND Code of Practice (DfE, 2014a);
  - ensure SEND provision is co-ordinated by a well-qualified SENCO;
  - provide relevant CPD for all staff in the school and that all staff have access to appropriate support and advice.

Requirements of the SEN Information Report

1. **The kinds of special educational need for which provision is made at the school**
   [Name of school] is [make clear whether the school is mainstream or special]. We make provision for [give some examples of the needs catered for. You might consider listing all the SEN needs recorded for your pupils on the latest census.]

   We ensure that our admission arrangements for students do not discriminate against or disadvantage disabled children or those with special educational needs.
2. **Information about the school's policies for the identification and assessment of pupils with special educational needs**
   At [name of school] we assess each student's needs on entry. We then use a range of assessments at various points [give examples of universal assessments] to monitor the progress of all pupils [x] times a year. Where progress is not satisfactory, we put extra support in place to enable the pupil to catch up. Examples of extra support are [list of examples].

   [You might wish to outline the assess→plan→do→review cycle to make clear how pupils' names are included in your school's SEND log. For example: 'If pupils continue to make inadequate progress, in consultation with parents we will use

a range of assessment tools to determine the cause of the learning difficulty. 'Inadequate progress' is that which:

- Is significantly slower than that of their peers starting from the same baseline
- Fails to match or better the child's previous rate of progress
- Fails to close the attainment gap between rate of progress
- Widens the attainment gap

SEN Code of Practice (DfE, 2014a: 6.17)

At [name of school] we are experienced in using the following assessment tools [list of individual assessment tools]. We also have access to external advisors who are able to use the following assessment tools [list of specialist assessments].

The outcome of this more detailed assessment will be shared with parents/families and the student, and we will discuss with them what additional resources and different approaches are required to enable the pupil to make better progress. We will put the outcome of this discussion into an SEN support plan and it will be reviewed regularly, and refined /revised if necessary. At this point we will have identified the pupil has a special educational need and make special educational provision for the pupil which is additional and different from what is normally available.

When a pupil is able to maintain good progress without the additional and different resources he or she will not be identified with special educational needs. When any change in identification of SEN is changed parents will be notified.

We will ensure that all teachers and support staff who work with the pupil are aware of the support to be provided and the teaching approaches to be used.

3. Information about the school's policies for making provision for pupils with special educational needs whether or not they have EHC Plans, including

(a) *How the school evaluates the effectiveness of its provision*
[Include here an outline of the school's systems and criteria for evaluating the effectiveness of its provision. You might wish to outline, for example, how each review of the individual SEN support plan will be informed by the views of the pupil, parents and class/subject teachers and the assessment information from teachers in order to see whether adequate progress is being made.

You might also wish to make reference to evaluations of all individual interventions and/or use of provision maps to ensure effectiveness, and/or evaluation of the effectiveness of the special provision at annual reviews for pupils with or without a statement of special educational needs/Education, Health and Care Plan, and evaluations of effectiveness that will be reported to the governing body.]

(b) *The school's arrangements for assessing and reviewing the progress of pupils with special educational needs*
Every pupil in the school has his/her progress tracked [number of times] per year. In addition to this, pupils with special educational needs may have more frequent assessments of reading, spelling, and so on to see if pupils are increasing their level of skills in key areas. [You might wish to add a list of assessments commonly used, or refer to the list above.] If these assessments do not show adequate progress the SEN support plan will be reviewed

and adjusted. We will make every effort to ensure that parent/families and the pupils will be actively involved at all stages in this process.

(c) *The school's approach to teaching pupils with special educational needs*
We make every effort to ensure high quality differentiated teaching in our classrooms for all our pupils. [Add an outline of the school's approach to differentiation, the use of individual plans, the matching of provision to individual needs, the approach to ensuring that teacher are aware of, and use, strategies to identify and support vulnerable pupils.]

In meeting the needs of individual students in classroom the school employs some additional teaching approaches [add examples of small group teaching, particular interventions designed to meet specific needs, and so on.]

(d) *How the school adapts the curriculum and learning environment for pupils with special educational needs*
[Outline how the school adapts the curriculum and learning environment, the reasonable adjustments made to meet the range of SEND, and how learning is planned, including group and individual adaptations. Also outline how account is taken of individual plans within the overall curriculum.]

(e) *Additional support for learning that is available to pupils with special educational needs*
The degree and kind of support required for each pupil with SEND to make good progress will vary. A full list of the interventions we offer is on our provision map. [Outline how resources are allocated, who is involved in decision-making and their role in this. Outline also how access arrangements are made for public examinations.]

The school is required to provide up to £6000 per year of resource for pupils with high needs, and above that amount the local authority should provide top up to the school.

(f) *How the school enables pupils with special educational needs to engage in activities of the school (including physical activities) together with children who do not have special educational needs*
All clubs, trips and activities offered to pupils at [name of school] are available to pupils with special educational needs. Where necessary, the school will use the resources available to it to provide additional adult support to enable the safe participation of the pupil in the activity. [You might also include information provided about support available during break times and the beginning and end of the school day.]

(g) *Support that is available for improving the emotional and social development of pupils with special educational needs*
At [name of school] we [outline the pastoral and social support that is available, the arrangements made to meet personal care needs, the support that is available to address unacceptable behaviour and/or attendance issues, make reference to the behaviour policy if appropriate, and ways in which the school ensures pupil safety. Also, if appropriate, include reference to access to a counsellor, referral to CAHMS, time-out space in the school for pupils to use, and so on].

4. **The name and contact details of the SEN Co-ordinator**
The SENCO at [name of school] is [name of SENCO], who is a qualified teacher, holds the National Award for SEN Co-ordination and additionally has the following qualifications [list of other qualifications].
Contact details for the SENCO are: [give telephone number or email address.If the SENCO is class teacher or part-time give best times for contact.]

5. **Information about the expertise and training of staff in relation to children and young people with special educational needs and how specialist expertise will be secured**
All teachers and teaching assistants have had the following awareness training [add a list of all awareness, training, and so on]. In addition, the following teachers have received specialist training as follows: [add list of members of staff, training received and qualifications gained]. If a training need is identified beyond our current staff specialisms we [outline theCPD programme, links with external specialists, and so on].

6. **Information about how equipment and facilities to support children and young people with special educational needs will be secured**
[Include here information about the school's accessibility for disabled students.]
Where external advisors recommend the use of equipment or facilities which the school does not have we [outline what the school will do in this situation].

7. **The arrangements for consulting parents of children with special educational needs about, and involving them in, their education**
All parents of pupils at [name of school] are invited to discuss the progress of their children on [number of occasions a year] and receive a written report [number of times per year].In addition [add any other opportunities for consultation with parents and families, for example new parents' visits, open days, and so on.]
In addition [add any other opportunities for families of children with SEND to discuss their progress with key staff that are additional to/different from opportunities for other families].
Parent/carers will be invited to all planning and reviews of provision for SEND and actively supported to contribute to assessment, planning and review. Wherever possible annual reviews will also include other agencies involved with the pupil. Information will be made accessible for parents.

8. **The arrangements for consulting young people with special educational needs about, and involving them in, their education**
When a pupil has been identified as having special educational needs s/he will be consulted about and involved in the arrangements made for them as part of person-centred planning.

9. **The arrangements made by the governing body relating to the treatment of complaints from parents of pupils with special educational needs concerning the provision made at the school**
[Name of school] has a formal complaints procedure for any complaint made by parents/carers. This procedure should be followed for any complaint about provision made for special educational needs. We encourage parents to discuss their

concerns with [give the list of school staff who are the first points of contact if a parent wishes to discuss something about the school or college. Also outline the school/college's general approach to resolving concerns prior to the parent/carer making the complaint formal to the Chair of the governing body.]

If the complaint is not resolved after it has been considered by the governing body, then a disagreement resolution service or mediation service can be contracted.If it remains unresolved after this, the complainant can appeal to the First–tier Tribunal (Special Educational Needs and Disability), if the case refers to disability discrimination, or to the Secretary of State for all other cases.

10. How the governing body involves other bodies, including health and social services bodies, local authority support services and voluntary organisations, in meeting the needs of pupils with special educational needs and in supporting the families of such pupils

The governing body have engaged with the following bodies:

[Add details of other professionals and organisations that provide support to children and young people at the school/college, of specialist staff working at the school, and any other services accessed by the school, including social care, health and therapies of various kinds.]

11. The contact details of support services for the parents of pupils with special educational needs, including those for arrangements made in accordance with clause 32 (Parent Partnership Services)

[Add details of the local authority parent partnership service here, and where to find details of the Local Offer.]

12. The school's arrangements for supporting pupils with special educational needs in transferring between phases of education or in preparing for adulthood and independent living

At [name of school] we work closely with the educational settings used by the pupils before they transfer to us in order to seek the information that will make the transfer is a seamless as possible. [Description of arrangements for seeking information from previous settings.]

We also contribute information to the next setting. [Description of arrangements for providing information to the next setting.]

13. Information on where the local authority's local offer is published.

The local authority's local offer is published on [web address]. We advise parents and families without access to the Internet to make an appointment with the SENCO for support to gain the information they require.

Approved by the GB on ______________________________

Next review on ______________________________

Appendix B8

Lesson observation pro-forma

Date:		Teacher:					**Lesson details: (topic/objectives)**			
Class/Year:		TA:								
Time from start of lesson (minutes)	Lesson part*	Predominant activity of TA					TA-supported pupil(s) (name, attainment level, SEN status)	Task differentiation for TA-supported pupils	Comments on teacher's role	Features of TA-to-pupil talk
		With pupil one-to-one	With group of pupils	Roving Classroom	Listening to teacher teach	Other task (tidying/admin)				
1										
2										
3										
4										
5										
[...]										
59										
60										
Total ✓										
Summary		%	%	%	%	%				
***Key for Lesson part: I = Teacher's main input T = Main learning task P = Plenary**										

Appendix B9

Whole-school needs analyses

Where possible, please discuss these Needs Analyses with your Line Manager, a member of the governing body, teaching and support staff and any others with an interest in the area of special educational needs, disability and inclusion.

Brief notes only are needed to complete these Needs Analyses.

Schools' policies and information reports relating to special educational needs provision, disability, access and inclusion

Check your policy documents on special educational needs and disability very carefully against the requirements.

- How does the SEND policy reflect the school's aims as set out in the school brochure?
- How does this policy link to the School Development Plan?
- When was the policy last reviewed and what was the review process?
- How are targets set in relation to this policy and what kinds of success criteria are used?
- To what extent is the policy a useful tool in evaluating and enhancing the quality of provision?
- Does the SEN Information Report on your school website include the information required by law about provision for special educational needs and disability?
- Do these documents meet the requirements? Is anything missing?

Overall areas of strength:

____

Overall areas for improvement:

____

Quality of teaching and learning for pupils with SEND

- To what extent is there evidence of differentiation in teachers' lesson planning?;
- To what extent is there evidence that teachers have taken account of individual learning plans for pupils with SEND?
- Does pupil grouping in classrooms enable pupils with SEND to develop their understanding through talk with other pupils with a range of abilities and levels of achievement?
- How far do teaching approaches and learning activities in mainstream classrooms enable all pupils to demonstrate what they know, understand and can do?
- To what extent do the marking and feedback of classroom teachers:
    - recognise and encourage the effort and achievement of pupils with SEND?
    - provide constructive advice, at an appropriate level, for future improvement?
- Is there obvious partnership working between classroom teachers and in-class support staff?
- Is the impact of additional/different provision in classrooms assessed on a regular basis?
- To what extent do all teachers know how to support reading/writing/numeracy skills in mainstream classes?

Overall areas of strength:

____

Overall areas for improvement:

____

Use of homework

- Is the homework set always appropriate for pupils with SEND?
- Are there clear procedures for assessing the appropriateness and value-addedness of homework?

Overall areas of strength:

____

Overall areas for improvement:

____

Use of support staff in classrooms and elsewhere

- What evidence do you have that your teaching assistants have
  - clear roles and expectations?
  - opportunities for CPD (either in-school or external)?
  - time for planning with class teachers?
  - regular access to pupils' individual (education) plans?
- Do teaching assistants contribute to records of individual pupils?
- Is there evidence of learning gain where the work of teaching assistants comprises part of the additional provision for pupils with SEND?

Overall areas of strength:

Overall areas for improvement:

Pupil voice

- To what extent do pupils with SEND have regular opportunities for giving their views on what helps and hinders their learning
  - in classrooms with class teachers?
  - in special sessions or individual/small group interventions?
  - in evaluations of their learning needs and planning for addressing these?
  - in setting targets?
- Do records for individual pupils include evidence of pupils' views?
- Are pupils always aware of their own learning plans and targets within them?
- Is there evidence of this?
- In what ways are pupils encouraged to express any concerns they may have about their own work and progress?

Overall areas of strength:

Overall areas for improvement:

Parent/family/carer involvement

- Do parents/families/carers of pupils with SEND have regular (at least twice yearly) opportunities to discuss the progress, and future plans for, their children in school?

- What is the procedure for parental/carers' complaints about the effectiveness of the special provision made to meet pupils' special learning needs?
- What opportunities are there for parents/carers to express a concern about a child's progress?
- How does the school respond?
- To what extent:
  - is clear account taken of parents'/families'/carers' views?
  - do pupils' files contain evidence of parents'/families'/carers' involvement?
- How are parents/carers informed of appropriate sources of support that may be available to them?

Overall areas of strength:

____

Overall areas for improvement:

____

Assessment of pupils' SEND

- Are there clear procedures for assessing pupils' needs on entry to the school?
- To what extent:
  - do forms of assessment of pupils' attainments allow for the progress and achievement of all children to be recognised?
  - are all staff aware of the agreed procedures for identifying and assessing the special learning needs of pupils?
  - are the arrangements for reviewing the progress of children identified as having SEND successful, including annual reviews for pupils with statements?
  - are links always made between the outcomes of assessment of SEND and plans made for individuals?
  - are pupils with SEND and their families always fully involved in discussions of needs and planning for individual provision?
  - is there evidence of all this?

Overall areas of strength:

____

Overall areas for improvement:

____

Record-keeping

- Do pupils' files contain evidence of progress:
  - from starting points?
  - in relation to additional provision/interventions?
- Does the school keep records of:
  - attainment and progress of pupils educated (wholly or partly) off-site?
  - literacy learning levels and progress across the whole school?
  - whole-school and/or group programmes to raise the level of literacy learning (if appropriate), and their outcomes?
  - numeracy learning levels and progress across the whole school?
  - whole-school and/or group programmes to raise the level of numeracy learning (if appropriate)and their outcomes?
  - individual case studies of assessment of pupils' difficulties, interventions and pupils' progress?
  - attainment and progress of different groups?

Overall areas of strength:

Overall areas for improvement:

Use of pupil premium

- To what extent:
  - are interventions clearly targeted at the designated pupils?
  - are there clear links between pupils' learning needs and decisions taken about spending pupil premium monies?
  - are the interventions clearly evaluated against their aims and objectives?
  - is there evidence of the impact of the interventions?

Overall areas of strength:

Overall areas for improvement:

Behaviour policies

- Does the school have a behaviour policy that has been recently evaluated and amended, where appropriate?

- To what extent does this policy contain all that is required (see Chapter 11)?
- Does the school behaviour policy include sections on
  - bullying?
  - cyber-bullying?
  - attendance and punctuality of pupils?
- Are all staff familiar with the behaviour policy?
- Are there procedures in place for monitoring the behaviour, attendance and exclusion rates of different groups of pupils?

Overall areas of strength:

Overall areas for improvement:

CPD in SEND

- How are staff development needs identified in respect of making appropriate provision for pupils with special learning needs?
- How are these staff development needs related to the school's overall staff development plan?
- Do staff have regular opportunities for CPD in SEND, either in-school or external?
- Is this CPD
  - clearly based on an analysis of staff needs?
  - evaluated against its aims and objectives?
- How does the induction of new teachers support them in fulfilling their responsibilities towards pupils with special learning needs?
- What opportunities exist for new and experienced staff to learn collaboratively?

Overall areas of strength:

Overall areas for improvement:

Resources to support learning needs, both human and material

- What is the school's budget for 'special educational needs'?
- What is the process by which the budget for 'special educational needs' is decided?
- How transparent is this process?
- How are decisions made about the allocation of resources to support pupils' learning needs from what is generally available in school?

- Which (if any) of the following criteria exist for allocating resources:
  - identified pupil learning need
  - the level of need in teaching groups
  - the needs of curriculum areas
  - values and principles expressed in the school's SEN policy
  - other?
- On what basis is support divided between:
  - individual pupils
  - in-class support
  - pupil withdrawal
  - curriculum support?

Overall areas of strength:

___

Overall areas of weakness:

___

Support services

- What information does the school have about the range of services available locally from the different support agencies: learning support, educational psychologist, educational welfare, health services, social services, voluntary organisations?
- What is the nature of the existing links the school has with these support services?
- How does the school assess its need for these services?
- Is external support targeted at individual pupils, groups of pupils, staff development, curriculum development, organisational development?
- How does the school monitor and evaluate the services it receives?
- How are staff included in discussions about the ways in which support services can work in the school?
- Does the school consult with other schools, including special schools, to maximise efficient use of resources and expertise in meeting pupils' SEND?
- How may the school need to develop its arrangements for linking with other agencies in the light of
  - the change in the law and the new (2014) Code of Practice?
  - views about the effectiveness of current arrangements?
- How will any such development be managed?

Overall areas of strength:

___

Overall areas of weakness:

___

Appendix B10

Behaviour Support Plan

Name:____________________ School: ____________________Primary ____________________

DOB:____________________

Class: Crystal Class teacher:____________________Teaching Assistants:____________________

Likes & dislikes

- Likes – sensory experiences that stimulate his hands and fingers e.g. keyboard, 'squidgy' toys, spreading sand on his skin, bubbles, iPad, colouring, music, familiar puzzles.
- Dislikes – going outside when it is cold and when the environment gets noisy.

Sensory issues

- Regularly 'plays' with hands and fingers and sometimes 'talks' to them. Sniffs hands and objects. Sometimes likes to put things in his mouth. Regularly places hands over ears, possibly to block out sensory stimulation. He doesn't like getting wet.
- Likes to spend time physically stimulating himself by spinning his body around on the floor or when standing.

Possible triggers

- Self-stimulatory
- Unable to control state of arousal
- Over or under sensory stimulation (auditory, visually, crowded spaces)
- Wants to interact with adults but doesn't know how to or how to communicate this need
- To gain adult attention
- To communicate his need for adult interaction
- Perhaps wants to be left alone

- The need to control a situation
- He wants to work on his own agenda
- Confused about what is expected, leading to stress and anxiety
- To escape a situation because he doesn't understand the purpose, therefore he has no motivation or desire to carry it out

Rewards/motivators

- Read above for what he likes and responds to. Special stickers and adult attention.
- Have two 'sensory' activity boxes. One for motivators and another for calming/relaxing. Include sensory motor toys, squeaky toys, balloons, play dough, smelly pens and lotions, etc.

General strategies

- Start the day with a sensory experience. Consider a sensory circuit. A few very familiar activities done in succession.
- Consider a mid-morning and mid-afternoon session of an intensive physical exercise circuit.
- Although he may use some verbal language and sometimes uses this to communicate, take into consideration he has significant difficulties with understanding communication and verbal language.
- Don't ask him to do something, *just TELL him*, very firmly and consistently and back up your verbal communication with something visual, if possible.
- Always respond to challenging behaviour in calm, controlled manner, confident that he will achieve the task and accept you may need to 'bring him back' after patterns of behaviour e.g. running away or saying 'No'.
- Limit the amount of verbal language adults use when giving instructions and provide plenty of time to help him process.
- Visual timetable – this may need to be portable rather than on a wall so it can be easily accessed in different areas.
- 'Now and Then' card – This needs to be consistently used. The 'Now' activity must be a motivator. He should be allowed to choose from a selection before the start of the activity.
- Accept that adult directed tasks or attention driven sessions and free play can only last for short periods of time. He must be kept busy by providing a range of short timed activities during the day.
- During each of the morning and afternoon sessions, provide plenty of opportunities for him to have some 'free play' and use this language and have a picture or symbol to back up the meaning. This provides him with opportunities to spend time on his own and work to his own agenda which can alleviate stress or anxiety.
- Do not insist on eye contact but insist that he looks at the visual cues, e.g. visual timetable and 'Now' and 'Then' cards.

Specific behaviours & strategies

- Hitting an adult and immediately running away. This can happen suddenly without warning.
    - To prevent or minimise this behaviour provide regular opportunities for him to 'communicate' and interact with adults during each morning and afternoon session by using 'Intensive Interaction' or games such as 'Peek a Boo' or 'Round and round the garden' or action nursery rhymes.
    - If the environment becomes 'busy' and noisy, keep a watchful eye and perhaps consider moving to a quieter area.
    - We need to teach him what to do rather than not what to do. Start to teach him how to communicate to an adult that he wants their attention. Read and show Social Story daily, am and pm. Practise using it to teach behaviour of gaining adult's attention e.g. tap an adult's arm, followed by verbal praise and a reward (sticker).
    - When he does hit, say 'No, that hurts', firmly but do not chase after him (otherwise you may be positively reinforcing the behaviour). It would be better for another adult to meet him at the place he has run to (if not, calmly walk and follow him) and gently move his arms and hands to his sides and say 'No hitting, that hurts'. If he is in a controlled state of arousal then take him to the adult he hurt and show him how to say sorry. If he is in an uncontrollable state then wait until he is calm before showing him not to hit and saying sorry.
    - Please make a written note of the situation for analysis and the adult who was hurt should have a debriefing of the incident with another adult.
- 'Melt down', out of control behaviour, screaming, throwing self on floor, running around.
    - To prevent or minimise this behaviour look out for early signs of stress or signs that he may go into a melt down and apply relaxing/calming strategies e.g. massage his back, ask him to lay on the floor looking up at the ceiling, play some calming music, take him to a large soft cushion to lie on. Try different strategies and make a note of the most effective.
    - If the relaxing/calming strategies do not work then accept that the 'melt down' needs to take its course, however ensure he is safe and protect others around him. Don't try to verbally communicate. Wait for him to come out of it and apply relaxation/calming strategies when judged to be an appropriate time, normally after he has gone quiet for a couple of minutes.
    - Please make a written note of the situation for analysis and the adult supporting him should have a debriefing of the incident with another adult.
- Suddenly becoming highly excited/aroused e.g. repetitive behaviours such as, laughing loudly, throwing arms around, and throwing self off chair.
    - First make a distinction between this behaviour being motivated by high arousal or used as a distraction strategy. If distraction then apply strategies for (4).
    - Stop the activity if it is an adult directed task. Stand back and allow him 2–3 minutes to see if he can self-regulate. If he isn't able to then take out a sensory calming down activity and use a very quiet voice and say 'Look' (bubbles) or 'Feel this' (a squidgy toy).

  - Allow him a few minutes to play or look at the calming object.
  - When he is calm return his attention to the adult directed task and remind him 'work first, then…' if the high arousal started during a task of his own choosing then allow him to continue saying 'free play'.
  - Please note he may repeat this pattern of behaviour a number of times, however ensure the adult directed task is completed before allowing him his motivator.
- 'Distraction' behaviours during an adult directed task e.g. playing with hands, singing, talking to self and turning attention away from task.
  - Ignore as much of this behaviour as possible, no matter how hard! It doesn't matter at this stage *how* the task is completed but he must know he needs to finish it.
  - Use minimal speech during the task, this helps him to focus on getting it complete. (Speech may in fact be an added sensory overload for him to process.)
  - If he does turn his head away from the task don't insist on him looking, just ensure he is at least using one hand to complete the task.
  - Perhaps try to introduce tasks in such a way that he needs to use both of his hands at the same time? Use hand over hand to model how to complete tasks.
  - Verbally say 'work first, then… (motivator)' and insist the task is completed.
  - Say 'all finished' just once and quickly provide the motivator.
- Refusing to carry out an adult directed task by saying 'No', turning body away or running away.
  - To prevent or minimise the behaviour, adult directed tasks that are low in motivation or are new, should be done in a low distraction room with the door shut with a powerful motivator.
  - If he says 'No', say 'work first, then (motivator)' repeatedly with visual cues.
  - Use hand over hand if necessary to complete the task.
  - If he runs away. Don't chase after him but calmly follow him and gently take him by the hand and say work first then ...
  - Insist that the task is completed, even if it means he needs bringing back after a number of times.

Medication/diet

- Needs to avoid all sugary foods and drinks as these cause him to become hyperactive.
- No medication.

Teacher: XXXXX SENCO: XXXX

Parent: XXXXX TAs: XXXXX

Plan started: April 20xx Review Date: September 20xx

References

Adams, C. and Lloyd, J. (2007) The effects of speech and language therapy intervention on children with pragmatic language impairments in mainstream school, *British Journal of Special Education*, 34(4): 226–33.

Aitken, S. (2000) 'Understanding deafblindness', in S. Aitken, M. Buultjens, C. Clark, J.T. Eyre and L. Pease (eds) *Teaching Children Who Are Deafblind*. London: David Fulton.

Aitken, S. and Millar, S. (2002) *Listening to Children with Communication Support Needs*. Glasgow: Sense Scotland.

Alborz, A., Pearson, D., Farrell, P. and Howes, A. (2009) *The Impact of Adult Support Staff on Pupils and Mainstream Schools: A Systematic Review of Evidence*. London: Institute of Education, EPPI Centre.

Ames, G. and Archer, J. (1988) Achievement goals in the classroom: students' learning strategies and motivation processes, *Journal of Educational Psychology*, 80: 260–7.

Assessment Reform Group (1999) *Assessment for Learning: Beyond the Black Box. Cambridge: University of Cambridge School of Education.*

Atkinson, M., Jones, M. and Lamont, E. (2007) *Multi-Agency Working and its Implications for Practice: A Review of the Literature*. Slough: CfBT Education Trust.

Audit Commission (1992) *Getting in on the Act: Provision for Pupils with Special Educational Needs*. London: HMSO.

Autism Education Trust/Centre for Research in Autistic Education (CRAE) (2011) *What Is Good Practice in Autism Education?* London: Autism Education Trust/CRAE.

Baer, D.M., Wolf, M.M. and Risley, T.R. (1968) Some current dimensions of applied behavior analysis, *Journal of Applied Behavior Analysis*, 1: 91–7.

Balshaw, M. (1991) *Help in the Classroom*. London: David Fulton.

Beattie, R. (2006) The oral methods and spoken language acquisition, in P. Spencer and M. Marschark (eds) *Advances in the Spoken Language Development of Deaf and Hard-of-Hearing Children*. New York: Oxford University Press.

Bell, D. (1967) *An Experiment in Education: The History of Worcester College for the Blind, 1866–1966*. London: Hutchinson.

Benn, C. and Chitty, C. (1996) *Thirty Years On: Is Comprehensive Education Alive and Well or Struggling to Survive?* London: David Fulton.

Bennathan, M. (2000) Children at risk of failure in primary schools, in M. Bennathan and M. Boxall (eds) *Effective Intervention in Primary Schools: Nurture Groups*, 2nd edn. London: David Fulton.

Bird, G. and Thomas, S. (2002) Providing effective speech and language therapy for children with Down syndrome in mainstream settings: a case example, *Down Syndrome News and Update*, 2(1): 30–1.

Birmingham City Council Education Department (1998) *Behaviour in Schools: Framework for Intervention*. Birmingham: City Council Education Department.

Bishop, D.V.M. (2000) Pragmatic language impairment: a correlate of SLI, a distinct subgroup, or part of the autistic continuum? in D.V.M. Bishop and L. Leonard (eds) *Speech and Language Impairments in Children: Causes, Characteristics, Intervention and Outcome*. Hove: Psychology Press.

Black, P. and Wiliam, D. (1998) Assessment and classroom learning, *Assessment in Education*, 5(1): 7–74.

Blatchford, P., Bassett, P., Brown, P., Martin, C., Russell, A. and Webster, R. (2009) *Deployment and Impact of Support Staff (DISS) Project*. London: London University Institute of Education.

Blatchford, P., Russell, A., Bassett, P., Brown, P. and Martin, C. (2004) *The Role and Effects of Teaching Assistants in English Primary Schools (Years 4 to 6) 2000 – 2003: Results from the Class Size and Pupil–Adult Ratios (CSPAR) KS2 Project*. Nottingham: DfES.

Blatchford, P., Webster, R. and Russell, A. (2012) *Challenging the Role and Deployment of Teaching Assistants in Mainstream Schools: The Impact on Schools. Final Report on Findings from the Effective Deployment of Teaching Assistants (EDTA) Project*. London: Institute of Education.

Borthwick, A. and Harcourt-Heath, M. (2007) Calculation strategies used by Year 5 children, *Proceedings of the British Society for Research into Learning Mathematics*, 27(1): 12–23.

Bowlby, J. (1952) A two-year-old goes to hospital, *Proceedings of the Royal Society of Medicine*, 46: 425–7.

Boxall, M. (2002) *Nurture Groups in School: Principles and Practice*. London: Paul Chapman.

Bradley, L. and Bryant, P. E. (1983) Categorising sounds and learning to read: a causal connection, *Nature*, 301: 419–21.

Brandon, M., Bailey, S., Belderson, P., Gardner, R., Sidebotham, P., Dodsworth, J., Warren, C. and Black, J. (2009) *Understanding Serious Case Reviews and their Impact: A Biennial Analysis of Serious Case Reviews 2005–07*. London: Department for Children, Schools and Families.

Brandon, M., Belderson, P., Warren, C., Gardner, R., Howe, D., Dodsworth, J. and Black, J. (2008) The preoccupation with thresholds in cases of child death or serious injury through abuse and neglect, *Child Abuse Review*, 17(5): 313–30.

British Psychological Society (BPS) (1996) *Attention Deficit Hyperactivity Disorder (ADHD): A Psychological Response to an Evolving Concept*. Leicester: BPS.

British Psychological Society (BPS) (1999) *Dyslexia, Literacy and Psychological Assessment*. Leicester: BPS.

Brooks, G. (2007) *What Works for Children with Literacy Difficulties? The Effectiveness of Intervention Schemes*. London: Department for Children, Schools and Families.

Bruner, J. (1966) *Toward a Theory of Instruction*. Cambridge, MA: Harvard University Press.

Bruner, J. (1996) *The Culture of Education*. Boston, MA: Harvard University Press.

Burman, D., Nunes, T. and Evans, D. (2006) Writing profiles of deaf children taught through British Sign Language, *Deafness and Education International*, 9: 2–23.

Buzan, T. (2000) *The Mind Map Book*. London: Penguin.

Byatt, L. (2014) Verbal presentation, at SENCo conference, Corn Exchange, Bedford, 2 July 2014.

Cameron, L. and Murphy, J. (2002) Enabling young people with a learning disability to make choices at a time of transition, *British Journal of Learning Disabilities*, 30: 105–12.

Campbell, C. (2011) *How to Involve Hard to Reach Parents: Encouraging Meaningful Parental Involvement with Schools*. Nottingham: National College of Teaching and Learning.

Canter, L. and Canter, M. (2001) *Parents on Your Side: A Teacher's Guide to Creating Positive Relationships with Parents*, 2nd edn. Bloomington, IN: Solution Tree Press.

Central Advisory Council for Education (1967) *Children and Their Primary Schools (Plowden Report)*. London: HMSO.

Childnet International/Department for Children, Schools and Families (DCSF) (2007–8) *Let's Fight It Together; What We Can All Do To Prevent Cyberbullying*. London: Childnet International and DCSF.

Children's Workforce Development Council (CWDC) (2009) *The Common Assessment Framework for Children and Young People: A Guide for Practitioners*. London: CWDC.

Clark, C., Dyson, A., Millward, A. and Skidmore, D. (1997) *New Directions in Special Needs*. London: Cassell.

Clay, M.M. (1993) *Reading Recovery*. Auckland: Heinemann.

Clay, M.M. (1998) *An Observation Survey of Early Literacy Achievement*. Auckland: Heinemann.

Cole, B.A. (2005) Mission impossible? Special educational needs, inclusion and the reconceptualization of the role of the SENCO in England and Wales, *European Journal of Special Needs Education*, 20(3): 287–307.

Cole, T. (1989) *Apart or A Part? Integration and the Growth of British Special Education*. Milton Keynes: Open University Press.

Cole, T. (1990) The history of special education: social control of humanitarian progress? *British Journal of Special Education*, 17(3); 101–7.

Collins, F. and McCray, J. (2012) Partnership working in services for children: use of the common assessment framework, *Journal of Interprofessional Care*, 26(2): 134–40.

Committee of Enquiry (1977) *A New Partnership for Our Schools (Taylor Report)*. London: HMSO.

Corbett, J. (1996) *Bad Mouthing: The Language of Special Needs*. London: Falmer Press.

Corby, B. (2006) The role of child care social work in supporting families with children in need and providing protective services–past, present and future, *Child Abuse Review*, 15(3): 159–77.

Cowne, E. (2000) Inclusive curriculum: access for all – rhetoric or reality? In *E831 Professional Development for Special Educational Needs Co-Ordinators*. Milton Keynes: Open University.

Cremin, H., Thomas, G. and Vincett, K. (2003) Learning zones: an evaluation of three models for improving learning through teacher/teaching assistant teamwork, *Support for Learning*, 18(4): 154–61.

Crozier, G. and Reay, D. (eds) (2005) *Activating Participation: Parents and Teachers Working Towards Partnership*. Stoke on Trent: Trentham Books.

Cruse (2015) Available at: www.cruse.org.uk

Dale, N. (1996) *Working with Families of Children with Special Needs*. London: Routledge.

Department for Education (DfE) (1994) *The Code of Practice for the Identification and Assessment of Special Educational Needs*. London: DfE.

Department for Education (DfE) (2010) *Statistical First Release: GCSE and Equivalent Attainment by Pupil Characteristics in England*, 2009/10. London: DfE. Available at: https://www.gov.uk/government/uploads/system/uploads/attachment_data/file/218842/sfr37-2010.pdf (accessed 1 June 2015).

Department for Education (DfE) (2011) *Review of Best Practice in Parental Engagement*. London: DfE.

Department for Education (DfE) (2012) *Provision Mapping*, available at: http://webarchive.nationalarchives.gov.uk/20130123124929/http://www.education.gov.uk/schools/pupilsupport/inclusionandlearnersupport/onetoonetuition/a00199972/provision-mapping (accessed 6 July 2015).

Department for Education (DfE) (2013a) *Provision Mapping*, available at: http://webarchive.nationalarchives.gov.uk/20130123124929/http://www.education.gov.uk/schools/pupilsupport/inclusionandlearnersupport/onetoonetuition/a00199972/provision-mapping (accessed 1 June 2015).

Department for Education (DfE) (2013b) *Use of Reasonable Force: Advice for Headteachers, Staff and Governing Bodies*. London: DfE.

Department for Education (DfE) (2014a) *Special Educational Needs and Disability Code of Practice: 0 to 25 Years*. London: DfE.

Department for Education (DfE) (2014b) *Schools' Guide to the 0–25 SEND Code of Practice*. London: DfE.

Department for Education (DfE) (2014c) *Supporting Pupils at School with Medical Conditions. Statutory Guidance for Governing Bodies of Maintained Schools and Proprietors of Academies in England*. London: DfE.

Department for Education (DfE) (2014d) *Behaviour and Discipline in Schools: Advice for Head Teachers and School Staff*. London: DfE.

Department for Education (DfE) (2014e) *Special Educational Needs and Disability (SEND): A Guide for Parents and Carers*. London: DfE.

Department for Education (DfE) (2014f) *Special Educational Needs and Disability Pathfinder*. London: DfE.

Department for Education (DfE) (2014g) *National Curriculum in England: Framework for Key Stages 1 to 4*. London: DfE.

Department for Education (DfE) (2014h) *Preventing and Tackling Bullying: Advice for Headteachers, Staff And Governing Bookes*. London: DfE.

Department for Education (DfE) (2015a) *Working Together to Safeguard Children*. London: DfE.

Department for Education (DfE) (2015b) *Keeping Children Safe in Education*. London: DfE.

Department for Education (DfE) (2015c) *What to Do If You're Worried a Child Is Being Abused*. London: DfE.

Department for Education (DfE) (2015d) *Information Sharing: Advice for Practitioners*. London: DfE.

Department for Education (DfE) (2015e) *Pupil Premium 2015 to 2016: Conditions of Grant*. London: DfE.

Department for Education and Skills (DfES) (2004) *Every Child Matters: Change for Children*. London: DfES.

Department for Education and Skills (DfES) (2006) *Primary Framework for Literacy and Mathematics*. Norwich: DfES.

Department of Education and Science (DES) (1978) *The Warnock Report: Special Educational Needs, Report of the Committee of Enquiry into the Education of Handicapped Children and Young People, Cmnd. 7212*. London: HMSO.

Desforges, C. and Abouchaar, A. (2003) *The Impact of Parental Involvement, Parental Support and Family Education on Pupil Achievement and Adjustment: A Literature Review*. Nottingham: DfES.

de Shazer, S. (1985) *Keys to Solution in Brief Therapy*. New York: WW Norton.

de Shazer, S. (1988) *Investigating Solutions in Brief Therapy*. New York: WW Norton.

de Shazer, S., Dolan, Y., Korman, H., McCollum, E., Trepper, T. and Berg, I.K. (2007) *More Than Miracles: The State of the Art of Solutions-Focused Brief Therapy*. New York: Haworth.

Devon Parent Partnership Service (n/d) *Look Out for EHPCs Near You*, available at: www.parentpartnershipdevon.org.uk (accessed 2 September 2015).

Dockrell, J. and McShane, J. (1993) *Children's Learning Difficulties: A Cognitive Approach*. Oxford: Blackwell.

Donaldson, M. (1984) *Children's Minds*. London: Fontana.

Douglas, G. and McLinden, M. (2005) Visual impairment, in B. Norwich and A. Lewis (eds) *Special Teaching for Special Children? Pedagogies for Inclusion*. Maidenhead: Open University Press.

Douglas, J.W.B. (1964) *The Home and the School*. St Albans: Panther.

Down, J.L.H. (1866) Observations on an ethnic classification of idiots, *Clinical Lecture Reports, London Hospital*, 3: 259–62.

Dunhill, A. (2009) *What Is Communication? The Process of Transferring Information*. Exeter: Learning Matters Ltd.

Dunn, L., Parry, S. and Morgan, C. (2002) Seeking quality in criterion referenced assessment, paper presented at Learning Communities and Assessment Cultures Conference, University of Northumbria, 28–30 August.

Dwivedi, K. and Gupta, A. (2000) 'Keeping cool': anger management through group work, *Support for Learning*, 15(2): 76–81.

Dykens, E.M. and Kasari, C. (1997) Maladaptive behavior in children with Prader-Willi syndrome, Down syndrome, and nonspecific mental retardation, *American Journal on Mental Retardation*, 102(3): 228–37.

Eden, G.F., Van Meter, J.W., Rumsey, J.M., Maisog, J.M., Woods, R.P., and Zeffrio, T.A. (1996) Abnormal processing of visual motion in dyslexia revealed by functional brain imaging, *Nature*, 382: 66–9.

Education Department (1898) *Report of the Departmental Committee on Defective and Epileptic Children (Sharpe Report)*. London: HMSO.

Ekins, A. (2011) *The Changing Face of Special Educational Needs*. London: Routledge.

Elkin, S. (2010) *Unlocking the Reader in Every Child: The Book of Practical Ideas for Teaching and Reading*. Winchester: Ransom.

Everatt, J. (2002) Visual processes, in G. Reid and J. Wearmouth (eds) *Dyslexia and Literacy: Research and Practice*. Chichester: Wiley.

Field, F. (2010) *The Foundation Years: Preventing Poor Children Becoming Poor Adults. The Report of the Independent Review on Poverty and Life Chances*. London: Cabinet Office.

Fisch, H., Hyun, G., Golden, R., Hensle, T.W., Olsson, C.A. and Liberson, G.L. (2003) The influence of paternal age on down syndrome, *Journal of Urology*, 169(6): 2275–8.

Fisher, G., Richmond, R. and Wearmouth, J. (2004) *Managing Behaviour in Schools: Study Guide Part 4*. Milton Keynes: Open University Press.

Florian, L. and Hegarty, J. (eds) (2004) *ICT and Special Educational Needs: A Tool for Inclusion*. Maidenhead: Open University Press.

Freeman, S.B., Taft, L.F., Dooley, K.J., Allran, K., Sherman, S.L., Hassold, T.J., Khoury, M.J. and Saker, D.M. (1998) Population-based study of congenital heart defects in Down syndrome, *American Journal of Medicine and Genetics*, 80(3): 213–17.

Friend, M. and Cook, L. (1996) *Interactions: Collaboration Skills for School Professionals*. White Plains, NY: Longman.

Fulcher, G. (1989) *Disabling Policies: A Comparative Approach to Educational Policy and Disabilities*. London: Falmer Press.

Furlong, V.J. (1985) *The Deviant Pupil: Sociological Perspectives*. Milton Keynes: OU Press.

Galloway, D.M., Armstrong, D. and Tomlinson, S. (1994) *The Assessment of Special Educational Needs: Whose Problem?* Harlow: Longman.

Galloway, D.M. and Goodwin, C. (1987) *The Education of Disturbing Children: Pupils with Learning and Adjustment Difficulties*. London: Longman.

Gamble, N. and Yates, S. (2008) *Exploring Children's Literature*. London: Sage.

Gamlin, R. (1935) *Modern School Hygiene*. London: James Nisbet.

Garner, P. and Sandow, S. (1995) *Advocacy, Self-Advocacy and Special Needs*. London: Fulton.

Gee, J. (2000) New people in new worlds: networks, the new capitalism and schools, in B. Cope and M. Kalantzis (eds) *Multiliteracies: Literacy Learning and the Design of Social Futures*. London: Routledge.

Gersch, I. (1995) Involving the child, in *Schools' Special Educational Needs Policies Pack*, London: National Children's Bureau.

Gewirtz, S., Ball, S.J. and Bowe, R. (1995) *Markets, Choice and Equity In Education*, Buckingham: Open University Press.

Glynn, T. (1982) Antecedent control of behaviour in educational contexts, *Educational Psychology*, 2: 215–29.

Glynn, T. and Bishop, R. (1995) Cultural issues in educational research: a New Zealand perspective, *He Pūkengo Kūrero*, 1(1): 37–43.

Glynn, T. and McNaughton, S. (1985) The Mangere home and school remedial reading procedures, *New Zealand Journal of Psychology*, 15(2): 66–77.

Glynn, T., Wearmouth, J. and Berryman, M. (2006) *Supporting Students with Literacy Difficulties: A Responsive Approach*. Maidenhead: Open University Press.

Goldberg, L.R. and Richberg, C.M. (2004) Minimal hearing impairment: major myths with more than minimal implications, *Communication Disorders Quarterly*, 24: 152–60.

Goodall, J., Vorhaus, J., Carpentieri, L., Brooks, G., Akerman, R. and Harris, A. (2011) *Review of Best Practice in Parental Engagement*. London: Institute of Education.

Goodlad, S. (ed.) (1998) *Mentoring and Tutoring Students*. London: Kogan Page.

Gordon, A. (1961) Mongolism (Correspondence). *The Lancet* 1 (7180): 775.

Grandin, T. (1996) *Emergence: Labelled Autistic*. New York: Warner.

Grauberg, E. (2002) *Elementary Mathematics and Language Difficulties*. London: Whurr.

Greeno, J.G. (1998) The situativity of knowing, learning, and research, *American Psychologist*, 53(1): 5–26.

Gross, J. (1996) The weight of the evidence, *Support for Learning*, 11(1): 3–8.

Hage, C. and Leybaert, J. (2006) The effect of cued speech on the development of spoken language, in P. Spencer and M. Marschark (eds) *Advances in the Spoken Language Development of Deaf and Hard-of-Hearing Children*. New York: Oxford University Press.

Hall, K. and Øzerk, K. (2008) *Research Briefing: Primary Curriculum and Assessment: England and Other Countries (Primary Review Research Survey 3/1)*. Cambridge: University of Cambridge Faculty of Education.

Hallgarten, J. (2000) *Parents Exist, OK!? Issues and Visions for the Parent–School Relationship*. London: IPPR.

Hanko, G. (1994) Discouraged children: when praise does not help, *British Journal of Special Education*.

Hargreaves, D.H. (1967) *Social Relations in a Secondary School*, London: Routledge.

Harris, M. and Moreno, C. (2006) Speech reading and learning to read: a comparison of 8-year-old profoundly deaf children with good and poor reading ability, *Journal of Deaf Studies and Deaf Education*, 11: 189–201.

Harris-Hendriks, J. and Figueroa, J. (1995) *Black in White: The Caribbean Child in the UK*. London: Pitman.

Hart, S. (1995) Differentiation by task or differentiation by outcome?' in National Children's Bureau, *Schools' Special Educational Needs Policies Pack*. London: NCB.

Hatcher, J. and Snowling, M. (2002) The phonological representations hypothesis of dyslexia, in G. Reid and J. Wearmouth (eds) *Dyslexia and Literacy: Research and Practice*. Chichester: Wiley.

Haylock, P. and Cockburn, I. (2009) *Understanding Mathematics for Young Children*. London: Sage.

Hertfordshire Special Educational Needs and Disability Pathfinder (n/d) *Local Networks and the Local Offer*, available at: http://www.hertsdirect.org/docs/pdf/s/faqs.pdf (accessed 9 March 2015).

Heubert, J.P. (2000) *High-Stakes Testing Opportunities and Risks for Students of Color, English-Language Learners, and Students with Disabilities*. New York: National Center on Accessing the General Curriculum.

Hornby, G. (2000) *Improving Parental Involvement*. London: Cassell.

Howard-Jones, N. (1979) On the diagnostic term 'Down's disease', *Medical History*, 23(1): 102–4.

Hudson, B. (2002) Interprofessionality in health and social care: the Achilles' heel of partnership? *Journal of Interprofessional Care*, 16(1): 7–11.

Irlen, H. (1991) *Reading by the Colors*. New York: Avery.

Joint Council for Qualifications (JCQ) (2014) *Adjustments for Candidates with Disabilities and Learning Difficulties*. London: JCQ.

Jones, C.A. (2004) *Inclusion in the Early Years*, 3rd edn. Maidenhead: McGraw-Hill.

Jordan, R. (1999) *Autistic Spectrum Disorders: An Introductory Handbook for Practitioners*. London: David Fulton.

Jordan, R. (2001) *Autism with Severe Learning Difficulties*. London: Souvenir Press.

Kanner, L. (1943) Autistic disturbances of affective contact, *Nervous Child*, 2: 217–50.

Kinder, K., Lord, P. and Wilkin, A. (2008) *Implementing Integrated Children's Services. Part 1: Managers' Views on Early Impact*. Slough: NFER.

Klin, A., Sparrow, S., Marans, W.D., Carter, A. and Volkmar, F.R. (2000) Assessment issues in children and adolescents with Asperger syndrome, in A. Klin, F.R. Volkmar and S. Sparrow (eds) *Asperger Syndrome*. New York: Guilford Press.

Lamb, B. (2009) *Report to the Secretary of State on the Lamb Inquiry Review of SEN and Disability Information*. London: DCSF.

Laming, Lord (2003) *The Victoria Climbié Inquiry: Report of an Inquiry by Lord Laming*. London: Crown Office.

Laming, Lord (2009) *The Protection of Children in England: A Progress Report*. London: HM Stationery Office.

Lave, J. and Wenger, E. (1998) *Communities of Practice: Learning, Meaning, and Identity*. Cambridge: Cambridge University Press.

LaVigna, G.W. and Donnellan, A.M. (1986) *Alternative to Punishment: Solving Behavior Problems with Non-Aversive Strategies*. New York: Irvington.

Leinonen, E. and Letts, C. (1997) Why pragmatic impairment? A case study in the comprehension of inferential meaning, *European Journal of Disorders of Communication*, 32: 35–51.

Lewis, A. (2002) Accessing through research interviews the views of children with difficulties in learning, *Supp ort for Learning*, 17(3): 110–16.

Lewis, S. (1996) The reading achievement of a group of severely and profoundly hearing-impaired school leavers educated within a natural aural approach, *Journal of the British Association of Teachers of the Deaf*, 20: 1–7.

Lifton, R.J. (2000) *The Nazi Doctors: Medical Killing and the Psychology of Genocide.* New York: Basic Books.

Lilley, C. (2004) A whole-school approach to ICT for children with physical disabilities, in L. Florian and J. Hegarty (eds) *ICT and Special Educational Needs: A Tool for Inclusion.* Maidenhead: Open University Press.

Lorenz, S. (1998) *Effective in-Class Support.* London: David Fulton.

Macfarlane, A. (1997) The Hikairo rationale: teaching students with emotional and behavioural difficulties: a bicultural approach, *Waikato Journal of Education*, 3: 135–68.

Macfarlane, A. (2000a) Māori perspectives on development, in L. Bird and W. Drewery (eds) *Human Development in Aotearoa: A Journey Through Life.* Auckland: McGraw-Hill Book Company.

Macfarlane, A. (2000b) The value of Māori ecologies in special education, in D. Fraser, R. Moltzen and K. Ryba (eds) *Learners with Special Needs in Aotearoa New Zealand*, 2nd edn. Palmerston North: Dunmore Press.

Mason, H. (2001) *Visual Impairment.* Tamworth: NASEN.

Mason, H., McCall, S., Arter, C., McLinden, M. and Stone, J. (1997) *Visual Impairment: Access to Education for Children and Young People.* London: David Fulton.

Massey, A. (2014) *Provision Mapping.* London: David Fulton.

McDermott, R.P. (1999) On becoming labelled – the story of Adam, in P. Murphy (ed.) *Learners, Learning and Assessment.* London: Paul Chapman.

McLeod, J. (1998) *An Introduction to Counselling*, 2nd edn. Buckingham: Open University Press.

Mehan, H. (1996) The politics of representation, in S. Chaiklin and J. Lave (eds) *Understanding Practice: Perspectives on Activity and Context.* Cambridge: Cambridge University Press.

Meichenbaum, D. and Turk, D. (1976) The cognitive-behavioural management of anxiety, anger and pain, in P.O. Davidson (ed.) *The Behavioural Management of Anxiety, Anger and Pain.* New York: Brunner/Mazel.

Mencap (undated) *About Profound and Multiple Learning Disabilities.* London: Mencap.

Merrett, F. (1985) *Encouragement Works Better than Punishment: The Application of Behavioural Methods in Schools.* Birmingham: Positive Products.

Milgram, S. (1974) *Obedience to Authority: An Experimental View.* New York: Harper and Row.

Miller, O. and Ockleford, A. (2005) *Visual Needs.* London: Continuum.

Ministry of Education (MoE) (1945) *The Nation's Schools.* London: MoE.

Ministry of Education (2005) *Effective Literacy Practice.* Wellington: Learning Media.

Moeller, M.P., Tomblin, J.B., Yoshinaga-Itano, C., Connor, C. and Jerger, S. (2007) Current state of knowledge: language and literacy of children with hearing impairment, *Ear and Hearing*, 28: 740–53.

Moore, D. (2004) Behaviour in context: functional assessment of disruptive behaviour in classrooms, in J. Wearmouth, R. Richmond and T. Glynn (eds) *Addressing Pupil Behaviour: Responses at District, School and Individual Levels.* London: David Fulton.

Moores, D. (2001) *Educating the Deaf.* Boston: Houghton Mifflin.

Moores, D. (2008) Research in Bi-Bi instruction, *American Annals of the Deaf*, 153: 3–4.

Morris, J.K., Wald, N.J., Mutton, D.E. and Alberman, E. (2003) Comparison of models of maternal age-specific risk for Down syndrome live births, *Prenatal Diagnosis*, 23(3): 252–8.

Murphy, S. (2002) Literacy assessment and the politics of identity, in J. Soler, J. Wearmouth and G. Reid (eds) *Contextualising Difficulties in Literacy Development: Exploring Politics, Culture, Ethnicity and Ethics.* London: Routledge.

National Association for Special Educational Needs (NASEN) (n.d.) *NASEN Help Sheet: Updating SEN Policy for Schools*. Tamworth: NASEN.

National Autistic Society (2015a) Position statement: Causes of autism. Available at: http://www.autism.org.uk/News-and-events/Media-Centre/Position-statements/Causes-of-autism.aspx

National Autistic Society (2015b) What is Asperger Syndrome? Available at: http://www.autism.org.uk/About-autism/Autism-and-Asperger-syndrome-an-introduction/What-is-Asperger-syndrome.aspx

National Deaf Children's Society (NDCS) (2008) *Acoustics Toolkit*. London: NDCS.

National Deaf Children's Society (NDCS) (2010) *Communicating with Your Deaf Child*. London: NDCS.

National Institute of Neorological Disorders and Stroke (NINDS) (2005) *Tourette Syndrome Fact Sheet*. Bethesda, MD: NINDS.

Nethercott, K. (2015) Understanding the use of the common assessment framework, unpublished PhD thesis, Bedford: University of Bedfordshire.

Norbury, C.F. and Bishop, D.V.M. (2003) Narrative skills in children with communication impairments, *International Journal of Language and Communication Impairments*, 38: 287–313.

Norwich, B., Cooper, P. and Maras, P. (2002) Attentional and activity difficulties: findings from a national study, *Support for Learning*, 17(4): 182–6.

Office for Standards in Education (Ofsted) (2010) *The Special Educational Needs and Disability Review*. London: Ofsted.

Office for Standards in Education (Ofsted) (2011) *Safeguarding in Schools: Best Practice*. London: Ofsted.

Office for Standards in Education (Ofsted) (2014) *Unannounced Behaviour Inspections: Guidance for Inspectors*. Manchester: Ofsted.

Office for Standards in Education (Ofsted) (2015) *School Inspection Handbook*. Manchester: Ofsted.

Oliphant, J. (2006) Empowerment and debilitation in the educational experience of the blind in nineteenth-century England and Scotland, *History of Education*, 35(1): 47–68.

Olweus, D. (1993) *Bullying at School: What We Know and What We Can Do*. Oxford: Blackwell.

Padden, C. and Gunsals, D. (2003) How the alphabet came to be used in a sign language, *Sign Language Studies*, 4: 1–13.

Palmer, C., Redfern, R. and Smith, K. (1994) The four P's of policy, *British Journal of Special Education*, 21(1): 4–6.

Panel of Enquiry (1985) *Child in Trust: The Report of the Panel of Inquiry into the Circumstances Surrounding the Death of Jasmine Beckford*. Brent: Brent Borough Council.

Phillips, C. and Jenner, H. (2004) *Inclusion at Bangabandhu Primary School: Inclusive Education: Learners and Learning Contexts*. London: David Fulton.

Piacenti, J., Woods, D.W., Scahill, L., Wilhelm, S., Peterson, A.L., Chang, S., Ginsburg, G.S., Deckersbach, T., Dziura, J., Levi-Pearl, S. and Walkup, J. (2010) Behavior therapy for children with Tourette disorder, *Journal of the American Medical Association*, 303(19): 1929–37.

Piaget, J. (1954) *Construction of Reality in the Child*. New York: Basic Books.

Piaget, J. (1964) Cognitive development in children, *Journal of Research in Science Teaching*, 2(3): 176–86.

Piaget, J. (1969) *The Child's Conception of Time*. London: RKP.

Pickles, P. (2001) Therapeutic provision in mainstream curricula, in J. Wearmouth (ed.) *Special Educational Provision in the Context of Inclusion: Policy and Practice in Schools*. London: David Fulton.

Pitchford, M. (2004) An introduction to multi-element planning for primary aged children, in J. Wearmouth, R.C. Richmond and T. Glynn (eds) *Addressing Pupils' Behaviour: Responses At District, School and Individual Levels*. London: David Fulton.

Pohlschmidt, M. and Meadowcroft, R. (2010) *Muscle Disease: The Impact: Incidence and Prevalence of Neuromuscular Conditions in the UK*. London: Muscular Dystrophy Campaign.

Pollard, A. (2002) *Reflective Teaching: Effective and Evidence-Informed Professional Practice*. London: Continuum.

Porter, J., Ouvry, C., Morgan, M. and Downs, C. (2001) Interpreting the communication of people with profound and multiple learning difficulties, *British Journal of Learning Disabilities*, 29(1): 12–16.

Poulou, M. and Norwich, B. (2002) Cognitive, emotional and behavioural responses to students with emotional and behavioural difficulties: a model of decision-making, *British Educational Research Journal*, 28(1): 111–38.

Qualifications and Curriculum Authority (QCA) Primary National Strategy (PNS) (2005) *Speaking Listening Learning: Working with Children Who Have Special Educational Needs* (Ref 1235/2005). London: QCA.

Radford, J. (2000) Values into practice: developing whole-school behaviour policies, *Support for Learning*, 15(2): 86–9.

Rapin, I. and Allen, D. (1983) Developmental language disorders: neuropsychological considerations, in U. Kirk (ed.) *Neuropsychology of Language, Reading and Spelling*. New York: Academic Press.

Reder, P. and Duncan, S. (2003) Understanding communication in child protection networks, *Child Abuse Review*, 12(2): 82–100.

Riddick, B., Wolfe, J. and Lumsdon, D. (2002) *Dyslexia: A Practical Guide for Teachers and Parents*. London: David Fulton.

Rix, J. and Simmons, K. (2004) *Inclusive Education: Listening to Others*. London: David Fulton.

Roaf, C. and Lloyd, C. (1995) Multi-agency work with young people in difficulty, *Social Care Research Findings*, 68.

Rochdale Borough Safeguarding Children Board (RBSCB) (2012) *Review of Multi-agency Responses to the Sexual Exploitation of Children*. Rochdale: The Rochdale Borough Safeguarding Children Board.

Rogers, B. (2013) Communicating with children in the classroom, in T. Cole, H. Daniels and J. Visser (eds) *The Routledge International Companion to Emotional and Behavioural Difficulties*. London: Routledge.

Rogers, J. (2007) Cardinal number and its representation: skills, concepts and contexts, *Early Childhood Education and Care*, 178(2): 211–25.

Rogers, W. (1994a) *The Language of Discipline*. Plymouth: Northcote House.

Rogers, W. (1994b) *Behaviour Recovery: A Whole School Approach for Behaviourally Disordered Children*. Melbourne: Australian Council for Educational Research.

Rogers, W. (1994c) Teaching positive behaviour in behaviourally disordered students in primary schools, *Support for Learning*, 9(4): 166–70.

Rogoff, B. (1990) *Apprenticeship in Thinking: Cognitive Development in Social Context*. New York: Oxford University Press.

Rose, J. (2009) Identifying and Teaching Children and Young People with Dyslexia and Literacy Difficulties, London: DCFS

Rosenthal, R. and Jacobson, L. (1968) *Pygmalion in the Classroom*. New York: Holt, Rinehart and Winston.

Roth, I. (2002) The autistic spectrum: from theory to practice, in N. Brace and H. Westcott (eds) *Applying Psychology*. Maidenhead: Open University Press.

Russell, P. (1997) Parents as partners: early impressions of the impact of the Code of Practice, in S. Wolfendale (ed.) *Working with Parents after the Code of Practice*. London: David Fulton.

Rutter, M. (1966) *Children of Sick Parents*. Oxford: Oxford University Press.

Rutter, M., Tizard, J. and Whitmore, K. (1970) *Education, Health and Behaviour*. London: Longman.

Selikowitz, M. (2008) *Down Syndrome*. Oxford: Oxford University Press.

Shah, M. (2001)*Working with Parents*. Oxford: Heinemann Educational Publishers.

Shapiro, S. and Cole, L. (1994) *Behaviour Change in the Classroom: Self-Management Interventions*. New York: Guildford Press.

Sheehy, K. (2004) Approaches to autism, in J. Wearmouth, R.C. Richmond and T. Glynn (eds) *Addressing Pupils' Behaviour: Responses at District, School and Individual Levels*. London: David Fulton.

Skinner, B.F. (1938) *The Behaviour of Organisms*. New York: Appleton Century Crofts.

Skinner, B.F. (1953) *Science and Human Behavior*. New York: Macmillan.

Smedley, M. (1990) Semantic-pragmatic language disorders: a description with some practical suggestions for teachers, *Child Language Teaching and Therapy*, 5: 174–90.

Snowling, M. J. (2000) *Dyslexia*, 2nd edn. Oxford: Blackwell.

Spencer, P. and Marschark, M. (eds) (2006) *Advances in the Spoken Language Development of Deaf and Hard-of-Hearing Children*. New York: Oxford University Press.

Spencer, P.E. and Marschark, M. (2010) *Evidence-Based Practice in Educating Deaf and Hard-of-Hearing Students*. Oxford: Oxford University Press.

Sproson, B. (2004) Some do and some don't: teacher effectiveness in managing behaviour, in J. Wearmouth, T. Glynn, R.C. Richmond and M. Berryman (eds) *Inclusion and Behaviour Management in Schools*. London: David Fulton.

Stanovich, K. (2000) *Progress in Understanding Reading: Scientific Foundations and New Frontiers*. London: The Guilford Press.

Steer, A. (2006) *Learning Behaviour Principles and Practice: What Works In Schools. Section 2 of the Report of the Practitioners on School Behaviour and Discipline*. London: DfES.

Strouse Watt, W. (2003) *How Visual Acuity Is Measured*. Available at: http://lowvision.preventblindness.org/eye-conditions/how-visual-acuity-is-measured (accessed June 2015).

Stuart, K. (2012) Leading multi-professional teams in the children's workforce: an action research project, *International Journal of Integrated Care (IJIC)*, 12: 1–12.

Tate, R., Smeeth, L., Evans, J. and Fletcher, A. (2005) *The Prevalence of Visual Impairment in the UK: A Review of the Literature*. London: RNIB.

Taylor, J. and Daniel, B. (1999) Interagency practice in children with non-organic failure to thrive: is there a gap between health and social care? *Child Abuse Review*, 8(5): 325–38.

Taylor, K. (2007) The participation of children with multi-sensory impairment in person-centred planning, *British Journal of Special Education*, 34(4): 204–11.

TEACCH (1998) Treatment and Education of Autistic and Related Communication Handicapped Children. Available at http://www.teacch.com/ (accessed 1 June 2015).

Tod, J., Castle, F. and Blamires, M. (1998) *Implementing Effective Practice*. London: David Fulton.

Tomlinson, S. (1988) Why Johnny can't read: critical theory and special education, *European Journal of Special Needs Education*, 3(1): 45–58.

Topping, K. (1995) *Paired Reading, Spelling and Writing: The Handbook for Teachers and Parents*. London: Cassell.

Underwood Report (1955) *Report of the Committee on Maladjusted Children*. London: HMSO.

UNISON (2013) *The Evident Value of Teaching Assistants*. Available at: https://www.unison.org.uk/upload/sharepoint/Briefings%20and%20Circulars/EVIDENT%20VALUE%20OF%20TEACHING%20ASSISTANTS%20%28Autosaved%29.pdf (accessed 1 June 2015).

Vernon, P. (1977) *Graded Word Spelling Text*. London: Hodder.

Vygotsky, L.S. (1962) *Thought and Language*. Cambridge, MA: MIT Press.

Watkins, C. and Wagner, P. (1995) School behaviour and special educational needs – what's the link? in National Children's Bureau, *Discussion Papers 1:, Schools' Special Educational Needs Policies Pack*. London: NCB.

Watkins, C. and Wagner, P. (2000) *Improving School Behaviour*. London: Paul Chapman.

Wearmouth, J. (1986) Self-concept and learning experiences of pupils with moderate learning difficulties. Unpublished Master's thesis. University of London Institute of Education.

Wearmouth, J. (1996) Registering special needs – for what purpose?, *Support for Learning*, 11(3):118–23.

Wearmouth, J. (2009) *A Beginning Teacher's Guide to Special Educational Needs*. Maidenhead: Open University Press.

Wearmouth, J. and Berryman, M. (2009) *Inclusion as Participation in Communities of Practice*. Palmerston North: Dunmore Press.

Wearmouth, J. and Berryman, M. (2011) Family and community support for addressing difficulties in literacy, in C. Wyatt-Smith, J. Elkins and E. Gunn (eds) *Multiple Perspectives on Difficulties in Learning Literacy and Numeracy*. London: Springer.

Wearmouth, J. Glynn, T. and Berryman, M. (2005) *Perspectives on Student Behaviour in Schools: Exploring Theory and Developing Practice*. London: Routledge.

Weavers, J. (2003) Dyslexia and mathematics, in M. Thomson (ed.) *Dyslexia Included*. London: David Fulton.

Whiting, M., Scammell, A. and Bifulco, A. (2008) The health specialist initiative: professionals' views of a partnership initiative between health and social care for child safeguarding, *Qualitative Social Work: Research and Practice*, 7(1): 99–117.

Wilkins, A.J., Evans, B.J.W., Brown, J.A., Busby, A.E., Wingfield, A.E., Jeanes, R.L. and Bald, J. (1994) Double-masked placebo-controlled trial of precision spectral filters in children who use coloured overlays, *Ophthalmic and Physiological Optics*, 14: 365–70.

Wilkins, M. and Ertmer, D.J. (2002) Introducing young children who are deaf or hard of hearing to spoken language, *Language, Speech and Hearing Services in Schools*, 33: 196–204.

Wilkinson, E. (1947) *The New Secondary Education*. London: HMSO.

Williams, H. (2004) *Behaviour in Schools: Framework for Intervention:* Birmingham: Birmingham City Council Education Department.

Wing, L. (1996) *The Autistic Spectrum: A Guide for Parents and Professionals*. London: Constable.

Wing, L. and Gould, J. (1979) Severe impairments of social interaction and associated abnormalities in children: epidemiology and classification, *Journal of Autism and Developmental Disorders*, 9: 11–29.

Wood, D., Bruner, J. and Ross, G. (1976) The role of tutoring in problem solving, *Journal of Child Psychology and Psychiatry*, 17: 89–100.

Wood, K.C., Smith, H. and Grossniklaus, D. (2001) Piaget's stages of cognitive development, in M. Orey (ed.) *Emerging Perspectives on Learning, Teaching, and Technology*, Atlanta, GA: University of Georgia Press.

World Health Organisation (WHO) (1992) *The International Statistical Classification of Diseases – ICD-10, WHO:* Geneva: WHO.

Wragg, E.C., Wragg, C.M., Haynes, G.S. and Chamberlain, R.P. (1998) *Improving Literacy in the Primary School.* London: Routledge.

Wray, D. (2002) Metacognition and literacy, in G. Reid and J. Wearmouth (eds) *Dyslexia and Literacy: Research and Practice.* Chichester: Wiley.

Wray, D., Medwell, J., Fox, R. and Poulson, L. (2000) The teaching practices of effective teachers of literacy, *Educational Review*, 52(1): 75–84.

Yoshinaga-Itano, C. (2003) From screening to early identification and intervention: discovering predictors to successful outcomes for children with significant hearing loss, *Journal of Deaf Studies and Deaf Education*, 8: 11–30.

Ysseldyke, J.E. and Christenson, S.L. (1993) *TIES-II: The Instructional Environment System—II.* Longmont, CO: Sopris West.

Ysseldyke, J.E. and Christenson, S.L. (1987) *The Instructional Environment Scale (TIES).* Austin, TX: Pro-Ed.

Yurdakul, N.S., Ugurlu, S. and Maden, A. (2006) Strabismus in Down syndrome, *Journal of Pediatric Ophthalmology and Strabismus,* 43(1): 27–30.

Index

Page numbers in *italics* refer to tables, *a* indicates appendix